RICHARD MUIR

Riddles
in the
British Landscape

with 148 illustrations and 4 maps

THAMES AND HUDSON

ACKNOWLEDGMENTS

Aerofilms Ltd 85, 87, 110, 119 l., 119 r., 121, 135 t., 148, 157; Airviews (M/cr) Limited 89; Alinari/Mansell Collection 28; J. Allan Cash Ltd 31; Avebury Museum, Photo Alexander Keiller 76; Bodleian Library, Oxford 41 t. (MS 764); Janet and Colin Bord 138; Bord Fáilte Photo 109, 183 t.; British Library 41 b. (Royal MS 2.B.VII), 156 (Cotton MS Nero D1); British Museum 17, 38, 39, 42 l., 96, 100, 120, 122 t.l., 133 t.l., 133 c.l., 155 b., 168; British Tourist Authority 26 b., 86, 94, 99, 116, 143, 160; Butser Ancient Farm Project Trust 103, 104; Cambridge University Collection: copyright reserved 10, 21, 62, 65, 82, 90, 122 t.r., 155 t., 171, 180; Peter Chèze-Brown 162 b.; Commissioners of Public Works in Ireland 12, 22, 23, 60, 61, 98, 164; By permission of The Masters and Fellows of Corpus Christi College, Cambridge 54 (M 194); Courtauld Institute of Art, London 174 b.; Crown Copyright Reserved 27 b., 52, 63; Foto Mas, Barcelona 15; Institute of Archaeology, London 35; Inverness Museum and Art Gallery, Photo N. Macleod 42 r.; A. F. Kersting 112; Murray King 107 t.; Dr E. W. MacKie 130 b., 135 b., 146 c.; Richard Muir 24, 27 t., 45, 47 t., 47 b., 50, 72 t., 72 b., 74, 91 t., 102, 107 b., 113 b., 128 (Ordnance Survey), 146 t., 158, 167, 174 t., 175, 177, 183 b.; National Library of Ireland 108; National Monuments Record. Crown Copyright 25, 46, 79 b., 105 t., 105 b., 172, 182; National Museum of Antiquities of Scotland, Edinburgh 129, 130 t.; Northern Ireland Tourist Board 185; Oxford University, Institute of Archaeology 122 b.; Crown Copyright: reproduced by permission of the Scottish Development Department 26 t., 131, 133 r., 134, 146 b., 147 t., 147 b., 162 t.; Scottish Tourist Board 71; Edwin Smith 1, 2, 6, 51, 73, 91 b., 118, 136, 153; Dr I. F. Smith 67 (redrawn by P. Bridgewater); Somerset Levels Project, Cambridge 37; Suffolk Archaeological Unit 115; H. Tempest Ltd, Industrial Photographers 93, 113 t.; *The Times* 124; Trinity College, Dublin 133 b.l.; Victoria and Albert Museum 55, 81; R. E. M. Wheeler 79 t.; Jeffery W. Whitelaw 183 c.
OTHER SOURCES: 43 *Beauties of Natural History*, Anon., 1777, pls 40, 72; 163 *The Ancient History of Wiltshire*, Vol II, R. C. Hoare, 1821, pl. 5; 54 *Camden's Britannia with Additions and Improvements*, E. Gibson, 1695; 32, 33 *The Forest Trees of Great Britain*, A. C. Johns, 1886; 166 *Mona Antiqua Restaurata*, H. Rowlands, 1723.
Maps drawn by Ian Thomson.

(*Half-title page*) The Neolithic tomb of Maes Howe in Orkney looking outwards along the entrance passage.

(*Title-page*) The exposed remains of the Lanyon Quoit tomb, Cornwall.

© 1981 Thames and Hudson Ltd, London

First published in the USA in 1981 by Thames and Hudson, Inc., 500 Fifth Avenue, New York, New York 10110

Library of Congress Catalog Card Number 80-54191

Filmset and printed in Great Britain by BAS Printers Limited, Over Wallop, Hampshire
Bound in Great Britain by
Webb Son & Co Ltd, Glamorgan

Contents

The ruins of Dun Carloway Broch on the Isle of Lewis.

Introduction

MOST PEOPLE ENJOY A GOOD PUZZLE and this is a book about unsolved puzzles which have frustrated the best efforts of a variety of gifted sleuths. All these mysteries have two things in common: they find some expression in the landscape of Britain (indeed, many of them can be seen in places where this landscape is at its most beautiful); and they also concern some aspect of the works of man. While these two strong threads run through the text, the riddles themselves come in a wide variety of forms, ranging from the stone circle to the hill figure, from the tombs of the Neolithic Age, to the earliest Christian churches.

A large number date from the prehistoric era, and very frequently our thoughts return to a single theme: we know that prehistoric people did some amazing things; but why they did them we can hardly begin to know. In some small way I hope that, despite its concern with mystery, this book will establish a link between the reader and the ancient inhabitants of these islands. If we imagine these people as outlandish savages engaged in preposterous tasks we will never begin to know them. If we visualize them as people who were born with minds identical to our own and who are only removed from ourselves by a fleeting moment of geological time, but who grew up in societies whose beliefs and priorities were often much different than those of the modern world, then the rudiments of understanding may lie within our grasp.

There are no chariots of the gods or other divine interventions in this story, nor any cause to think that human intelligence was implanted from another world. What does emerge in each succeeding chapter is that the ancient populations of the British Isles were far more talented, and their undertakings infinitely better organized and co-ordinated, than we once thought. Moreover, with all these resources and abilities, time and again we find the people who lived by peasant subsistence-farming devoting incredible energies to the construction of burial mounds, stone circles and other monuments which yielded them absolutely nothing in the way of material wellbeing.

One way to approach the mysteries described in this book involves logical deduction and the assumption that things were done for rational reasons. This approach may sometimes produce the most sterile conclusions, for one only needs to look at the behaviour of modern men to realize that human actions may be anything but rational, while in other cases the rationality involved may be part of an unfamiliar system of logic. For example, the moated manors of medieval East Anglia may seem to represent a sensible approach to the problem of defending a home, until one looks closely at the surrounding moat and sees that it is generally narrow and often breached by open causeways. Perhaps, then, the moats are a response to the problem of ill-drained ground? In fact, one finds streams being diverted from their natural courses to top up the moats. Logic seems to produce no rational answer until one realizes, as did my friend Chris Taylor, that the moats belong neither to a defensive, nor to an economic system, but to a social one – the moats are status symbols. The purposes of human behaviour, often highly elaborate and – in many eyes – completely irrational, may be quite beyond retrieval by archaeological means. Who, discovering a brass hunting horn a thousand years from now, could postulate (and be believed) that it was an artefact from a sub-culture in which members of a twentieth-century landed élite, who wore red coats (which they insisted were pink), pursued an inedible animal and daubed initiates with its blood?

Archaeological evidence is severely limited in providing solutions to many of our puzzles. Although one cannot rule out the possibility of new discoveries to rank with those of the dating revolutions of the 1950s and 1960s (described in Chapter 1), excavations often yield only fragments of the most durable knick-knacks of material lifestyle, which tell us next to nothing about the beliefs, priorities, society or politics of the men and women who once owned them. It is probably true to say that archaeology on its own (as opposed to the historical study of contemporary documents) is unable to demonstrate that a Norman conquest of England took place in 1066. If the entombed evidence for an event so recent and so much a watershed in the development of the nation is obscure, it is sobering to think of what momentous prehistoric revolutions might be lost to modern man. The members of the public at large, who directly or indirectly fund British archaeology, are seldom interested in the typologies of different kinds of pot or urn, but they are generally eager to learn about the beliefs or day-to-day lifestyles of bygone societies. These are the very questions which archaeology is often least able to consider.

Many archaeologists would also regard them as being the most important questions, but those bold diggers of the past who were not afraid to speculate were as often as not spectacularly wrong. With the postwar upsurge in the outpourings of a band of authors described by the professionals as 'the lunatic fringe', a stereotype of the academic or serious part-time archaeologist has been created which is quite unjust. The expert is cast as a Blimplike figure, bound to the conservative vested interests of establishment science and wilfully blind to the revelations of the fringe doctrines. In fact, while most workers in or around the discipline could nominate one or two scholars whose arrogance and intolerance are legendary, such figures are unrepresentative of the profession. Approaching archaeological questions from a background in geography, I am surprised by how adventurous many archaeologists are prepared to be. The subject regularly produces figures who are ready to paint on a broad canvas and speculate on the basis of the few facts that are available to them. Gordon Childe from the last generation of academics and Euan MacKie from the present are two of those whose writings fire the imagination.

Many readers may be surprised that more of the fringe theories are not represented in this book. The answer is simply that they do not stand up to rigorous objective enquiry, and if a mystery has no real existence outside the uncritical imagination, it is not a mystery at all – or at least not one of the kind with which we are concerned. No notion has been rejected because it is controversial or upsets any sacrosanct applecarts; considerable numbers have been bypassed because they are unconvincing and the only mystery concerns the gullibility of their adherents. If we look at the achievements of bygone cultures, we can only conclude that fact is far more exciting, thought-provoking and amazing than fiction.

Throughout the writing of this book I have been conscious of the potential contribution that the keen and gifted reader might be able to make in the solution of the various riddles described. Some fields of enquiry are so technical and complex that even the acknowledged world experts are unable to agree upon techniques, let alone results. This is one of the reasons why I have not allowed the section on prehistoric astronomy to dominate the text. There are other areas, however, where the mystery might yield to new insights by an informed outsider. I would place the code of the Pictish symbol stones in this category, though it has remained unbroken through almost a century of concentrated enquiry.

A word of explanation is necessary on the presentation of dates in this book. These are all calculated according to the Carbon-14 dating methods described in Chapter 1 (pp. 16–19), where I also analyse the recent discovery that such dates are usually to be revised upwards, sometimes making archaeological finds far older than was originally thought. The work of recalibrating Carbon-14 dates according to comparison with the tree-rings of the bristlecone pine has so far been taken back only to about 5000 BC; so dates prior to this, and any later ones that have not been recalibrated, have been taken as estimates of the latest dating possible, and not as 'true dates'. In order to keep the presentation of dates as clear as possible for the general reader, however, it was decided to avoid loading the text by expressing dates, as is conventional in the specialist literature, either in years 'BC' (meaning recalibrated or 'true dates') or in years 'bc' (meaning simple Carbon-14 dates). The familiar 'BC' has been used throughout, but is prefixed with the word 'before' if the date is not a recalibrated one. In general, the further back one goes, the greater the margin of error; so while a Carbon-14 date of 1000 BC might be recalibrated to 1200 BC, a date of 3000 BC might become 3800 BC. Earlier dates may prove to follow the same pattern, but it would be unwise to assume too much at this stage. Pending the results of further work on this subject it would be wrong not to warn the reader of yet one more riddle that still awaits its answer.

The former administrative counties have been retained in this text because, particularly where Scotland is concerned, they provide a much finer network of areas and often relate more closely than their modern counterparts to the old man-land associations.

Measurements of distance and size have been given as a rule in imperial units. The only exceptions to this are when figures are quoted from publications in which the decimal system is used. In such cases it seemed superfluous to convert all the figures to the other standard, and cumbersome to provide both forms.

Perhaps one more point deserves to be made. The words 'heritage' and

'conservation' recur in many clichés, but one doubts that the public is fully aware of how desperately underfinanced and understaffed the conservation of the British heritage really is. While a few professional archaeologists and their invaluable part-time assistants desperately engage in rescue digs, scurrying like frightened rabbits in advance of motorways, airports and the other paraphernalia of modern civilization, hardly any major excavations are in hand. By and large, the remnants of Britain's past are not being conserved at all, but destroyed at an unprecedented rate. In the week that this introduction was written, the Ministry of Agriculture announced its intention to sell off its land holding at Laxton in Nottinghamshire, where a unique survival of medieval strip farming is visited by 10,000 schoolchildren each year. An expert on farming systems, Dr Joan Thirsk of Oxford University, declared the site to be as irreplaceable as Stonehenge. We cannot assume that the monuments which make up Britain's incomparable assemblage of ancient manmade features will always be here to impress and astonish.

Those who attempt to write books whose topics span a variety of subject boundaries may agree that there tend to be two types of experts: those who reply to letters giving a wealth of assistance which is much more than the enquirer had any right to expect, and those who do not reply at all. From the former category I would like to thank Cherry Lavell, the editor of *British Archaeological Abstracts*; Euan MacKie of the Hunterian Museum, Glasgow; Hugh L. Porteous of Sheffield City Polytechnic; Alan Small of Dundee University; and finally the Warden of Wandlebury. Any mistakes are entirely my own, and as our knowledge of landscape history progresses, doubtless some more will be revealed.

Each chapter of this book is followed by a Gazetteer section, containing a list of sites which are discussed in the chapter, and some directions on how to reach them. The list of sites is by no means exhaustive, but is intended to help readers discover at least a few of the sites for themselves, and to understand this writer's own fascination for the British landscape and its history.

The remnants of medieval strip farming at Laxton in Nottinghamshire.

Chapter 1

Time and the tombs

DURING THE FIRST HALF of this century, archaeology did not paint a very flattering picture of Britain. The islands were cast as an Atlantic backwater of Europe, far removed from the mainstreams of development and depending on continental invasions for the periodic injection of new ideas. The Continent of Europe in its turn was seen as a generally backward area which derived its stimuli from the dynamic theatres of action in the Mediterranean and Middle East. Underpinning many of the concepts involved was the doctrine of diffusionism, which held that few discoveries were made independently and that most important advances could be traced back via invasion or trade routes to a civilized heartland.

Carried to extremes the argument attributes the great American civilizations to Egyptian culture bearers. During the interwar period Elliot Smith attempted to link Egypt with cultures as widely removed as those of Peru, Japan, New Zealand and Madagascar. More recently it has become fashionable to assume that if one can sail a bundle of reeds, balsa wood or old newspapers from one place to another without drowning, then prehistoric contacts have been demonstrated.

During the last three decades, two complete revolutions in scientific dating techniques have set some old systems of belief on their heads. West European advances in building and technology, which were thought to be based on degraded civilized prototypes, are sometimes found to be older than the supposed originals, and Britain begins to emerge as a place with its own dynamic and inspiration.

The old system of dating relied heavily on the expert study of typologies, according to which similar objects share the same source. It also rested on the assumptions of backwater and heartland diffusionism, and consequently any artefacts or techniques unearthed in the 'backwaters' were judged younger than the 'civilized' prototypes. For the theories to fit the facts, very elaborate chains of connection were necessary to link the 'younger and degraded' products of Atlantic Europe to their assumed originals. In the absence of an objective and reliable archaeological clock, typological study linked to diffusionism was the best method of dating that was available. In fact, it was no better than the often misleading assumptions upon which it rested.

Many of the artefacts unearthed in the civilized world of the pre-Christian era could be dated; in the nineteenth century the script of the ancient Egyptians was decoded and the thirty-one Egyptian dynasties and other events recorded by the ancient scribes were anchored in time in a chronology which now extends back to 3100 BC, the beginning of the

Interior of the megalithic tomb at Knowth in Ireland.

13

Egyptian Old Kingdom. The resulting timescale formed a tolerably stable pillar set in a morass of temporal uncertainty and diligent efforts were made to link distant cultural developments to this support.

According to the old system (which was current until at least the mid-1950s, and survived in some recognizable form into the next decade), in about 2000 BC, Atlantic Europe – then thinly populated by the hunting and fishing peoples of the Mesolithic period – received a visitation and large-scale settlement by seaborne colonists. The impact of these peoples, who introduced farming and buried their dead in imposing collective tombs, was more profound than anything that could have been accomplished by people in Western Europe before or since. The Atlantic margins were launched culturally from a nearly stagnant position, circumscribed by the vicissitudes of the hunting life, on a course of development which continues to the modern age.

If this version of prehistory is correct, then a thousand years after the dawn of the Old Kingdom in Egypt, Western Europe remained a backward place, its meagre population of savages struggling to survive by gathering shellfish and grubbing for roots, fishing the rivers and swamps and pursuing the reindeer while knowing nothing of pottery or agriculture. The arrival of a seaborne colonization by a people with the ability to sail the oceans, raise crops and erect massive monuments in stone must have resulted in a dazzling explosion of progress and change affecting European development more profoundly than the Renaissance or the Reformation.

Scholars were not entirely in agreement as to who these remarkable immigrants were, or whence they came. They called them 'The Megalithic People' (from the Greek: *megas* = big and *lithos* = stone) because they were believed to be responsible for the construction of structures such as the chambered tombs, which incorporated stones of great size. It was widely accepted that the colonists were engaged in a great missionary movement, perhaps the devotees of a Mother Goddess religion. It was also generally believed that the megalithic rite of collective burial originated in the eastern Mediterranean; that the first westerly landfall by the missionaries from a civilized world occurred in Spain and Portugal; and that from Spain there was a movement to pioneer Atlantic seaways, exporting the megalithic culture and beliefs to Brittany, Denmark, France, Britain and the western Baltic. Some students of the typology of tombs concluded that there might have been two megalithic movements, the first current moving along the Atlantic seaways from Spain and Portugal to export simple tombs or dolmens to the northern lands, and the second taking the more sophisticated 'passage grave', with its central burial chamber and entrance corridor, from Los Millares in the south-east of Spain to Brittany and thence to Ireland and, ultimately, Orkney.

Given the prevailing diffusionist outlook, a place of origin for the megalithic missionaries had to be found. Several researchers thought that this could be located in Early Minoan Crete, where circular stone tombs were known to date from 2500 BC. All the assumptions of current thinking required a civilized or semi-civilized homeland for the migrants and the general area of the Aegean seemed the most likely, though the actual evidence for contact between Spain and the Aegean was rather thin and ambiguous. While the details often seemed to be blurred, most students in the 1960s were (like myself) taught the remarkable saga of the megalithic missionaries, who plied the oceans to bring the seeds of advancement, the first agricultural revolution and a compelling religion to lighten the darkness of Atlantic Europe.

One effect of the dating revolutions is simply this: to show that the oldest of the European megalithic tombs date from well before 4000 BC and are found not in Spain, but in Brittany, while Britain has many examples which are older than 3000 BC. The first Egyptian stone pyramids were not constructed until about 2700 BC and it is clear that, instead of the old vision of an Atlantic backwater which received its first push in the direction of farming and civilization from the Aegean via Spain around 2500–2000 BC, we find a number of Western European provinces pioneering the building of massive stone structures. The oldest of these structures which has so far been dated (at Kercado, in Brittany, dated to 4800 BC) precedes the Egyptian stone pyramid by perhaps a little more than 2000 years.

The edifices built on the old chronologies crumbled during the 1960s in the face of new dating evidence. In his book *Before Civilization*, published in 1973, Professor Colin Renfrew summarized the case against the old diffusionist assumptions, and presented the case for a culturally far more advanced prehistoric Europe. But this did not dispel the mysteries concerning the diffusion of tomb types within Europe – in Brittany, Ireland and the British mainland.

At least the old version of Neolithic development in Europe was organized around some sort of near consensus, but its demolition encouraged all manner of unanswered questions. There is no longer much point in questioning the broad outlines which the new datings have established, even if the controversy concerning the precision of the new techniques is not completely resolved. Diffusionism itself is not dead and plainly it is possible for an innovation to be attributed to trading contacts or colonization rather than to independent invention. However, if the civilized East is to be credited with a megalithic movement, some older heartland than Crete has to be found. A completely revamped interpretation of the Atlantic tombs in terms of Mediterranean and Near-Eastern influences and origins was duly developed by the Scottish archaeologist Euan MacKie himself a leading exponent and advocate of the new dating techniques.

Of course, the problem with the Neolithic tombs of Atlantic Europe, examined from a neo-diffusionist point of view, is that they are too old for most known civilized societies of the Near East and eastern Mediterranean to have played any part in their introduction. Even so, a number of workers believe that, despite some fairly obvious regional variations, there are sufficient similarities between the tombs of Spain, Portugal, Brittany, Britain and Denmark for some sort of international movement to have been essential for their dispersion. The ideas which Dr MacKie advanced in 1977 are far from proved and are based on many different factors, including C. D. Darlington's ideas about the stimulating social effects of genetic and cultural mixing; highly controversial notions concerning standardized international systems of prehistoric measurement (explained pp. 63–4), as well as new dating material recently available from ancient Mesopotamian cities.

Inside the large megalithic tomb of Cueva de Menga in Spain.

Dr MacKie revives the idea of a religious revolution as the motive force for the diffusion of the rite of collective burial, but the origin of the revolution is placed far enough back in time not to affront the new dating systems. His theories suggest that a religious revolution took place in Mesopotamia in the fifth millennium BC, in an area where agriculture was already established. A professional priesthood, he believes, developed within the Mesopotamian peasant society and its beliefs and customs were then exported as the movement gained in strength. Members of this priesthood took their advanced ideas on astronomy and numerology, their doctrines and institutions to Western Europe. There, they mixed with the priestly orders of the barbaric tribal societies, invigorating the local populations both culturally and genetically. Although the exported religion provided an underlying unity, it was probably not possible for regular maritime contacts with the Mesopotamian heartland to be maintained, while the survival of local customs and beliefs is said to account for variations between various collective tombs and their associated rites.

The tombs themselves are regarded as the temples and graves of the priestly caste. Dr MacKie believes that, early in the third millennium BC, the advanced Neolithic people of Portugal, vitalized by renewed contacts with the Aegean and Near-Eastern worlds, moved northward to undertake a fruitful fusion with the leading castes in the British Isles, producing a dynamic theocracy centred on southern England. These leaders, he believes, were responsible for the construction of the great stone-circle temples. The distinctiveness of Western Europe according to this thesis is due not so much to the Roman heritage as to the progress and unity established in the course of the Neolithic religious revolution.

'Diffusionism' and 'independent development' are not very exciting words, but they represent fundamentally opposed outlooks on many prehistoric problems. The real crux of the matter lies in whether one can regard the different types of megalithic tomb which appeared in most parts of Western Europe within a timespan of one-and-a-half millennia as the products of local inventiveness and minimal cross-cultural influences, or whether they represent local variations on a common theme of international religion and custom which can only have been dispersed by seagoing missionaries. Within the timespan allowed, did a number of Atlantic cultures converge independently upon the practice of burying their dead collectively in massive and imposing tombs, and are the variations between the different tomb forms sufficiently small to be explained as local preferences and responses to different geological conditions? Ironically, while the new dating techniques anchor the tombs to a timescale, these questions tend to revolve around the old methods of typological study.

What then is this dating revolution which has upset so many learned applecarts? In fact, like the Russian Revolution of 1917, there are two revolutions, the second of which intensified the radicalism of the first. The initial revolution was based on the discovery and application of the radio-carbon dating technique, of which many readers will know a little. The second revolution involved the linking of Carbon-14 dates to a tree-ring calendar and forced them to be reappraised and recalibrated. When the first C-14 dates became available, many learned reputations were jolted and their

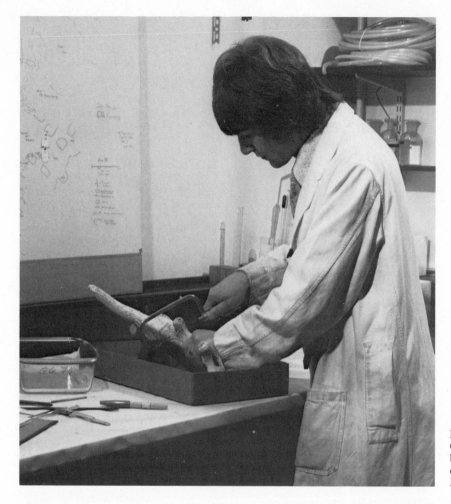

Piece of antler from the Grimes Graves Flint Mines, Norfolk, being prepared for Carbon-14 dating analysis in the British Museum.

owners severely ruffled, because much was shown to be older than had previously been proclaimed. The tree-ring revolution heaped insult on injury because the older C-14 dates in particular were shown not to be too old, as had been claimed, but too young.

Archaeologists had always dreamed of possessing a clock which could date the objects which they unearthed with an accuracy free of all the uncertainties, controversies and subjectivity which the stratigraphical and typological methods involved. Few would have dared believe that a technique so wonderful as C-14 dating might ever be developed.

Radio-carbon dating is made possible by the fact that all living organisms absorb carbon from their air or sea environments and convert it to carbon-dioxide, which is returned to the environment. A minute proportion of atmospheric carbon is in the form of the radioactive isotope Carbon-14, which is created in the upper atmosphere through the bombardment of nitrogen nuclei by cosmic rays to produce carbon atoms having extra neutrons in their nuclei. The excess of neutrons makes the C-14 atoms unstable; eventually the nuclei disintegrate and the atoms convert to atoms of Nitrogen-14. This process of decay takes place at a fixed rate: after about

5730 years – according to most scholars – half of the C-14 has decayed; and after a further similar period, half of the remaining half has decayed; and so on. It follows that any material which was once living and absorbing C-14 from its environment can be dated by measuring the remaining level of C-14. The first dating revolution followed the discovery of the C-14 method by Professor W. Libby of the University of Chicago in 1949 and the application of the technique shortly afterwards to fragments of organic material, such as charcoal or grain, which had hitherto been undatable.

Many shocks ensued. The date of the development of farming in the Near East was pushed back 3000 years beyond the previously accepted date of 4500 BC; the Neolithic in Britain, which was thought to have commenced around 2000 BC, was predated by at least another thousand years; and in Greece the beginning of farming was found to be almost twice as ancient as the experts had believed.

The C-14 dates depended upon very precise laboratory techniques for the measurement of the C-14 residuals in the scraps of organic material sent for analysis and did not claim to provide exact calendar dates – only probabilities that a measured date lay within a stated timespan. Nevertheless, by the early 1960s most archaeologists had come to recognize the worth of the unexpected clock which nuclear physics had provided and, though the turmoil and trauma had not completely subsided, the second dating revolution began to gather momentum.

It was common knowledge that the stages in the growth of trees were charted by the formation of annual rings. It was also known that in favourable years a tree will make a more substantial growth than in a year of drought, late frosts or cool summers. It was therefore easy to deduce that a succession of years with a particular combination of good and poorer growth conditions would leave an individual fingerprint in the pattern of tree-rings which are formed, and it seemed highly unlikely that any long forty- or fifty-year sequences would be exactly alike. These simple deductions laid the foundations for tree-ring dating.

The technique is especially valuable in two ways. Firstly, growth patterns can be obtained from timbers of known age and long series of tree-ring fingerprints can be strung together to produce graphs of growth patterns which span many centuries; the ring patterns discovered in undated timbers can then be compared along the graph until a 'best fit' zone is found which represents the age of the undated timber. Secondly, and more central to our theme, the extension of the tree-ring sequence backward through time provides science with a yardstick against which C-14 dates can be tested.

One of the assumptions upon which the C-14 method rested was that the level of C-14 in the atmosphere was always constant. Events proved this invalid. The evidence that the C-14 clock needed to be reset came from research on the remarkably long-lived bristlecone pine, a tree which grows in the White Mountains of California. Examples of these trees were discovered which were up to 4900 years old, while the tree-ring record of the bristlecone pine has now been extended beyond 6000 BC by using the evidence of dead as well as living trees. The growth-rings of the bristlecone pine provided organic material of a known antiquity against which the dates offered by C-14 analysis could be compared.

By 1967 it was clear that the simple clock of C-14 needed considerable adjustment. The amount of C-14 in the environment is known to have fluctuated, though over the past 1200 years these fluctuations have been small. The further one goes back, however, the greater seems to be the discrepancy between past and present C-14 levels. The effect of the tree-ring based recalibration of the C-14 clock was not, however, to reduce the dates which many had thought to be too old, but just the reverse – the prehistoric dates were pushed even further back in time, and the older the date, the greater its readjustment.

The exact amount of recalibration necessary in relation to any particular date given in a C-14 laboratory is somewhat questionable, and various slightly different recalibration curves have been published. They take the form of graphs with both C-14 and tree-ring curves shown; the curves themselves are not standardized: some show an even C-14 line, others show it full of little variations which may represent short-term fluctuations in the atmospheric C-14 content; at a few points, more than one recalibrated date is possible. Further complications may result if the C-14 level in the environment has fluctuated from region to region, as well as from time to time.

There is no doubting the revolutionary impact of the C-14 clock, described by Professor Glyn Daniel as 'perhaps the greatest breakthrough in the development of archaeology'. When the C-14 information is added to the tree-ring evidence the effect is plainly to show that the prehistoric peoples of Britain produced achievements in the pacification of the landscape whose important consequences were experienced at dates when they were once judged to be savages. After the close of the last Ice Age and its bitter periglacial aftermath came the Mesolithic period, during which a relatively thin population struggled to survive following the northward migration of the herds which had flourished on the open plains of the Arctic-like tundra. Before the dating revolutions it was seen as an almost interminable period during which there only emerged the faintest awareness of the possibilities of raising livestock and moulding the environment. Now it appears as a stepping stone between the hunting cultures of the Palaeolithic on the one hand, and the farmers and raisers of mighty monuments of the Neolithic on the other. In 1954 a learned and gifted archaeologist dated the beginning of this Neolithic Age to 2000 BC. Radio-carbon dating methods produced uncalibrated dates of up to 3795 ± 90 BC, while the recalibration of these dates suggests an age which began in about 4580 BC. Similarly, the earliest Bronze Age date is now given as *c*. 2600 BC, more than 1000 years older than the experts of the 1950s would have allowed.

This chapter began with the saga of the megalithic tombs; there is one tomb, however – if, indeed, it is a tomb – that is particularly mysterious: Silbury Hill in Wiltshire. It is surely the most neglected of the mighty prehistoric monuments of the British Isles, and why this should be so is not easy to understand. At the height of the tourist season of 1979 I arrived at the Avebury stone circle quite early in the morning in advance of the anticipated throng of visitors. By late morning the car-park at Avebury was packed with coaches bearing visitors from many parts of the world. From

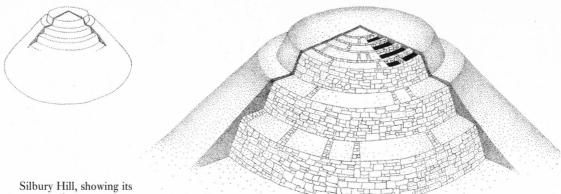

Silbury Hill, showing its construction.

this car-park the unnatural cone of Silbury Hill is plainly seen, yet the enormous manmade mound had attracted only two visitors. In the course of three hours in the middle of the day I doubt that more than a dozen tourists came to gaze at this largest of prehistoric monuments; meanwhile, nearby Avebury was thronged with people and Stonehenge, I am sure, must have positively swarmed with them. This latter monument would, incidentally, sit quite comfortably on the flat Silbury summit.

Nearly everything about Silbury is known except the answer to the most important question of all – its purpose. Since an excavation by Professor R. J. C. Atkinson in the years 1967–70, we even know the time of year when the work was begun – late July or early August – for ants equipped with wings which develop at this time of the year were preserved in the turf core. The calibrated C-14 date suggests that the work took place in about 2660 BC, though other systems of calibration could produce a date which is a century or so older. We know how the work was accomplished, and that it was carried out in a series of stages. First, a ring of stakes was used to mark out a circular area 66 feet in diameter; a central mound of clay and flints about 16 feet wide and 3 feet in height was built; and the area within the stakes was then filled with layers of earth, turf, gravel and chalk, raising the work to a height of 17 feet. In the second stage, the diameter of the mound was increased to 240 feet, using chalk blocks. A change of plan came at the end of the second stage when it was decided to raise the height of the mound. A second quarry ditch was opened up further away from the mound and the initial ditch disappeared beneath the expanding hill. The final mound had the structure of a stepped cone and the faces of the steps were reinforced with a revetment of chalk blocks; the steps were then filled to give a smooth sloping profile, with the exception of the uppermost step where the terraced form is still clearly visible. The hill has a total volume of $12\frac{1}{2}$ million cubic feet, of which $8\frac{3}{4}$ million represent material quarried for construction work, while the remainder is composed of a natural pre-existing chalk spur nucleus. Silbury stands 130 feet above the surrounding fields and covers $5\frac{1}{4}$ acres of land.

The stupendous nature of this prehistoric achievement is obvious when we consider the amount of labour involved in its construction. The excavation of building materials alone would have been sufficient to occupy a labour force of 1000 men for around 6 months. The complete task, involving the raising of the mound and all the necessary organization, might have employed 700 men continuously for 10 years, or alternatively, if the work had been done on a seasonal basis, 500 men might have been at work for 30 to 50 years. Clearly, Silbury Hill was not built by ignorant savages; here was a highly organized force of men working under a system of political control which was sufficiently powerful and sophisticated to ensure not only a massive and prolonged system of recruitment, but also the provision of the many essential back-up services that are a vital part of all massive constructional operations. The whole represents an almost incredible accomplishment.

The hill has experienced a number of excavations but has not so far yielded its main secret. There have been six excavations since the late eighteenth century. In 1776 the Duke of Northumberland launched a force of Cornish tin miners to sink a shaft from top to bottom of the mound, while in 1849 a tunnel was driven horizontally along the former ground level at the base of the mound to meet the vertical shaft of 1776 at its centre. No great discoveries were made. Professor Atkinson's excavations included the cutting of a tunnel at a higher level, which then broke into the nineteenth-century tunnel and followed it to the centre of the mound. As a result of these excavations, detailed insights into the constructional techniques and much else were derived. There had been hopes that a tomb might be discovered, but this was not the case.

Archaeological opinion still inclines to the view that Silbury Hill is a gigantic tomb, in some ways a remarkable British equivalent of the pyramids of Egypt. The fact that no tomb has been discovered by no means invalidates this belief. The evidence of other prehistoric burials shows that there is no reason to expect that the burial would be made at the exact centre of the mound, the area explored by the tunnels, and any number of these shafts might be sunk before an eccentrically placed burial could be found. Other explanations apart, the Hill is an enormous proclamation of political muscle and perhaps this function was not lost upon the initiator of the operations. The proximity to the vast Avebury ring, Windmill Hill causewayed camp and the West Kennet long barrow can hardly be coincidental.

An air-view of the earthen mound which covers the burial chambers at West Kennet in Wiltshire.

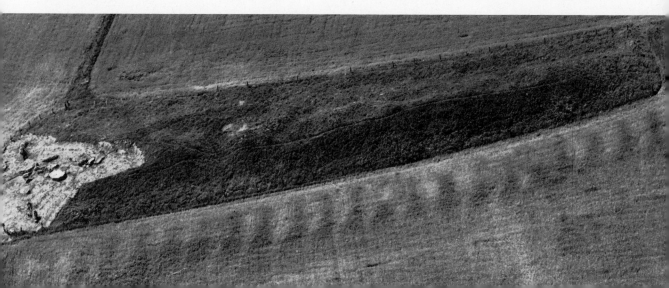

Earlier in this chapter I remarked that clues to the likelihood of a unified megalithic religious revolution may be gained from a typological study of the different forms of tomb used in the rite of collective burial – with all the subjectivity which such study involves. The question of the relationship between the different forms of collective burial is still a matter of great debate and examples of different tomb types are given in the gazetteer section at the end of this chapter. Earthen long barrows may have a pear-shaped plan; occasionally they have a very attenuated form and are known as 'bank barrows', but a very common design is wedge-shaped. Trapezoidal houses of this kind have been discovered in northern and central continental Europe, and it can be argued but not proved that the British long barrows sometimes imitate this form and are thus 'Houses of the Dead'. Sophisticated recent excavation techniques have discovered evidence of wooden or turf mortuary houses within the barrows, obscured by the collapse of the perishable structures. Most skeletons which are found in long barrows consist of a jumble of disarticulated bones and it may be that corpses were left to decompose in the mortuary houses before the final covering of earth was cast up. Not all Neolithic tombs have an elongated form and the famous examples of Newgrange and Maes Howe have a circular inspiration; recent excavations at Mid Gleniron (Wigtownshire) and Camster Long (Caithness) reveal a probably older tradition of burial in simple circular cairns, from which the circular designs may derive.

Neolithic decorations carved on the megaliths at Newgrange passage grave in Ireland.

The corbelled roof of the Knowth burial chamber in Ireland.

The megalithic chambered tomb consists of one or a series of burial chambers set within a mound of earth or stone. While the earthen long barrows were sealed by the enveloping earth mound, the chambered tombs could be re-opened for later interments. Scant respect was then given to the remains of older occupants, which were often roughly swept aside. Sometimes, as in many of the tombs of the Severn valley and Cotswolds area, the tombs have forecourts and galleries from which side chambers lead to the left and right; in some cases false entrances were built, perhaps to deceive tomb robbers. The 'gallery grave' form of chambered tomb has no clear-cut distinction between the entrance passage and the burial chamber proper and the mound is generally elongated, while the mounds which cover 'passage graves' often tend to be circular and there is a clear distinction between the narrow entrance passage and the funerary chamber. The 'portal dolmen' form of chamber tomb is most common in Ireland, but there are examples in Wales and western England. The small, narrowing burial chamber is approached between two vertical stone slabs; another may close the entrance, while a horizontal slab or capstone roofs the structure.

To delve further into the forms of Neolithic burial would be to enter a labyrinth of typological debate in which little is certain and controversy abounds. Experts do not agree on the extent to which local traditions and differences in the geological resources of a region influenced the construction of tombs, or on the stages used in the diffusion of different types, or on whether migration and missionary work played any great part in the adoption of the ritual of collective burial.

Enormous sarsen stones provide the façade at the entrance of the West Kennet long barrow.

It seems that burial in a Neolithic collective tomb was the right of a privileged few, and Dr G. Wainwright estimates that only a handful of Wessex people died each year who merited interment in one or other of the tombs. Although some long barrows continued to be used in the Bronze Age, after about 2500 BC a ritual of individual burial under round barrows began to be adopted; again this form of burial seems to have been reserved for an élite, for even in areas with a dense scatter of Bronze Age barrows these monuments may only have been erected once every two years or so.

Although the reset radio-carbon clock ticks more accurately than before, the measurement of time alone will not solve the mystery of the tombs or tell us whether one of the most formative stages in British development was the product of an alien cult, indigenous ingenuity, or a merging of the two. In the case of the rich interplay of English Church architecture with that of the Continent, the historical records enable us to understand the development of each variant. We find different Romanesque styles adopted by the Saxons and by the Normans, and we can find Continental parallels for the medieval Early English and Decorated styles; while England goes its own way in adopting the Perpendicular manner of the late medieval period. These national styles are conditioned by regional preferences and available building materials in each locality – and a diversity of lovely buildings is the result. But we have no written evidence to help us to unravel the mysteries of the tombs of the Neolithic Age. However, the tombs do tell us of capable and creative peoples, who were so well adjusted to their environments that dozens of peasant farmers could be released from agriculture for weeks on end to construct local mausolea, without bringing about the collapse of their subsistence farming economy.

Addington and Chestnuts Tombs. The village of Addington lies 7 miles WNW of Maidstone in Kent. The Addington tomb is at the W end of the village near the entrance to the Park Farm drive. Its outline is traced by the sarsen stones which formed its kerb. The large stones at the end were its burial chamber. The Chestnuts tomb lies 50 yds to the NW. There is a small entrance fee. It became a rabbit warren until ploughing removed most of the earth covering. The large stones of the burial chamber have been preserved.

Belas Knap. Lies 2 miles S of Winchcombe (7 miles NE of Cheltenham) in Gloucestershire, at the end of a long uphill walk, signposted at a lay-by on the minor road running S towards Charlton Abbots from the A46. Dating from about 3000 BC, it is one of several Neolithic long barrows with false entrances. This one faces a forecourt lying between a pair of horn-shaped banks. Its burial chambers contained 31 skeletons. A man and 5 children seem to have been sealed behind the false entrance in the Early Bronze Age. Restored 1930–1.

Carrowmore. In the Glen of Knocknarea, accessible by a lane circling the S slopes of Knocknarea, in the small peninsula just SW of Sligo (NW coast of Ireland). A remarkable collection of dolmens rivalled only by the assemblage at Carnac in Brittany. Most of the tombs have had their earth covering removed, exposing the stones of the burial chambers.

The Dwarfie Stone. Lies in an isolated valley in the Orkney island of Hoy. This unusual Neolithic tomb has been cut out of a lump of solid rock. A passage 7 ft long, 2 ft 4 ins high and 3 ft wide, with cells to either side, was hewn into a fallen block of red sandstone. It was originally sealed with a slab.

Kits Coty House. Only three massive uprights and a capstone remain of the burial chamber of this long barrow. The mound was once almost 180 ft long. It is signposted from a lay-by on the A229, 1 mile N of Aylesford (between Maidstone and Rochester) in Kent. The jumbled sarsen stones of a chambered tomb, known as Lower Kits Coty or the Countless Stones, lie about 500 yds further S.

Maes Howe. Lies on the mainland island of Orkney, 9 miles W of Kirkwall, beside Loch of Harray. Probably the finest chambered tomb in Europe. The workmanship of the smoothly dressed slabs is unique. The domed mound, 115 ft in diameter and 24 ft high, is surrounded by a shallow ditch. Burial cells adjoin the 15-ft square central chamber, reached by a 36-ft long passage. Its high corbelled roof was destroyed either by Viking plunderers in the 12th cent. or tomb robbers in 1861. The walls bear the world's finest collection of runic inscriptions, left behind by the Vikings, who describe themselves as crusaders.

Men-An-Tol. This peculiar arrangement of stones lies beside a track

The curious stones of the Men-An-Tol monument in Cornwall.

25

The stone partitions in the Mid Howe stalled cairn, Orkney.

The remarkable mound of Silbury Hill in Wiltshire.

near the Madron to Morvah road and opposite the road which leads to Chun Castle (2 miles NW of Penzance) in Cornwall. The origin of the stones is uncertain; they have possibly been moved from a Neolithic burial chamber. The central stone is in the shape of a large upright ring, and folklore holds that victims of back ailments can be cured by passing through it; other legends claim that the stone cures rickets in children.

Mid Howe. This type of Neolithic burial is known as a 'stalled cairn', since upright slabs project from the sides of the central alley, and provide 12 burial compartments along its length. The remains of oxen, sheep and birds found in the tomb are perhaps associated with funeral rites. It was not full when it went out of use. Lies in the Orkneys on the W of Rousay, by Scabra Head cliffs, with Mid Howe broch nearby.

Newgrange. Upstream from Old-bridge in Ireland's Boyne valley (17 miles NW of Dublin). Take the lane leading off the Slane road. It is arguably the most impressive of all megalithic tombs, and is part of a remarkable assemblage known as the Brugh Na Boinne. It is surrounded by a stone circle and a Stone Age cemetery. The Newgrange tomb is 280 ft in diameter, and close to the mound of Dowth, another tomb, 208 ft in diameter. The third gigantic tomb in the area is at Knowth. It was excavated in 1962 when the 114-ft long passage to the central chamber was revealed; a second passage was discovered in 1968. The standing-stones lining all these passages were unusual in being intricately decorated.

Silbury Hill. This enormous man-made mound lies beside the A4, 1 mile S of Avebury (10 miles S of Swindon on the M4). The Roman road makes a detour around the hill. There is a car-park $\frac{1}{4}$ mile away on the A361 between Beckhampton and Avebury, and a lay-by on the A4 serving the West Kennet long

barrow. Both are within easy walking distance.

Three Cornish Quoits. Cornwall contains a number of imposing quoits – the remains of Neolithic tombs which have been stripped of their covering earth mounds. They are known in other parts of the country as dolmens. Lanyon Quoit lies to the N of the road from Madron to Morvah (3 miles NW of Penzance) and was reconstructed in 1824. It consists of an enormous horizontal capstone supported by a trio of massive uprights. Trethevy Quoit is well signposted to the W of the B3254 near St Cleer (3 miles N of Liskeard, 15 miles NW of Plymouth). In appearance if not in its setting it is the most impressive of the quoits, and its seven huge stones support the vast sloping capstone of a burial chamber. A track from the B3306 leads to Zennor Quoit, which lies about 1 mile NW of Zennor (5 miles N of Penzance). The capstone has slipped, but the upright stones define the main burial chamber and its small antechamber.

Wayland's Smithy. A local legend tells that Wayland the Smith forged shoes for the chalk-cut White Horse of Uffington and would mysteriously re-shoe the horse of any traveller who left a silver groat upon the tomb. It can be reached by walking along the Ridgeway where it runs S from the B4507 (1 mile NE of Ashbury, 6 miles E of Swindon on the M4). Particularly significant in the history of Neolithic tombs, because shortly after 14 interments were made in the timber burial chamber of the earlier chalk barrow in 3600 BC, a stone tomb was built over it, consisting of a chamber, 2 transepts, and an impressive facade of upright monoliths. Small stones marked its trapezoidal outline. A 180-ft long mound was constructed of earth excavated from the 2 side ditches. During excavations in the 1920s, 8 skeletons were found near the entrance. The Uffington hillfort and the White Horse are within easy walking distance, and there are magnificent views from the Ridgeway.

West Kennet Long Barrow. It is 350 ft long and one of the largest long barrows in Britain. Remained in use for many centuries, well into the Bronze Age. The line of huge sarsen stones across the entrance dates from the sealing of the tomb, perhaps as late as 2000 BC. Two pairs of chambers flank the gallery that leads to the main chamber. Excavators uncovered at least 46 skeletons and an unceremonious jumble of flints and pottery. The sarsens have been smoothed where they were used to sharpen stone or bronze axes. The tomb can be reached on foot from the lay-by S of the A4, about ½ mile W of the junction with the B4003 to Avebury (10 miles S of Swindon on the M4). There is a fine view of Silbury Hill.

The Whispering Knights. These remains of a portal dolmen form a group of inward inclining uprights and one fallen capstone. Held by local legend to be a group of traitors conspiring against the 'army' of the Rollright stone circle (Chap. 3, p. 72), all petrified by a local witch. Part of the Rollright Stones, they lie beside the minor road which links the A34 and A44 via Little Rollright (3 miles NW of Chipping Norton, 20 miles NW of Oxford); the Whispering Knights stand in a field 350 yds to the E of the circle and are clearly visible from the road.

Wayland's Smithy tomb on the border of Oxfordshire.

The view down the entrance passage of the West Kennet long barrow in Wiltshire.

Legionaries engaged in constructing a Roman road, from Trajan's Column in Rome.

Chapter 2

The vanished wildwood

THE NATURAL FOREST OF BRITAIN – the wildwood – has certainly gone, though few realize the completeness of its disappearance. Much remains mysterious about the manner and timing of its going and, indeed, the very appearance and contents of the ancient forest. It is generally thought, and in many schools still taught, that our prehistoric ancestors were ill-equipped to cope with the serried giants of the lowland forest; their primitive attempts at farming were confined to clearings on the thin soils of the lightly wooded uplands and of the heathlands, where they scratched out a meagre living on the chalk downs and sandy heaths. The Romans, this vision concedes, cleared some farmland from the forest, but the real pioneers, the makers of the British farmland landscape, were the Anglo-Saxons, who brought axes, determination and the heavy plough to bear upon the vast expanses of virgin lowland woodland and initiated a programme of forest clearance which continued right through the Middle Ages. Modern research has begun to paint a very different picture; it portrays a landscape which was in many areas of Britain scarcely more forested when the Saxons arrived than it is today. Moreover, a great deal of this deforestation is seen to date not from the Iron Age or even from the Bronze Age, but to have been accomplished during the Neolithic period, and in some places, even earlier still.

Banished must be the vision of the Stone-Age farmer who, tossed about on nature's tide, ekes out a precarious living in tiny clearings above the dark and unyielding wildwood. The origins of much in the British landscape must be sought not in the days of Bede and Alfred but in the fourth millennium before Christ.

But when had the wildwood itself first developed? After a false start in the centuries before 12,000 BC, which was followed by a sharp deterioration, the climate of Britain began to warm quite rapidly sometime before 8300 BC. The decaying remnants of glaciers disappeared from the northern highlands and the landscape which emerged from the last Ice Age was a wasteland of shattered, ice-scoured rocks in the mountains, with mounds and plains of mud, sand and gravel in the lowlands. Temperatures increased for a thousand years and for the two thousand years which followed Britain was a warm and relatively dry land; in this period it was warmer than it is today, but it became gradually moister until an optimum climate was achieved around 4000 BC. A cooler and drier climate then developed until the onset of a marked deterioration, with an increase in rainfall, which began around 1400 BC and has persisted with fluctuations to the present. There is every reason to suppose that this deterioration will culminate in the very distant future in a new Ice Age which, in the absence of important discoveries in the manipulation of climate, will obliterate our cities and turn the countryside of Britain into an ice-encrusted wilderness; but that is another story and not a problem for our generation.

During the millennia which followed the disappearance of the glaciers, waves of plant species which had been displaced southwards by the advancing ice returned to Britain, and – along with the small and hardier plants which had survived in southern England – they moved northwards across the low-lying plain still connecting Britain to the land mass of the Continent. The first trees to enter Britain on this northern green migration were those which could best tolerate the chill of the post-glacial climate: the birch and the pine. But during the next thousand years they were progressively displaced to the cooler northern uplands by the deciduous species which thrive in a temperate climate.

One of the most important notions in the conceptual armoury of the botanist and ecologist is that of 'climax vegetation': given stable conditions and a sufficient period of competition between rival claimants, the species of vegetation which will become established in any particular environment will be those which are best adapted to its conditions; the climax vegetation will then maintain itself so long as the environment remains stable. Questions about the wildwood, the virgin forests of Britain, are therefore questions about climax vegetation, and they are beginning to yield some surprising answers. As we have seen, during the two millennia leading up to 4000 BC, conditions in Britain were warm, moist and fairly stable and a climax wildwood was established; but by the close of the period, man had begun to make a significant impact upon the forest which so became progressively less 'natural'. Just how significant this impact was remains something of a mystery.

Many of the questions about the natural wildwood are still unanswered, but such researchers as Dr John Birks have now provided us with the basis for a sketch. In England, but only on the northern coastal fringe of the Lake District, in the Highlands of Scotland and over the western mountains of Ireland, the wildwood was dominated by those hardy rivals, the birch and the pine; elsewhere in Ireland, in south-western Wales, and perhaps in Cornwall, the hazel and the elm were the leading species, while the uplands of northern and western England, the remainder of Wales, Scotland south of the Highlands and the foothills of Ireland's western mountains were shaded by oak and hazel.

The evidence for southern and midland England has proved difficult to obtain, but as pieces are added to the jigsaw, some surprises emerge. The woodland here must have been varied, with ash, maple, hornbeam and elm among the many species represented. Traditionally, and until quite recently, it was assumed that the lowland wildwood was dominated by the oak; this was the tree so often chosen to symbolize English virtues, which for thousands of years provided the framework for British homes and which for centuries was the backbone of the fleet. It appears in fact that the commonest, the most dominant tree in the lowland wildwood was none of those that we have mentioned, but that unobtrusively graceful tree, the lime, which began its widely victorious advance across the English countryside some 8–9000 years ago. When the town makers of the last hundred years

The Major Oak in Nottingham's Sherwood Forest.

selected the stately lime to add grace to so many English avenues they can scarcely have realized that in a small way they were re-creating a morsel of the vanished wildwood. They favoured the lime in part for its speed of growth and its resilience, and – though it is far from being our commonest tree today – these qualities must have helped it to gain mastery in many a woodland contest. Of the other common British trees, the alder was an early arrival, establishing itself strongly on the damper lands; the beech and the holly seem to have been assisted in their dispersion by human interference with the natural forest; the sweet chestnut was a Roman introduction; and the now widespread sycamore did not arrive until the Middle Ages.

The wildwood must have been a beautiful place, with towering limes, elms and oaks, with hazel and elder fruiting in the underwood while deer fed in sun-dappled glades. It must also have been as far removed from the sombre sterile monotony of the modern commercial plantation of close-packed conifers in aspect as it is in time. As the recent biographer of the wildwood, Oliver Rackham, points out, we would be in a better position to reconstruct the appearance of the wildwood if we knew more about the way in which dead trees rotted under natural British conditions. If they rotted rapidly at the base, then the calm of the forest would have been punctuated by the crashing of dead trees and the glades which were blasted out by the falling giants would have been a frequent feature of the woodland landscape.

From *The Forest Trees of Britain*, Johns, 1886. The Lime Tree.

The Ash.

(*Above left*) The Purley Beeches.

(*Above*) The Elm.

The Scots Pine.

33

On the other hand, if the trees decayed gradually in an upright position, the glades would have been smaller and the woodland more continuous. Areas of even, near-natural temperate forest are few and far between in the modern world, and none of them reflects exactly the subtle conditions of the British wildwood, which cannot be reconstructed by analogy. As Rackham points out, we do not know how open the wildwood was, or whether it consisted of patches of trees all germinating, maturing and dying together, or whether there was an intermixture of trees of all ages, sizes and species.

Another approach to the problem has been provided by D. P. Kirby, who asks, 'What then would it have been like to have penetrated into an Old English forest?' His analysis runs as follows:

There will in fact have been an infinite variety of trees and shrubs, as indicated by place-names, and we should probably think in terms of what has been called 'the constantly moving mosaic' of the forest. Close canopy woods will probably have been free of undergrowth and dark and humid even on a clear day. In some parts there is likely to have been a ground layer of dead wood, or a deep tangle of dead trees, together with patches of matted undergrowth where fallen trees let in light. . . . A more open canopy oakwood on clays and loams would provide a rich habitat for a variety of woodland plants (e.g. creeping buttercup and meadow sweet in wetter areas, or wild hyacinth (bluebell), primroses, violets, wood anemones, lesser celandine, and wood forget-me-not). Festoons of twining honeysuckle, curling up and round trees, are actually causing distortion in some cases, and creeping, climbing ivy draping itself round trees to the extent of handicapping growth, would be familiar features.

This last environment is likely to have been the most attractive form of forest, for where the leafy canopy was more open still, the undergrowth was likely to be more formidable: 'Thorn bushes and holly trees or a ground cover saturated with briar, bramble and some bracken, liberally impregnated with stinging nettles, forming an ever extending mass of prickly vegetation ranging from two feet to twelve feet high, could present an intractable barrier.' While medieval woodland was carefully tended and manicured and would seem very tidy to our eyes, the wildwood, though often beautiful, would have seemed an untidy place.

In the course of this century, scientists have learned how to decipher the evidence left in physical traces of the vanished wildscape, while the development of radio-carbon dating techniques allows some of the evidence to be located in time through their association with datable organic remains. Insects, such as beetles, and molluscs, such as snails, are both very sensitive to environmental conditions and particular species will only flourish within a narrow range of conditions and surroundings. The presence of their chitinous skeletons and shells within datable layers of soil may allow a reconstruction of former environments, though by far the most useful evidence for the wildwood and for man's assault upon it has come from the analysis of ancient pollen grains, which are abundantly preserved in the soil layers of old bogs and ponds.

The pollen record is not, however, completely straightforward: the number of trees of different species which grew in a particular area at a particular time is not simply proportional to the number of different types of pollen grain that we may count in a datable layer of soil. Pollen may drift into an area from outside on the wind, while some varieties are more resistant to decay than others; some trees, such as oak, produce a superabundance of pollen and this may tempt one to exaggerate their presence in a landscape. In contrast to the oak, lime relies not on the wind, but upon insects for the dispersion of its pollen; it produces much less and is under-represented in a simple pollen count. In spite of all these difficulties, many of the secrets of the prehistoric landscape are beginning to yield themselves to the pollen analysts and it could well be that no single specialist branch of science will do more to assist our understanding of British prehistory during the remaining years of this century.

The pollen evidence tells us much about the species of tree in the wildwood, and a little about its appearance. Lowly but light-loving plants, such as grasses and willow-herb, are present in the prehistoric pollen record and point to the existence of open glades within the wildwood. Many of these glades must have been rent open by a toppling giant, a lime, an oak or elm, and preserved as open herbage by grazing animals – red deer and roe deer, aurochs and perhaps the elk or moose – which nibbled out the saplings which attempted to reclaim the glade for the forest.

Other evidence suggests that, at least in some places, the trees were quite densely packed and obliged to soar upwards in order to reach the light; this competition between neighbours urged trees to reach heights seldom if ever attained in the parkland or hedgerow. The most substantial relics of the wildwood are the blackened bog oaks of the East Anglian fenlands, which regularly emerge as ploughing and peat-consuming bacteria lower the level of the land. The well-preserved trunks are not only those of oak, but include yew, pine and willow; the trees are the remains of forest which died by suffocation as a result of increasing dampness associated with peat accumulation about their roots around 5000 BC. Some of these trunks shot upwards for 60 or 70 feet before the first branch was reached.

As the wildlife and vegetation returned to Britain after the last Ice Age, they were met and followed by man; at first he must have been little more than a part of the natural order, a gatherer of fruit and berries – but primarily a hunter and fisherman – competing for the ample resources of deer, wild oxen, wild boar, small game and fish with other predators, the bear, lynx, wolf and otter, all of which must have avoided him as best they could. Before too long, however, man began to break the ecological links which held nature in equilibrium and slowly he bent the environment to his will.

During the past decade a body of evidence has built up which suggests that man was delivering a sustained and considerable onslaught upon the natural woodland of the British Isles not only in the Neolithic period, but also before, during the Mesolithic.

The evidence of Mesolithic forest clearance is insufficient for us to construct a clear picture of its extent, but excavations at site after site, from the Pennines to Sussex and from Suffolk to Dartmoor, are revealing traces of charcoal of Mesolithic date or of the Mesolithic displacement of forest by plants which can survive after burning, such as grasses, bracken and hazel. The evidence of fire is widespread and indisputable, and while fire will devastate wide areas of dried-out coniferous forest under natural conditions,

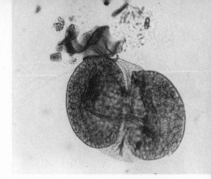

This pollen grain of the Scots Pine comes from Palaeolithic deposits at Broxbourne.

A modern pollen grain of the Scots Pine.

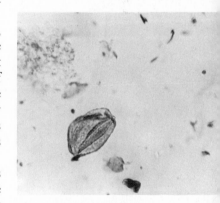

A Bronze Age pollen grain of the oak, from Sutton Hoo.

A modern oak pollen grain.

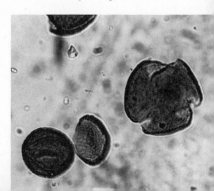

it does not seem to make much impact without a considerable amount of human assistance upon deciduous forest of the kind which blanketed much of Mesolithic Britain.

Fire was the servant of man from distant Palaeolithic times and, if Mesolithic man used fire to clear away large areas of the wildwood, it seems reasonable to suggest that burning was an invaluable means of flushing out game as part of his hunting drives. It might be suggested that man was deliberately seeking to create open hunting ranges, devoid of wooded refuges, and grassy plains which would support a heavier population of game. There may, however, be an even more remarkable solution, for evidence from the Continent seems to show that the domestication of livestock, which marks the beginning of man's career as a farmer, dates back beyond the Neolithic period and into the Mesolithic. With this in mind, some excavations carried out in the late 1950s at Oakhanger near Selborne (Hants) may prove to be a small landmark in British archaeology, for a Mesolithic level in the soil revealed a remarkable concentration of ivy pollen. Such an accumulation is quite unnatural, since ivy produces very little pollen, and the only convincing explanation which has been offered suggests that the ivy was gathered in large quantities as winter fodder. Ivy is not poisonous to livestock and one animal that relishes it in winter is the red deer.

The possibilities of Mesolithic interference go further still. It was once thought safe to assume that, as one form of climax vegetation or another established itself in the various parts of Britain, each enjoyed several millennia of natural stability before man took a hand in the affairs of nature. However, Mesolithic man arrived in Britain with the returning woodland and the effects of his systematic burning may have prevented forest from ever establishing itself in some areas where it would, in the natural order of things, have flourished. Research published in 1976 seems to show that, through his calculated use of fire, Mesolithic man prevented the natural forest from gaining a foothold on the upper slopes and plateaux of the Pennines above 1000 feet, where one would have expected it to be found. The whole question of the natural or unnatural origins of the upland moorlands of Britain is a matter of some mystery at present; one school of thought holds that the replacement of the upland forest by grasses and moorland plants was a natural event brought about by an increase in rainfall which occurred before 5500 BC and caused the forest to be engulfed in spreading blanket bog. Supporters of Professor G. W. Dimbleby's ideas, on the other hand, argue that the blanket bog spread because man had removed the trees which drained the land through transpiration, with each mature oak absorbing through its roots, and liberating through its leaves, an average of seven gallons of water each day.

One final item, which leaves us in a state of tantalizing uncertainty, is worth pondering before we turn to the equally controversial realms of the Neolithic. Between the great Ice Ages, more than 150,000 years ago, human families lived at Swanscombe near the Thames estuary; their remains include general purpose flint axes and they are associated with flints that show signs of burning. Interglacial remains of human occupation at Hoxne in Suffolk include flint tools which were found with charcoal, while the

A Neolithic timber routeway across the marshes of the Somerset Levels: the Abbot's Way.

pollen evidence depicts a decline in forest and a rise in grassland pollen. It could be that man was manipulating the British landscape in the temperate era before the last Ice Age had even begun.

About 4000 BC, or a little later, just after the dawn of the Neolithic Age and at the time when Britain was basking in its best ever post-glacial climate, a curious and remarkable event took place; this is known as the Elm Decline. It occurred with great suddenness and was remarkably widespread. In pollen studies made throughout the country it is reflected in a drastic decline in the elm and dramatic increase in the abundance of uncommon farm weeds, such as the nettle and plantain. The most obvious explanation for this might seem to be a prehistoric outbreak of Dutch elm disease such as now blights the British countryside. The elm, however, is fortunate in having a great capacity for recovery and will regenerate itself through suckers and shoots. Thus the only credible agency for the Elm Decline is man. Wooded areas yield little grass for grazing animals, but cattle will quite happily browse on the leafy shoots of the elm. We have good evidence that man was deliberately removing the wildwood during the Mesolithic and there is equally good evidence emerging that during the Neolithic he was practising quite skilful woodland management. If the elm is pollarded, or if it is shredded by removing its lateral branches, it will produce an abundance of leafy young shoots suitable for cattle fodder. The Elm Decline may not reflect the selective removal of the elm, but the systematic cropping of its shoots on a short rotation, which would prevent the trees from flowering and producing the pollen which is so notable in its absence in the Neolithic soils. Apparently conclusive evidence of the development of woodland husbandry at this time comes from the Somerset Levels.

Here, for centuries man constructed 'corduroy roads' of poles and brushwood to assist his passage across the soggy ground. The best-built example of these roads is the Abbot's Way, which dates from 2500 BC; it shows different types of timber being used for the special purposes for which they were most suited – alder and ash for poles, oak for heavy logs and birch for a brushwood mat and retaining pegs. The construction of these roads required a far greater volume of straight poles than the natural wildwood could provide and there is every reason to believe that Neolithic Stone-Age man was operating an organized programme of coppicing. The timber was cut low to produce a stool which would throw up straight new shoots; every five to ten years the resulting poles were removed, thus preparing the way for a new crop. Twenty miles of thick alder poles and 80,000 yard-long pegs would have been needed to produce one mile of the Abbot's Way, and thirteen miles of such track are known.

We are learning more about the time when man removed the wildwood; we know the tools which he used; but much uncertainty remains concerning the methods employed, for there are various effective ways of clearing land. Some of the primitive farming communities studied in twentieth-century Africa, for example, practise a shifting agricultural economy based on rotation. The fertility of their cleared plots falls rapidly after a brief period of cultivation and abandonment is followed by the return of the forest; the farmers then wait twenty or more years for a recovery of natural fertility before the land is cleared anew. Other communities plan ahead and kill the trees slowly by removing a ring of bark in plots earmarked for future use.

It may be significant that the Neolithic British were mixed farmers. The fertility of natural woodland soils is not great, and only a brief period of arable farming would be sustained; however, if livestock were turned on the abandoned farm plots to graze, they would nip out the young shoots which would otherwise regenerate the forest, while their manure would assist the return of soil fertility. Fire almost certainly played an important part in the Neolithic farming system; the plants which invade a burnt area of forest – thistles, daisies, dandelion and plantain – are different from those which colonize natural forest clearings, and their presence is abundantly recorded in the pollen evidence. The pollen of hazel and aspen, which both spring from roots which are resistant to burning, become increasingly numerous in the Neolithic pollen record.

It is highly probable that after the woodland was cut down the trunks and brushwood were piled around the stumps and burnt, with the intention of generating sufficient heat to kill the forest roots while providing valuable wood ash fertilizer for the soil. In a Danish experiment, an area of forest was cleared using primitive tools; two experimental plots were produced, one being burnt and the other not. Both plots were hand sown with wheat and barley, raked, hoed and weeded. Scarcely any crop was produced on the unburnt ground, but the burnt plot produced a good crop in the first year, though the declining yield of the second harvest suggested that the time had come to turn livestock on to the ground.

The stone axe is often presented to schoolchildren as a symbol not of the remarkable ingenuity of early man but as proof of his backwardness. In the Yukon a contest was held between the users of steel and stone axes. The stone axes were used as wedges to chisel out splinters, rather than in the conventional manner, and they emerged victorious. Many experiments have been carried out using stone axes, and while in some accounts they appear to

A Palaeolithic hand-axe found near Maidenhead.

38

perform with the speed of a bulldozer, on balance there seems to be little to choose between the stone and the steel axe when applied to the softer woods, although considerably more energy is expended in wielding the stone version. In Denmark, 3 men armed with Neolithic-style axes cleared 600 square yards of forest in 4 hours, so that a single farmer might have been expected to clear about half an acre of wildwood in a week. During the 1960s experiments were carried out in Czechoslovakia and in Russia; in the Czech experiment it took 7 minutes to fell a tree 6 inches in diameter using a polished stone axe, while in Russia a polished nephrite axe cut down a 10-inch pine in 20 minutes.

Stone axes of one kind or another have been used in Britain for hundreds of thousands, if not millions of years. Early in the Neolithic, the axe business became highly organized, having more points of contact with modern industry than with aimless fumblings and chance finds of rock. There were factories, specialist miners and craftsmen, skilled production techniques, spoil heaps and a developed distribution network. At Grimes Graves in Norfolk during the third millennium before Christ there was extraordinary activity; an area of 34 acres was developed for mining and up to 400 pits were sunk. These miners were not merely scratching the surface for flints, for they were prepared to sink shafts of 30 to 40 feet in depth in order to reach a particularly fine seam of flint known as the floorstone. From the base of these pits half a dozen or more galleries radiated outwards for distances of up to 40 feet. The miners used the antlers of red deer to prise the flints from the chalky matrix and carried lamps made from chalk cups containing grease to illuminate the galleries. Each complex of pit and galleries was produced by the removal of 10,000 cubic feet of flint and debris, and it is probable that a three- or four-man mining team would accomplish this work within a six-month mining season. We can speculate that perhaps no more than a dozen miners worked the site, and even they may have farmed for half the year. Nevertheless, they were specialist industrial workers; their output of axes must have been much more than the local market required and we can imagine axes being roughed out on the site for trading far and wide.

Only a small proportion of British rocks have the necessary qualities of hardness and workability required by the axe-maker and woodcutter. Mines have been discovered elsewhere in Norfolk at Lynford and Massingham among other places, in the flint of Sussex at Cissbury, Blackpatch and Harrow Hill, and in Wiltshire at Easton Down. High up on Great Langdale in the Lake District volcanic rocks which can be worked in the same manner as flint were mined and probably sent to the coast for finishing and polishing. An axe factory operated at Craig Lwyd in north Wales, and at Tievebulliagh in Co. Antrim a mountain seam of porcellanite rock was quarried. In the age of wildwood clearance there must have been an intense and widespread demand for the products of these factories; the axes of Tievebulliagh crossed the Irish Sea and have been discovered in north-east Scotland and the Thames valley, while those of Great Langdale also reached the Thames and have turned up in the Hampshire basin. Apart from anything else the discovery of these widely dispersed products reveals the existence of long-distance trading routeways, involving travel by sea as well as by land.

Polished axes in different types of stone set in reconstructed shafts.

39

The purposeful removal of the wildwood continued through the Bronze and Iron Ages; we do not know its extent at different periods or the degree to which truly natural woodland had been replaced by woodland pasture and productive coppiced woodland. Only the existence of extensive tracts of open country would permit the construction of prehistoric alignments, such as the Late Neolithic or Early Bronze Age Dorset Cursus, which extends across the Wessex landscape for more than 6 miles in a series of near-straight sections that could only be sighted in an unforested countryside. The fragmented wildwood lingered into the historical era in those parts of the countryside which were rejected by the prehistoric farmers: the coarse, leached soils of some modern moorlands and the heavy intractable clays of parts of the English Midlands which experienced no prehistoric farming or were abandoned as soon as the thin coating of forest humus was worked out.

Some clay lands surrendered to the heavy, furrow-turning plough of the Romans, and Domesday Book of 1086 records only sufficient woodland for 20 swine – about 30 acres – on the very heavy clay lands of Stevington parish in Bedfordshire. The forest must have made its last stand in areas like the tacky boulder clay of west Cambridgeshire, and here we can record its surrender with some certainty. These clays are associated with a concentration of place names which end in -ley and denote Anglo-Saxon clearings; Domesday Book shows the heavier woodland to have been removed, and by 1300 it is estimated that only 2 per cent of the area of west Cambridgeshire clayland carried woodland. The woodland historian, Oliver Rackham, suggests that while the descriptions of boundaries given in Anglo-Saxon charters seem to portray a landscape which was a little more wooded and rather less hedged than today, in many places trees were valued resources. A decree of the sixth-century King Ine of Kent values a modest tree under which 30 swine could stand at 60 shillings.

Along with the wildwood went the larger wild beasts (though some were preserved for hunting) and their going reveals in a rough and ready fashion the stages in the pacification of the landscape. Only rarely is a definitive date available, as it is for the killing of the last British wolf near Findhorn in Scotland in 1743. Loneliness cannot have improved the animal's disposition, for it consumed two schoolchildren on the day before its death. The subject of the lost beasts of Britain has recently been meticulously studied by Anthony Dent, though much will never be reconstructed. For example, there is ample evidence for British bears, which are indicated by place names containing the Celtic word *arth* in Wales and which were exported to fight in Roman arenas; however, there is little good information about them in Britain after the eighth century and the Bear Ward who appears among the household officers of Henry I was almost certainly a bear keeper and not a hunter. Moose horns provided tools for the Mesolithic hunters, but the animal was hunted out in this or the Neolithic period, while the beautiful fallow deer was a Roman introduction. The reindeer is not included among the many stylish animal carvings of the Dark Age Picts of Scotland, but it may just have retained a toehold in Caithness until the ninth century.

The imposing British wild ox or auroch provides another mystery, though the ceremonial auroch drinking horns of the Saxons, which include a

celo.

Deer from an English bestiary of the twelfth century.

The bearward and his charge from an English manuscript of the fourteenth century.
By this time the native bear was long extinct.

Fluent Pictish carving portrays a bull on this stone slab from Burghead in Morayshire, dated to the seventh or eighth century.

A stone inscribed with the figure of a wolf, from Ardross in Inverness-shire

fine example from the Sutton Hoo ship burial, were probably Scandinavian imports. The auroch may survive in Britain in a variant form; the white park cattle are conceivably the descendants of white sports of the wild red and white auroch, which may have been adopted for ceremonial purposes by a prehistoric priest cult and were then taken over by the early monastic communities. The monks who kept these semi-wild cattle before the Reformation allowed only royalty to hunt them. The lynx, on the other hand, was hunted out in Britain well back in the prehistoric period; its niche was filled by the now rare and protected wild cat, which probably survived in England in the Hambledon Hills and perhaps in Somerset until a century ago and still manages to outwit some unscrupulous gamekeepers in Scotland – but only just.

The widespread distribution of the wild boar in Saxon times is shown by the many place names, such as Eversden and Everley, which are derived from the Saxon boar word *eofor*. The last wild boar south of Yorkshire was killed on Cannock Chase in Staffordshire in 1676, but on various occasions from Tudor to Victorian times the New Forest was artificially restocked: the wild boar shot there at the beginning of this century was certainly a descendant of beasts brought in from Brunswick in the time of Prince Albert. Although the boar was probably poached out of existence by the swineherds or starved to extinction by domestic woodland herds, its passing is not a reliable indicator of the disappearance of the wildscape, because it was artificially maintained and protected for hunting.

One animal that even the most passionate huntsman could not afford to preserve was the wolf. Its disappearance roughly marks in turn the disappearance of large tracts of truly wild (if not strictly natural) country. The evidence has been studied by Dent, who notes that the rents of some holdings in Baysdale (Yorks.) were paid to the monks of Rievaulx Abbey in wolf skins during the fourteenth century. By the end of this century the wolf had probably gone from England south of the Pennines, although the prior of Whitby paid a tanner to dress no less than 13 wolf skins in 1396. The last Welsh wolf probably perished in the region of Brecon at the start of the seventeenth century, while the remarkable event of the killing of an Irish wolf by the Carlow Foxhounds at the beginning of the last century may well have involved an animal that had escaped from an unrecorded private collection. Dent believes that in England the wolf may have made its last stand not in the forest, but in the marshy 'carrs' of Holderness and Pickering in Yorkshire, and he guesses that the last pack may have perished around Flixton Wold in the reign of Henry VIII.

Wolves and bears, boars and aurochs are not quite the whole story, for one of the least publicized of Britain's lost beasts is the beaver; it is commemorated by place names such as Bewerley and Beverley in Yorkshire, and despite having a very desirable coat of waterproof fur which was favoured by the hat trade, it survived in northern and western Britain until the twelfth century.

The lynx and the beaver, from a natural history book of 1777.

The evidence for woodland clearance following the Norman Conquest is generally clear-cut although myths, as Rackham points out, are slow to die. The medieval period was not so much one during which unwanted forest provided a safety valve for the expansion of farming, as one in which woodland was a valued, carefully managed and expertly husbanded resource. Had this not been the case, the enormous demand for timber (a farmhouse might require the timber of over 300 trees) could never have been sustained – certainly not by the progressive removal of natural forest. Towards the end of the Middle Ages, a good oak tree was worth around £75 in modern prices. The charcoal-based iron industry of areas like the Weald and the Forest of Dean would not have committed suicide by destroying the woodland which provided its fuel. The industry encouraged the planting and husbandry of forest and it declined only in the face of Swedish competition. Neither did the shipyards of the British Navy decimate the forest, for Rackham's survey of timber prices showed that the cost of British oak was stable until 1813 and it largely satisfied the domestic demand until 1860.

The process of woodland clearance which began in the Mesolithic period must have climaxed in the Bronze Age, when most English landscapes assumed their open and thinly wooded appearance. An important and so far insoluble mystery confronts those engaged in research on the appearance of early medieval landscapes. It is clear that medieval woodland was a large, carefully managed and valuable resource. At the same time one of the most important sources of royal revenue came from the issue of licenses and imposition of fines for illegal assarting, or forest clearances. Most assarting seems to have taken place in areas which were farmed in Roman times, as the discovery of Romano-British villas and villages shows. One can only conclude that during the Dark Ages numerous forests were re-established on lands deserted by the farmers. We do not know whether this return of the woodland resulted from the traumas of Roman withdrawal, from Saxon settlement and Viking raiding, from the decimation of population by plague, or from some other environmental cause. Until the mystery is solved we will not properly understand the making of the medieval landscape. In a recent lecture, to commemorate the 25th anniversary of Professor Hoskin's *Making of the English Landscape*, the archaeologist Christopher C. Taylor pointed out that 'by the 3rd century AD there is no doubt that England had not only a much larger population than that of the late 11th century [i.e. the time of Domesday Book] but that that population existed in a much more organized and tamed landscape'.

The decline in craft industries during the last century brought a collapse of the centuries-old demand for carefully grown timber, and a drastic fall in standards of woodmanship followed. However, the real culprits for the destruction of our ancient (but not natural) forests are not to be found in the ranks of the Wealden iron masters, the Tudor builders or the Georgian shipwrights. They are found in the modern generation in an age when the demand for carefully coppiced hardwood timber has dropped to almost nothing, when taxation and inheritance laws discriminate against any small long-term gains which might be won from hardwood plantations, and when forests with pedigrees extending beyond the medieval period are being grubbed out to provide farm or building land or ground for growing the rows of ugly but swiftly maturing conifers. In 1975 a survey showed that 42 per cent of the woodland which made up the ancient Rockingham Forest in Northamptonshire had been grubbed out in the years since 1946, while in the same period, 46 per cent of the Lincolnshire woodland had disappeared; elsewhere the picture is much the same.

There is a large – if tragically declining – number of woods in Britain still occupying almost the exact boundaries which they filled in the Middle Ages and, in many cases, probably for a much longer period before. These are ancient woods, but they are by no means the tattered remnants of the wildwood. They are not natural forest, since for most of their history they experienced expert management; they were comprehensively farmed with the encouragement of some species and patterns of growth and the removal of others. Were you to ask me to show you an area of truly natural environment, I would have considerable difficulty – the estuary of an unpolluted river, or some remote coastal sand dunes, perhaps. Some important questions of conservation are thereby raised; what the lovers of our countryside seek to preserve are not natural, but manmade landscapes. Our best-loved landscape may be that of the Lake District, with its green slopes and stone walls: a legacy of centuries of upland sheep farming, now a precarious pursuit at the best of times. If small-scale hill sheep farming were to lose its viability altogether, the price of preserving its landscape against the pressures of commercial forestry or ranching would be enormous. The near destruction of the wild Brecklands landscape, an area of heath and woodland on the Norfolk–Suffolk borders, following the collapse of the sheep and rabbit economy, is a cautionary example.

The reader will want to know when the last remnants of the true wildwood perished, but the answer is largely a mystery. The Forest of Dean appears to have been virgin forest at the time of Domesday. In the years which followed it must have been in full retreat, but in the middle of the thirteenth century Henry III donated oaks from Dean for the construction of a friary for the Dominicans at Gloucester. The timbers of these gigantic oaks can be seen there today in fifty-foot lengths of good, solid timber. Here, and also in the bog oaks of the Fens and just possibly in the upright timbers which form the walls of the Saxon church at Greensted-juxta-Ongar (see p. 183) in Essex, you can reach out and touch the wildwood. During the

Dark Ages the Picts advanced into the wildwood of the great forest of Plater in the valley of the South Esk in Scotland, but to the north and west in the Highland interior of Scotland, a little spoiled wildwood of pine and birch may have survived in Speyside until the Union of the English and Scottish crowns at the beginning of the seventeenth century. In a remote fringe of the Scottish mainland which faces the northern part of the Isle of Skye is Loch Maree, well known to geologists for the remarkable antiquity of its schist rocks. Loch Maree should be equally famous for the age of its woodland, for the tattered remains of pine and oak wood forest which skirt the Loch are the last of the British wildwood, a living relic of the Mesolithic period.

The wildwood may have resembled this long-undisturbed wood at Knapwell in Cambridgeshire, with trees of all sizes and ages.

Cissbury Flint Mines. Four miles N of Worthing (10 miles W of Brighton) in West Sussex. Follow the narrow road E from Findon, to the small car-park. They were being worked in about 3500 BC. Most of the 200 flint mines were later included within the imposing Iron Age hillfort, appearing as hollows in the SW of the oval enclosure. Only 40 lie outside it. Some shafts are over 40 ft deep, with radiating galleries that follow the seams of flint. They were excavated by General Pitt-Rivers in the 1870s.

Clifton Hampden. Near the Thames, 6 miles S of Oxford, a 12th-cent. relief of a boar hunt, showing the boar being gripped by a hound as the hunter approaches. Built into the N wall of the church, on a steep river bluff overlooking the thatched cottages below. It may originally have been a lintel.

Epping Forest. On the N outskirts of London, flanking the A11 between Chingford and Epping. Pollarding over the centuries has restricted the growth of the oaks, and some of only medium size may be 400 years old. The oaks are giving way to beeches in some parts. The abandonment of pollarding, following the Epping Forest Act of 1878, which required the Corporation of London to preserve the 'natural' aspect of the forest, has radically changed its traditional appearance. One of the first areas to be managed as a wild, public open space. Enfield Chase, 7 miles to the W beyond Enfield, was an enormous tract of wood pasture once extending 9 miles between Enfield and Hatfield. It was grubbed out at the end of the 18th

cent., but a fragment remains at Monken Hadley Common.

Felsham Hall Wood. A private wood NE of Long Melford and SE of Bury St Edmunds, in Suffolk: Oliver Rackham believes that an $18\frac{1}{2}$ ft, 1000-year-old ash stool there may be one of the oldest living things in Britain. It can be seen from the top of the famous medieval church tower at Lavenham, 4 miles NE of Long Melford, which offers a remarkable view of the countryside, dotted with ancient woods and divided by hedgerows. Many of the boundaries were set in the Middle Ages, and several of the woods occupy their ancient boundaries.

Glen More Forest Park. About 6 miles E of Aviemore (25 miles SE of Inverness). It contains some Scots pines of the kind which grew in the ancient Caledonian wildwood. The forest has not survived unchanged. Cattle-grazing land was traditionally improved by the burning of heather, and by the late 17th cent. the remaining timber was such a valuable resource that those who burned too close to it were nailed by their ears to the gallows. Wolves were found here until the start of the 18th cent.

Great Langdale Axe Factory. In the Lake District National Park. The factory lay on the northern screes below Pike of Stickle, right down into Great Langdale valley. Axes were roughed out from the volcanic rock at a height of 1800 ft and were probably sent down to the Cumberland coast for finishing and polishing before being exported to other

Medieval carving of a boar hunt from Clifton Hampden in Oxfordshire.

parts of Britain. The site was identified in 1947 by the scattered flint flakes and rejected axes on the scree. Other workshops were later found on Loft Crag, Harrison Stickle and Scafell Pike. An axe-finishing site was discovered in the 1870s at Ehenside Tarn, near the villages of St John and St Bridget Beckermet, 7 miles SE of Whitehaven on the Cumbria coast, with axes in various stages of completion and grindstones for polishing them. One finished axe was found in its beechwood haft.

The Great Yeldham Oak. Beside the A604, 6 miles NW of Halstead in Essex (12 miles NW of Colchester), at the road junction in Great Yeldham village. The trunk of an oak which must have been a large and venerable specimen in the 18th cent. is preserved on the green.

Grimes Graves Flint Mines. One of the most famous prehistoric sites in Britain. A flint knapper worked until very recently nearby at Brandon. Signposted 6 miles NW of Thetford (30 miles SW of Norwich), S of the B1108 near the junction with the A134. Cars can be parked at the pock-marked site, where antler picks and a reconstructed axe are on show and booklets can be bought. Steel ladders have been installed in the shafts open to the public, but the galleries are barred. Photographers will need a flash.

Loch Maree Wildwood. Two miles NW of the village of Kinlochewe (about 50 miles W of Inverness, on the A832). The Scots pine and oak forests are the last tattered remnants of the Highland wildwood, and resemble that which grew on the northern margins of the Lake District. A beautiful area, with Skye visible from the nearby coast.

The New Forest. Covers much of S Hampshire, W of Southampton Water. Parts of it are wood pasture: heavily grazed for centuries and coppiced in the

Middle Ages. It was primarily an ancient royal hunting ground, decreed by William the Conqueror in 1079 and ruthlessly protected by hunting laws. A vestige of medieval forestry survives in the meetings of the Verderers, whose court still upholds commoners' rights. The New Forest was exploited for naval timber in the 17th cent.

The Norfolk Wildlife Park. Lies 12 miles NW of Norwich, N of the B1067 between Lenwade and Sparham. Founded in 1961 as the first wildlife park in Europe, it contains a very large collection of European birds and mammals, including many of the vanished beasts of the British wildwood: a wolfpack, the European brown bear and bison, wildcats, lynxes, boars and beavers.

The Ripley Boar. Situated 17 miles N of Leeds, just past Harrogate on the A61. Turn W to Ripley at the first roundabout after Killinghall. Ripley castle was given to the Ingilby family 700 years ago as a reward to Thomas Ingilby for saving the King's life by diverting a wild boar during a hunt in Knaresborough Forest. The event is commemorated by the statue of a boar posing angrily near the castle gate. At Barnborough in S Yorks., 17 miles NE of Sheffield (2 miles N of Mexborough), is the tomb of Percival Cresacre, reputed to have been killed by a wildcat in about 1460. At the foot of his tomb is a carving of the guilty party. Vigorous medieval carvings of a boar hunt are preserved in the parish church of Liverton, 2 miles S of Loftus (17 miles E of Middlesbrough) on the N Yorks. coast.

Tievebulliagh Axe Factory. On the E face of Tievebulliagh Mountain in the Mountains of Antrim N of Belfast. Axe workings have been found on the steep slopes, with mounds of waste chippings, and several roughed-out axes made of stone extracted from a seam of porcellanite rock.

The stump of an ancient oak preserved in the road junction at Great Yeldham in Essex.

The Ripley Boar, under an icing of snow.

Chapter 3

Stones, circles and stars

THE PREHISTORIC STONE CIRCLES of Britain have made a profound impact upon the imagination and intellect of modern man. As long ago as 1876, William Long remarked that the literature on Stonehenge alone 'would fill the shelves of a small library'; and such a library would be dwarfed by one which contained the speculative and scientific literature of the century which has followed. Of the many issues raised by this debate, perhaps the most important are:

Did the builders of the circles intend them to be used as astronomical observatories?

Were the circles built according to precise geometrical models, including not only the perfect circle, but also the flattened circle, 'egg-shape' and ellipse?

Was a standard unit of measurement – the Megalithic Yard – employed in the layout of these monuments?

What was the function of the circular timber buildings of vast proportions which have been recognized at a number of important Neolithic sites?

How were the mighty megaliths transported and erected at monuments such as Avebury and Stonehenge?

As each quest unfolds, the searcher is taken from one learned journal to another, from the quicksands of one theory to the pitfalls of a second, third or fourth and into a world where gifted astronomers are not only at odds with archaeologists, but with each other. Although one hopes for firm answers or consensus views, very few will emerge in this chapter.

Before we embark upon this mystery tour, there is the problem of putting the circles in their proper perspective. They are by far the most widely known and most frequently visited of British prehistoric relics and many, like the Rollright Stones, Stonehenge or the Callanish circle, will fill the onlooker with awe. Consequently, it is easy to assume that the circles exerted a completely dominating influence in the lives of those who built them. These builders were very largely peasant farmers and herdsmen and, it is plausible to suppose, reluctant conscripts to the task at hand. There must have been many Neolithic and Bronze Age peasants who never even saw a stone circle, let alone helped to build one. How frequently other peasants visited or worshipped at one of these temples is unknown, but it is not unreasonable to suggest that rather more mundane problems of survival must often have filled their thoughts. There is a great danger of judging people remote from ourselves in terms of their most enduring relics. Were our distant descendants to judge this civilization by such a standard we might be commemorated as the Plastic Bottle People (perhaps a fitting epitaph, after all!). This said, the stone circles are a remarkable testament to

Stones in the Ring of Brodgar circle, Orkney.

The Rollright stone circle, Oxfordshire.

the intellect and capabilities of their makers. One archaeologist has compared the social effort in the making of Avebury to that surrounding the Apollo space programme.

There can be little doubt that the stone circles are a manifestation of the spiritual beliefs of their makers and even the most cautious and sober of archaeologists refer to them as temples. The absence of large amounts of refuse argues against their use as domestic sites and, where they are surrounded by banks and ditches, there are usually open causeways and the ditch is generally situated within the bank, making a defensive function unlikely. None of this rules out some political function, for any chief or theocrat who could assemble and discipline the labour involved to build the gigantic structures of Stanton Drew in Somerset, or Avebury in Wiltshire (see pp. 73, 71) displayed a formidable development of political muscle. Moreover, the mixing of workers from many localities and backgrounds in the course of circle-making might have hastened the evolution of broad and coherent political territories.

At the same time, it is hard to imagine that the circles served any obvious economic role. If, as it has been suggested, the circles acted as date-fixing observatories, the dates must have concerned ritual occasions rather than the needs of farming. Any British farmer who ties his operations to a rigid calendar is asking for trouble in such an uncertain climate. Like the modern farmer, the prehistoric peasant doubtless arranged his sowing according to ground temperature, accumulated knowledge and intuition; until quite recently, the bare bottom was judged an excellent instrument for judging the critically important temperature of the ground.

Our first key question concerns the possible astronomical functions of the circles, and invites speculation on the existence of a sophisticated prehistoric astronomical and mathematical science. Various important heavenly events might have interested prehistoric peoples. The rising and setting positions of the sun at the solstices could be linked to key events in the calendar by using a feature such as a standing stone, distant hillside notch or pinnacle as a foresight, and a stone as a backsight. As the rising or setting sun approached the positions so marked, people would be aware of the imminence of a turning-point in the year. Societies which were closely adjusted to the farming seasons might attach great importance to the midwinter death of the old year and the birth of the new. The prediction of eclipses, on the other hand, requires a sophisticated knowledge of the mathematics of astronomy, and the stones which could be used to predict an eclipse would have some of the qualities of a computer. As Rider Haggard suggested in *King Solomon's Mines* (1886), any individual or priestly caste who possessed the ability to predict eclipses might be regarded as godlike by members of an illiterate society. The earliest records of ancient civilizations, such as the Babylonians, Egyptians and Chinese, reveal considerable interest in the calculation of astronomical events, while the Bible itself shows how people like shepherds who spent nights on guard over their flocks developed an intimate knowledge of the heavens. However, before we attribute great feats of mathematical astronomy indiscriminately to all early peoples we should note that recent work suggests that the Norman conquerors of England seem to have had difficulties in forming perfect right-angles in their churches.

The Callanish stone circle on the island of Lewis.

51

Sunrise at Stonehenge viewed from the south-west.

The modern age was quick to notice that the circles might have been built for astronomical purposes. As early as 1740, the antiquary William Stukeley observed that Stonehenge was orientated to the sunrise at the midsummer solstice, and Godfrey Higgins's *Celtic Druids* (1827) anticipated the modern suggestion that Stonehenge might have had a lunar significance. More advanced ideas were put forward by the astronomer Norman Lockyer at the start of this century; he believed that Stonehenge and some other megalithic monuments embodied important alignments, including mid-solstice markers, and were involved with May year worship. Although he was an important pioneer astronomer, much of his astro-archaeological work was sloppy, and tainted by irrelevant borrowings from folk mythology, Egyptian and Druidical connections and by an imperfect understanding of archaeological evidence. As the editor of *Nature*, Lockyer was able to publish free from the rigour which academic referees impose upon less privileged contributors. By the end of the nineteenth century, Stonehenge had been heavily garlanded in literary claptrap and judged by different cranks to be, among other things, a Saxon gallows for the execution of defeated British chieftains, a solar temple, an astronomical calendar, a Buddhist temple and a planetary model.

Conflicting astronomical theories continued to be advanced during the first half of this century, but professional archaeologists were anxious to escape the extravagances of their discipline's nursery days and on the whole they did not feel great need to pay much attention to the astronomical claims. However, the profession was obliged to take note when an article on the astronomy of Stonehenge appeared in the prestigious journal *Nature* in 1963. The author, astronomer Gerald Hawkins, had employed an IBM 7090 computer to determine significant alignments for the horizon positions of the rising and setting sun, stars, moon and planets. Stellar and planetary significance was discounted, but when the computer examined the solar and lunar events for *c.* 1500 BC, it seemed that the monument was ideally designed to record the winter and summer solstices and the four extreme positions of the moon at this date. Strangely, the lunar and solar relationships were in some respects anticipated by the late C. A. Newham in 1962. The publication of Newham's discoveries was a catalogue of disaster, which culminated in the destruction by fire of the print shop in which his booklets were to have been published – at the author's expense. When publication eventually came in 1964, the astro-archaeological thunder had been stolen by Hawkins and *Nature*. A later exposition of Newham's theories (more lucid than most such works) is sold at the Stonehenge shop.

When Hawkins' theories appeared, the public at large and many professional prehistorians were still mesmerized by the computer: to some, the astronomer's estimate that the odds against coincidence explaining his findings were more than 1 : 100 million seemed insuperable proof. Not all archaeologists were beguiled; and when the response came, it was peppery and spiced with a soupçon of the extra chilli that members of the profession save for interlopers from outside the discipline. The initiative, however, remained with the astronomers, who had much still to offer. Impressed by additional ideas supplied by Newham (who had discovered a possible new alignment, '94-stone hole C', which had been missed by the computer), and by R. S. Newall (who had drawn attention to the roughly 19-year Metonic cycle of the moon and the 19 bluestones), Hawkins returned to the Stonehenge problem in 1964.

New data fed into the computer produced new suggestions. Most staggering was the evidence that the circle could be used as a device for predicting eclipses occurring at just over 18-year intervals. In the course of an 18.61 year nodal period, the winter full moon moved from a maximum to a minimum north declination across the Heel Stone from stone D to stone F and back again, while the full moon of midsummer swung to and fro on viewing lines through the central 'trilithon' (three-stone) arch. Moreover, the stones of the circle were known to be surrounded by a ring of 56 pits called the Aubrey Holes, after the antiquarian who discovered them. These could themselves be related to the mathematics of eclipses.

In his second *Nature* article, which appeared in 1964, Hawkins introduced some highly complex mathematics to suggest that if counters or markers of some kind were moved anticlockwise from one Aubrey Hole to the next each year (preferably using 3 stones of one distinctive form and 3 of another, with the 6 placed at intervals of 9-9-10-9-9-10 holes), then the prehistoric observer could compute the arrival of many significant lunar

Stonehenge illustrated in an English history of the world of the fourteenth century.

Stonehenge, Wiltshire, from Camden's *Britannia* with additions and improvements by Edmund Gibson, London, 1695.

events over a period of centuries according to the juxtaposition of the stones.

Stonehenge as portrayed by Constable in the summer of 1820.

The celebrated British astronomer Fred Hoyle both liked and disliked the Hawkins thesis, and *Nature* again provided a forum in 1966. The 56 pits were, he felt, an eclipse cycle computer, but not quite in the manner that Hawkins had specified. The Hoyle computer relied on a different and more complex system of moving markers, some going 3 holes clockwise each day, some 2 holes anticlockwise each day and others 2 holes anticlockwise every 13 days. Superimposed upon these complex operations was the need for regular corrective manipulations (one does not envy the prehistoric operator his task). To add a little teleological icing to this heavy numerological cake, Hoyle speculated that the moving markers were symbols of a divine trinity of sun, moon and the invisible god; when the sun and moon were eclipsed, the invisible god remained.

By this time, the ideas were coming thick and fast, the problems of Stonehenge astronomy producing theories, rejoinders, modifications and critiques and becoming in the process almost incomprehensibly complex. Despite the worldwide publicity which followed the publication of Hawkins' book, *Stonehenge Decoded*, in 1966, one very much doubts that there existed as many as two dozen people in the world who were really *au fait* with all the astronomical and archaeological arguments involved. The more intricate the computer became, the more difficult it was to imagine that the Neolithic people, who dug ditches with antler picks and left no signs of literacy, possessed the level of numeracy necessary to conceive such an instrument.

Newham now directed attention to a series of post holes which had been found arranged in 6 ranks in the Stonehenge causeway entrance. These, he suggested, might have held markers which delimited the winter full-moon swing over a period of 6, approximately 19-year cycles. Such markers might have been employed to discover the 19-year Metonic cycle in which the same phases of the moon are repeated, to within an hour or so, on the same date of the year. They might also have been related to the 18.61 year nodal cycle which governs eclipses.

Holes were in the news in 1966 when an extension of the Stonehenge carpark revealed the traces of 3 large post-holes. Newham suggested that tree trunks placed in these holes could be aligned with important horizon setting positions of the sun and moon when observed from the detached Heel Stone and from the 4 station stones of the outer ring which mark the corners of a large rectangle. Meanwhile, some support had accompanied claims by Newham and G. Charrier, a French architect, that the latitudinal position of Stonehenge (51° 2′N) was deliberately chosen in such a way that the extreme northerly and southerly rising and setting positions of the sun were seen at right angles to one another in accord with the rectangular plan embodied in the station stones.

The reticent but influential apostle of megalithic astronomy and measurement, Professor A. Thom, did not focus his attentions upon Stonehenge until 1974. He then carried out his own precise survey of the monument and gave support to the view that Stonehenge was a pioneer lunar observatory which might have inspired the establishment of other astronomical centres elsewhere in the islands. He also believed that the circle contained ample evidence of the use of advanced geometry and the standardized system of megalithic measurement which we shall encounter later in the chapter.

During the 1960s the initiative for interpreting Britain's most impressive prehistoric monuments had passed from the archaeologists to the astronomers – in the public mind, at least. It should be remembered that before the last war there were very few independent departments of archaeology in Britain and most archaeologists in the postwar period had received little, if any, formal training in mathematics. A good proportion had studied Classics, including some archaeology, but usually with a strong Mediterranean bias. Others had trained in geography in the days when a mastery of French and German was highly valued, but numeracy was thought to be of little consequence. On the whole, the archaeological profession not only disliked the implications of astro-archaeology, but also, not surprisingly, it did not understand them.

One notable exception to this rule was Professor R. J. C. Atkinson, a leading figure in the subject, a member of the team which excavated Stonehenge in the early 1950s and a man who proved capable of meeting the mathematicians on their own ground. In 1966 he published his eagerly awaited review of the astronomical debate in *Antiquity*, under the suggestive title 'Moonlight on Stonehenge'. The article was primarily a rejoinder to Professor Hawkins' book, *Stonehenge Decoded*. Atkinson found much of which to disapprove, ranging from the unauthorized use of copyright illustrations, some very sloppy background archaeology and the use of plans which were never intended to meet the demands of accuracy placed upon them, to inaccuracy in the calculation of probabilities and margins of error. He was unconvinced by the notion that the Aubrey Holes could have been used over a number of 56-year cycles as tally holders, since their excavation had shown that they were filled in shortly after being dug and seemed to have contained cremation remains. Despite his very severe critique, however, Atkinson thought that 'it must in justice be made clear' that the book does contain some suggestions of positive value'. The notion that, whenever an observer at the centre of the circle saw the full moon nearest the winter solstice rise roughly over the Heel Stone, an eclipse of the sun or moon would follow, was 'the best explanation of the Heel Stone so far put forward' – though only half the eclipses so predicted would in fact be visible at Stonehenge. He thought that 'We must be grateful [to Hawkins] for quickening the interest of prehistorians in the early development of observational science and metrology.' The idea, made previously by Newham, that the latitude of Stonehenge was deliberately chosen, moreover, did seem to account for the rectangular geometry of the station stones.

Subsequent editions of *Antiquity* contained a succession of articles by the leading contenders. Those who had always doubted the astronomical conclusions were able to gain ammunition from an article which appeared in *Nature* in 1967, written by R. Colton and R. L. Martin. They revealed that unrecognized errors in the astronomy and mathematics invalidated Hawkins' arguments regarding the use of the Aubrey Holes for the prediction of eclipses. In addition, since half of the eclipses predicted by the Hoyle method would not have been seen in the Stonehenge area, they could thus have been of little interest to the people of Wessex; and much simpler means of eclipse prediction would have worked without the complicated structures at Stonehenge. The observer notes when the sun and moon are diametrically opposed and when the moon rises less than 30 minutes before the sun sets: if these two conditions are fulfilled, an eclipse of the moon will follow. At the very most it seemed that the Aubrey Holes might have served as a simple protractor to measure the diametrical opposition of the sun and moon. Colton and Martin suggested that many stone circles could have served such a function.

While most archaeologists looked on in some bewilderment as their hereditary stamping grounds became the battlefields of interlopers, the public response was one of superficial fascination – superficial because only the most adept astro-mathematicians could evaluate the real nature of the issues at stake. Although herself somewhat bemused by the numbers games, the archaeologist Jacquetta Hawkes came forth with the very shrewd observation that people got the sort of Stonehenge that they wanted: in the nineteenth century, when druids were the rage, Stonehenge was a druid temple, while in the space and computer age, it was an astronomical computer. Too much respect for the use of computers in finding 'answers' reflected a failure to grasp that the machines were no more clever than the weakest assumptions in their manmade programmes. Much of their apparent objectivity was illusory; for example, it was for the programmer to guess what constituted a tolerable margin of error for observed alignments, while the Hawkins programme did not include constraints derived from archaeological evidence, such as was available from the excavation of the Aubrey Holes. If it had, then the probability that the excavators' conclusions were correct should have been calculated – and no astronomer could assess such a question.[1]

It is probably fair to say that at this stage in the continuing debate most prehistorians accept the possibility that some stone circles were built to include astronomical alignments. Each particular claim must be judged on its own intrinsic merits and in many cases it will always be impossible to say whether a specific alignment was intentional or coincidental. When Hoyle lent his prestige to the argument that the Aubrey Holes represented an eclipse computer the case seemed all but proven, but this now seems to be one of the weakest of the astronomical possibilities.

Although the debate has focused on Stonehenge, this is by no means the only monument with astronomical potential. Since early in the postwar period Professor Thom has been engaged in the meticulous surveying of megalithic circles and standing stones throughout Britain and Brittany. His position as an Oxford professor (of engineering), the precision of his techniques and the sobriety of his publications have earned him the respect of those who reject his interpretations. He believes that he has discovered alignments at a host of megalithic locations. In some cases these are incorporated in circles of complex construction, but in others a simple stone seems to have been erected as a backsight, and this would be brought into line with a prominent horizon feature (like a natural notch in a hillside) to serve as a foresight. The resultant apparatus would be sighted on the position of a significant 'astronomical event'.

In his *Megalithic Lunar Observatories*, first published in 1971, details of 32 lunar and solar sites are given. One of his most famous locations is at Kintraw in Argyll. Here, at the midwinter solstice in about 1700 BC, the sun would have been seen to set behind Beinn Shiantaidh, to be followed by a flash of green light, which would have been seen as the rim of the setting sun reappeared in the valley notch between the mountain and its neighbouring mass of Beinn á Chaolais. The observer of this important event was almost thirty miles away from the twin peaks, which are on the isle of Jura, and Professor Thom believes that the sunset flash was watched from an artificial hillside platform, with 2 standing stones and a cairn providing marking sights.

At Ludin Links in Fifeshire there are 3 stone pillars which are delightfully described by the archaeologist Aubrey Burl: 'Ringed in battered iron railings on a golf course, they huddle like captured triffids.' Professor Thom believes this to be an important lunar astronomical site, used for observations of the minimum moonrise and moonset, using the Bass Rock and a tumulus silhouetted on Cormie Hill as foresights.

The reader in astro-archaeology is likely to be swung back and forth by the proponents of different interpretations. The case against some, if not all, astronomical alignments is as convincing as many of the astronomical

[1]The complicated and controversial nature of the evidence was underlined in September 1979 when a Russian geologist, Vladimir Avinsky, claimed to have discovered that Stonehenge was based on a pentagram, the five-pointed star with occult connections, and that it carries information on the size of the planets and models planetary correlations to within a one per cent margin of error. The reader will recall that the Hawkins computer discounted any planetary significance.

claims; it underlines the need for caution. Apparently significant alignments will almost certainly be found in any random assemblage of stones. Aubrey Burl, author of a magnificent guide to British stone circles, demonstrates the problem using the Cumberland circle of Grey Croft as an example. The circle contains only 12 stones and an outlier. This produces 132 possible sighting lines between members of the circle – one for every 2.7° of the horizon. The figure can be multiplied by 3 for the extra sighting possibilities if stone side edges as well as stone tops are used; a further 36 sight lines can be produced from the circle centre to the tops, left and right side edges of each stone. Many additional alignments would be possible if the outlier is used as a foresight or backsight and there are additional foresight possibilities provided by the various horizon hills and hollows. There is also a vast array of possible targets: 6 significant sun positions, 40 significant lunar alignments and an almost infinite number of potential star targets. Taking just the sun, moon and 9 prominent stars, it is estimated that of the 360° of horizon, no less than 136° might be utilized in a search for ancient alignments. For any single random line, the odds of a 'significant' alignment being found are less than 3:1 against.

When these statistical possibilities are taken into account, it is clear that alignments will be found whether or not they were intended by the makers of a stone ring. Cautionary analogies can be taken from the proponents of 'ley-lines'. Discounting the arbitrariness of including features which can be lined up and the exclusion of those which cannot, the laws of statistical probability decree that large numbers of prehistoric burial mounds, standing stones or medieval moats will lie on lines. The superficial attractions of ley-lining tend to evaporate with the publication by sceptics of 'ley-lines' joining up Victorian railway stations, telephone call-boxes in the Chiltern Hills, public lavatories and public houses, while an Oxford don has recorded the (humorous) discovery that the distribution of Inner London Roman Catholic churches forms a perfect logarithmic spiral.

There is clearly much in the debate which supports the maxim that there are 'lies, damn lies and statistics'; and doubtless many new twists to the problem are still to arise. What has certainly not been established by either side is the *relative* importance of astronomy within the total complex of stone circles and it is quite feasible that an astronomical alignment could be included in a circle as a secondary rather than a primary feature. Indeed, had such alignments been the main objective, one would not have expected to find circles, but pairs of foresights and backsights, with timber poles providing finer sighting markers than broad and bulky hunks of stone. From the circular positioning of the stones, one might reasonably infer that they – or the frequently found encircling ditch – demarcated the limits of a sacred area; in this view, the stones provided a dramatic backdrop to the rituals performed within the ring and the circles were primarily temples. In any case, the searcher for alignments must always bear in mind that the stones in a circle are not always in their original positions. Members may have been systematically destroyed, as at Avebury, removed for building material, as at Rollright, or re-erected after some natural catastrophe.

Before we proceed to explore new aspects of the stone circle mystery, it should be noted that astronomical theories are not peculiar to the rings.

This decorated stone lies at the entrance to the Newgrange Neolithic tomb in Ireland.

Superstitions relating to the rising and setting of the sun may explain the fact that most (but by no means all) megalithic long barrows are orientated in a generally easterly direction. One of the most convincing cases for astronomical orientation concerns the Newgrange passage grave, described in *Nature* by J. Patrick in 1974. The tomb is about 30 miles to the north northwest of Dublin and dates from about 3100 BC; it is a remarkably fine example of its kind and contains a unique wealth of Neolithic geometrical carving. The most singular and interesting feature, however, is the 'roof box', a slab-lined opening slot above the entrance passage roof; this is exactly aligned so that the midwinter sunrise casts a beam of light directly down the passage which leads to the interior of the tomb. Whatever the alignments at Stonehenge may be, the most important of those proposed were anticipated by a millennium at Newgrange.

The cursūs monuments, which are found as far apart as Stonehenge and Rudston, near Bridlington, are a completely mysterious set of linear earthworks, elongated features consisting of a strip of land bounded by banks and ditches, sometimes several miles long. Their functions remain unknown; they were originally thought to be race courses – hence the name – and subsequently it was suggested that they were prehistoric processional ways. In 1973, A. Penny and J. E. Wood published an account of the Dorset cursus complex in the scholarly *Archaeological Journal*. A part of the function of the cursus was, they thought, 'to indicate, by means of the parallel banks of what were originally gleaming white chalk, the approximate direction in which to look for the distant sight'. The distant sight was an astronomical event, and barrows were often used as foresights. Associated with the cursus are a number of burial mounds and, following

One of the many decorated stones in the Kerb at Newgrange.

the application of some complex astronomical analysis, the authors concluded that they might be employed to determine the day of the winter solstice, to track the motions of the winter moon and to predict lunar eclipses. Six detailed case studies of alignments were given. For example, an observer standing at the end of the section known as the Gussage cursus, at a place called the 'Wyke Down Terminal', would see the last flicker of the midwinter sunset of 2500 BC at the end of a silhouetted long barrow which is listed as 'Gussage St Michael III'. If an observer were to stand on this barrow and if a bonfire were lit on the other extremity of the cursus – the 'Thickthorn Terminal' – it would serve as a foresight aligned on a maximum moonset declination.

Setting the astronomical questions aside, it has been suggested that many stone circles embody quite sophisticated geometry in their layouts. Any people with the ability to transport and erect massive stones would surely be able to mark out a perfect circle – a length of cord anchored to a central peg is all that is required. But a large number of stone rings are not circular and so it might be assumed that geometrical form was not considered important and that stones were set up in a rough-and-ready ring. In 1961, however, Professor Thom produced convincing evidence that the imperfect circles were in fact complicated geometric forms with different properties – flattened circles, ellipses, egg-shapes and compound rings. Then, in 1970, Thaddeus M. Cowan published an article in *Science* which demonstrated how these forms might have been marked out on the ground. Thom had thought that rods or (megalithic) yardsticks (see pp. 63–4) were used, but Cowan showed how ropes and stakes could have been used to great effect.

The 'Type A flattened circle', one example from many, suggests an advanced knowledge of geometry. A perfect circle forms two-thirds of the circumference, but the remaining third is flattened and the figure appears to be based on an internal equilateral triangle, a figure which can be described using 3 ropes or rods of equal length. A stake might have been anchored in the centre of the triangle, with others at 2 of the corners. A rope attached to the centre post, swung through two-thirds of the circumference of a circle, would mark out a perimeter; but swung further, it would inscribe narrower circumferences when it rested against the pivot posts in the corners of the triangle, so that 2 heart-like lobes would be drawn in the remaining third of the circle. A line extended from the anchor post through the un-posted angle of the triangle would then cut the circumference of the circle. At this point, if a second anchor post with a rope attached was inserted, the rope extended until it reached the furthest points on the heart lobes and then swung, the rope would describe the most flattened portion of the circumference. Different systems of geometry also employing ropes, anchor posts and pivot posts might have been used to mark out the other types of ring.

Why these distortions of the circular form might have been employed is difficult to imagine. It has been suggested that the audience at the circle rituals might have gathered along the flattened portion of the circumference the better to view the rituals performed by priests standing at the unflattened or more pointed sections. Aubrey Burl, however, notes that the distortions are only apparent when the circles are seen in plan and they may not be evident to viewers at ground level. Thaddeus Cowan offers the interesting speculation that the flattening of circles might have represented attempts to escape from the mathematical complexity of the relationship between the radius and circumference of the perfect circle and to produce figures whose circumferences were exactly divisible by their radii.

An air-view of the Ring of Brodgar stone circle in Orkney, showing the surrounding earthworks.

Burl has taken the question a little further by suggesting that there is a time relationship between the age and shape of the rings. The oldest rings, dating from before about 2600 BC, are largely circular, although some flattened circles appear; in the second phase, ending about 2000 BC, circles remain in the majority, flattened circles are not evident, but ellipses and egg-shapes have developed; in the most recent phase, up to 1400 BC, ellipses are by far the most popular form and circles are about as numerous as the flattened circles and egg-shapes combined. The supporting dating evidence is far from complete, and other variables are superimposed on the data. For example, the ellipses always seem to have diameters of less than 100 feet, while the circles are often larger; the ellipses, moreover, are concentrated in north-east Scotland and south-west Ireland.

We must return to Professor Thom for our third major field of enquiry, which concerns the question of a standardized system of megalithic measurement. Ancient systems of measurement have been advocated in the past – Piazzi Smyth's 'pyramid inch', Flinders Petrie's 'Etruscan foot' and William Stukeley's 'Druid cubit', for example. These supposed units – particularly the notorious pyramid inch – have provided the basis for intricate and tendentious flights of fancy; they have been shown to be based on unsound mathematical and surveying practices (a follower of Smyth was even discovered chipping at a boss in the Great Pyramid to help to make the fact fit the theory!). Consequently, prehistorians have not been well disposed towards the publicists of measurement theories and their readiness to explore and, in a few cases, to accept Professor Thom's system is testimony again to the seriousness of his approach.

Once more we are cast on a sea of mathematical uncertainty. The essential quest concerns a search for 'quanta' or basic units which may be hidden within a series of measured dimensions. For example, were we to measure a series of modern international sports stadia and apply mathematical analysis to our results we would expect the use of the metre to emerge from the data, while were the same methods used on older British, Commonwealth or American stadia, the yard would appear. From his measurements of hundreds of megalithic monuments, Professor Thom believes that he has discovered a standardized prehistoric system of measurement involving the megalithic rod of 6.80 feet; there is also a megalithic inch, which is said to be found in cup and ring marks (described on pp. 117–18), and a megalithic fathom consisting of 2 megalithic yards. But most publicity has attached to the Megalithic Yard of 2.720 ± 0.003 feet. The mathematics involved in the evaluation of the quanta content of measurement data is far too complicated to be introduced here (anyone who doubts this might refer to the article 'Hunting Quanta' by D. G. Kendall in the 1974 *Transactions of the Royal Society of London*).

The convolutions of the different mathematical arguments apart, one cannot simply accept the Megalithic Yard and leave the matter there. Believers in the Yard must also subscribe to the existence of some sort of Megalithic Standards Institute – a body responsible for guarding the standard and, presumably, for issuing measuring rods of the set length, as well as organizing their distribution throughout the country. Even if such an

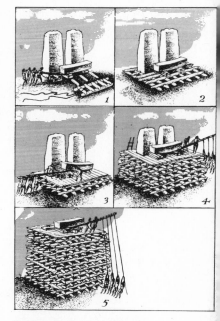

Raising the horizontal lintels at Stonehenge – one version of the method used.

organization existed, one wonders how it could have maintained its continuity over successive centuries; and credulity is stretched to the limits by the claims by the Scottish archaeologist, Euan MacKie, that Megalithic Yard quanta are to be found in measurements of Scottish brochs (see pp. 141–5). This would extend the unit's period of use from the Neolithic to the Roman occupation of England.

In fact, there may be a much more prosaic solution. Quanta may indeed be apparent in megalithic monuments, but as Dr Hugh L. Porteous (among others) has pointed out in his 1973 article in the *Journal of Historical Astronomy*, 'Megalithic Yard or Megalithic Myth?', the explanation may be simple. The Megalithic Yard bears an uncanny resemblance to the human pace! Here I can add some speculations of my own. The first concerns accuracy, for it could be argued that a standard pace could not be maintained with a precision sufficient to produce quanta which would be recognizable in measurement data. However, commercial geologists or field archaeologists often use pacing in simple surveys. With a little practice the pace can be controlled to an accuracy of well within 2 per cent. Moreover, the pace can easily be adjusted to produce either Imperial or metric surveys, as circumstances require!

The second speculation relates to the height of the pacer – if the pace of modern man is roughly equivalent to a yard, then shorter people might have been expected to take shorter steps: the MY falls short of the yard by 0.280 foot. There is a popular misconception that prehistoric people were minute; it may be due partly to the survival of many suits of armour which were made for young teenagers, and partly to the dramatic increases in height of the last couple of generations, particularly in the USA – doubtless the result of improved nutrition and of intermarriage between immigrant communities. Certain historical figures – Thomas à Becket and Richard the Lionheart, for instance – may have been gigantic by any standard, while Bronze Age immigrants to Britain included many burly men who would easily match the physical requirements of the modern police force. The Neolithic people whose skeletons are found in dozens of barrows and cairns are noticeably light in build, shorter than the British of today by a few inches, but by no means dwarfs. Perhaps their average pace was around 2.7 feet long. . . .

There are few more convenient ready-made units of measurement than the human pace and it is not surprising that pacelike units are often found; P. L. Brown, for example, has listed the Roman pace, the Valencian *vara* of 35.55 inches, the *vara* of Castile of 32.94 inches, the Bavarian ell of 32.77 inches and the Austrian ell of 30.78 inches.

The reality of the next mystery is beyond dispute and for the first time in this chapter we can be absolutely certain that we are not tracking a chimera. The problem concerns the gigantic timber buildings whose traces have been discovered in association with two of the most important British circles. The story may begin at Woodhenge in Wiltshire, less than a couple of miles from Stonehenge. Its discovery in 1925 was one of the early coups of air photography, and it was thought to be a large disc barrow – a type of Bronze Age round barrow surrounded by an open space and then by a ditch. But when the site was excavated between 1926 and 1928, it was shown to have consisted not, as was thought, of a barrow, but of a bank and internal ditch surrounding a series of concentric rings of vertical posts. The jocular name 'Woodhenge' stuck, for it was thought that the monument was a wooden version of Stonehenge and that the timber posts had supported wooden crosspieces or lintels. In 1940, however, Professor Stuart Piggott pointed out that the remains might more sensibly be interpreted as the supports for a gigantic roofed timber building.

Although the purpose of such a building is controversial, postwar enquiry has revealed similar structures elsewhere in Wessex and detailed excavations have been undertaken. At Woodhenge, a ditch 6 feet deep and up to 16 feet wide was surrounded by an external bank. Inside the ditch, the outlines of the timber structure are traced by 6 concentric oval rings of posts, 60, 32, 16, 18, 18 and 12 in number from outside to centre. A possible dedicatory sacrifice of a three-year-old child, whose skull had been split, was at the centre of the site. The long axis of the timber structure was aligned with the midsummer sun. Professor Thom suggests that the circle perimeters approximate (with considerable inexactitude) to 140, 100, 80, 60, 60 and 40 MYs and that the oval forms are an attempt to create π values of radii to circumferences as close as possible to three. (The Cunningtons, on the other hand, who undertook the original excavation, chose as their quantum the 'Woodhenge Foot' of $11\frac{1}{2}$ modern inches.) After the wooden structure had decayed, a recumbent sarsen stone was placed near its centre, probably as a memorial.

Woodhenge lies much too close to the Durrington Walls complex for coincidence, being just 63 yards from the banked and ditched enclosure of 30 acres. Inside the enclosure at least two comparable timber structures

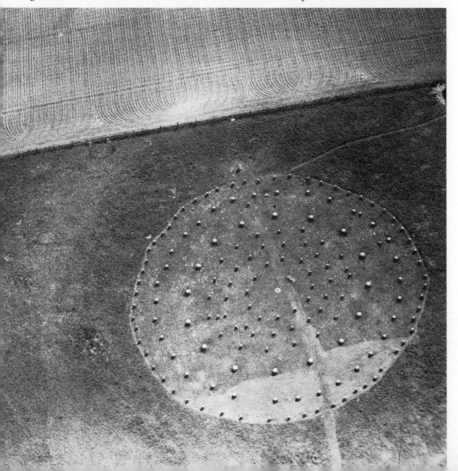

Concrete stumps mark the positions of the timber posts at Woodhenge in Wiltshire.

existed, the largest being 41 yards in diameter and formed of 5 concentric rings of timber uprights. Durrington was a major undertaking; the excavation of the ditch was a sufficient task to occupy 200 workers for almost 15 months, while about 9 acres of natural oak forest might have been scoured to furnish the building timbers. The ditch was dug in around 2570 BC and, as archaeologists only excavated a strip across the large enclosed area, there is every possibility that the unexplored portions were packed with massive round buildings. One or more large roundhouses may have stood there before the ditch was dug, while Woodhenge nearby seems to have been constructed just a little later.

In 1970, Professor G. J. Wainwright's rescue dig at Durrington (catalysed by road-widening operations) was followed by his excavation of a comparable site at Mount Pleasant, just east of Dorchester. Here there is a massive oval enclosure of 14 acres, defined by a bank and internal ditch which is breached by 4 entrances; the ditch dates from *c.* 2500 BC and may have been slightly preceded by the erection of a large timber building, again about 41 yards in diameter and formed of 5 concentric rings of posts. In *c.* 2100 BC 11 acres of the surrounding hilltop area were enclosed in a vast palisade of vertical tree trunks, each about a foot thick and standing perhaps 16 feet above the ground. Ninety acres of forest may have been utilized to provide the necessary timber. When the circular wooden house decayed, an open-sided square of sarsens was erected at its centre: like the house at Woodhenge, it seems to have merited a stone memorial. This excavation had been preceded by another at Marden, close to the River Avon (which flows past Durrington), and only 10 miles to the north. Here there was a bank and internal ditch enclosing 35 acres and breached by 2 causeway entrances. A simple wooden roundhouse was discovered inside the enclosure, though the large site may have held many more; Professor Wainwright's date for the construction was *c.* 2560 BC.

Finally, there is the case of the Sanctuary at Avebury, less than 1½ miles to the south-east of the great ring. Although the site was largely destroyed in the eighteenth century, it is still possible to discern the pattern of 6 concentric post rings and 2 rings of stone. The initial nucleus seems to have been a hut structure of slender posts with a diameter of 14 feet. Then a larger timber house 38 feet in diameter, its roof carried on 2 rings of posts, was set up on the same centre; a third and even larger building 66 feet across then surrounded the second building and at this time, or a little later, a 45-foot diameter circle of standing stones was erected inside the structure, with a second circle of stones 130 feet in diameter enclosing the whole. The standing stones of the West Kennet Avenue seem to form a processional way which leads from the Sanctuary to the great Avebury circle; and the Sanctuary building phases date from about 2500 to 2300 BC.

The dating and constructional similarities between these massive wooden buildings are obvious. They also seem to be linked to the paramount stone and earthen temples of Wessex: the Sanctuary with Avebury, and Durrington Walls/Woodhenge and possibly Marden with Stonehenge. They all date from around 2500 BC and were generally in use for a few successive centuries. They slightly postdate the construction of Silbury Hill, overlap with the period of use of some earlier and long-lived

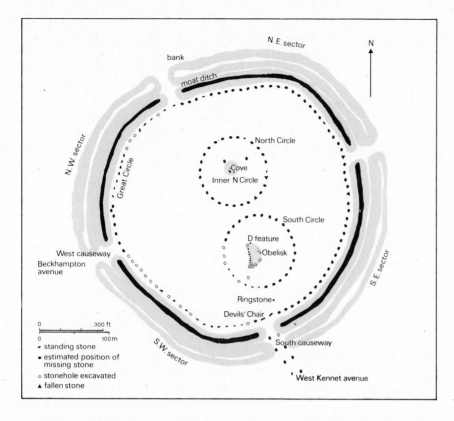

A plan of Avebury.

causewayed camps and barrows (such as Windmill Hill and West Kennet) and they are roughly contemporary with the initial stages of construction of the great stone monuments of Avebury (undated but thought to have been begun around 2500 BC) and Stonehenge (around 2700 BC). The sort of occupation at the great wooden roundhouses is not known, but they are clearly not representative of the normal homes of the period, of which scant traces have been preserved (see pp. 97–8, 101).

Although immense labour was expended upon the construction of the surrounding ditches, the ditch at Durrington was never cleared out and its position inside its dump bank and the provision of causeway entrances argue strongly against a defensive function. If the ditch was simply intended to prevent the straying of livestock the makers would seem to have taken a sledgehammer to crack a walnut. Speculation has focused on the occupants of the timber buildings and it is reasonable to suppose that special buildings had special inmates – particularly when the proximity to the megalithic temples is taken into account.

The foremost excavator of these sites, Professor Wainwright, is inclined towards secular interpretations: he thinks that the massive roundhouses may have been public buildings of some kind, which may have been surrounded by less spectacular domestic huts. The surrounding earthworks can be interpreted as either livestock enclosures or perimeters defining a sacred area. The liberal scatter of human debris obtained at these sites – pottery, stone fragments and animal bones – could represent either the accompaniments to ceremonial and ritual feasting, or mundane domestic refuse. At the same time, a purely secular use is difficult to reconcile with the apparent commemoration of the great buildings by stone monuments.

A more adventurous interpretation is provided by Euan MacKie. The great roundhouses cannot be dissociated from their period, during which Wessex men were undertaking prodigious construction works which served few practical functions. MacKie sees them as the residences of a priestly caste of astronomers, magicians and wise men, who inhabited the enclosures with their families and retainers and were provided with food as tribute by the surrounding peasant farmers. The priests were, he thinks, the same people who standardized the Megalithic Yard and established the various astronomical alignments. He supports his case by reference to the debatable mathematical and astronomical complexity of the Woodhenge building. But if one accepts the astro-archaeological case, it is hard to avoid the belief that there must have been in Neolithic and Early Bronze Age Britain a super-numerate élite to supervise the building of monuments. Such an élite presumably would not have shared their lot with the surrounding peasantry, but might perhaps have lived in unusual ceremonial and residential complexes. Whatever the roundhouses were, they were not ordinary homes and they can only have been built with considerable effort and ingenuity for very specific and important reasons.

To keep matters in perspective, it may be as well to note that it cannot even be proved that the post circles did support a roof – although most experts think that they did. The largest such structure stood at Durrington, and was more than 41 yards in diameter. One might imagine a conical roof, rising from eaves perhaps 9 feet above the ground to an open centre 43 feet above ground, with a pitch of 25°. When sunlight flooded into a central space and was glimpsed through a forest of tree trunk pillars, the sight must have been most impressive. But whether the buildings were trading centres, palaces, temples or the monasteries of a gifted élite, we simply do not know.

Let us give the last (but not conclusive) word on the subject to the veteran archaeologist Glyn Daniel. He sees the post rings as an intermediate stage between hypothetical forest clearings used for sacred and secular gatherings and the erection of stone circles, with the wooden posts reconstructing the ethos of the clearing. The datings marginally allow the post rings to precede most circles, but his thesis is no more proven than others which he dislikes.

Lastly, we confront the question of how the great temples like Stonehenge and Avebury were built. Considerable light has been cast on such problems by projects in experimental archaeology. On the whole, the picture which emerges suggests that organized and disciplined labour was involved, that there was the expenditure of vast quantities of brute force, and the use of simple handtools, as well as effective, if not particularly sophisticated, engineering techniques.

We know that the ditches which surrounded many ritual enclosures were dug with simple handtools: antler picks and probably shovels made from the scapulae of large herbivores, baskets of wicker being used for the removal of earth. A quantity of antler picks, doubtless discarded by the workforce when the digging was complete, was found in the ditch at Durrington. The hills and forests were probably systematically scoured for the annually discarded antlers of the red deer. Although the tools were primitive, they were not ineffective and replicas have not suffered in field tests against modern handtool equivalents. None the less, it is clear that stupendous amounts of labour were essential for the success of the major megalithic projects. Rough calculations of the man hours involved can be made as a result of the achievements of volunteers at modern experimental earthworks. Thus, for example, it is estimated that the removal of more than four million cubic feet of chalk from the enclosure ditch at Avebury represented the work of 1,560,000 man hours – sufficient to occupy a gang of 200 labourers for 780 days. Even if all the astronomical and numerological possibilities relating to the major stone circles should be disproved, the circles would still be monuments to the remarkable civil-engineering capabilities of their prehistoric makers.

Much popular interest has also been focused on the assembly of the gigantic sarsen blocks displayed at Stonehenge and Avebury. As the largest of the Avebury sarsens weigh 40 tons, they could not have been moved by simple lifting – 400 men would have been needed to lift such stones and there is insufficient space around them for a fraction of this number. The most probable form of transport resembles that used by the ancient Egyptians, involving the lashing of the stone to a sledge which was propelled along tree-trunk rollers. It would have taken a workforce of 880 men hauling on ropes, with others shifting rollers from behind to the front of the sledge, to move the largest of the Stonehenge sarsens two-thirds of a mile in one day. It can be calculated that the removal of the 81 Stonehenge stones from their origin on the Marlborough Downs to their destination 20 miles away might have occupied 1500 labourers for 5 years.

At Avebury, the sarsens are undressed, but those at Stonehenge have been smoothed. Sarsen stone may be twice as hard as granite and it has been suggested that 50 masons pounding and grinding for 10 hours each day might have been occupied at Stonehenge for 3 years.

We can speculate on how the great stones might have been raised, beginning with the digging of the socket at a 45° slope. The socket faces the sarsen, which is positioned on rollers. The stone is then gently rolled forward until it tips into the hole, resting against the angled side. Next, sheerlegs are positioned on the opposite side of the hole, a crossbar lashed to the sarsen top and roped to the sheerlegs. A force of less than 200 men might then be able to raise the stone to the vertical by hauling back on the sheerlegs. The raising of the stone lintels, which were morticed to the tops of the vertical stones, presented a more difficult problem. It is possible that a timber crib and a system of levers was employed. Men with levers would raise one end of the lintel and insert a wooden bearer and the procedure would be repeated at alternate ends until the stone was sufficiently raised to be slithered horizontally into position.

The question of the origin of the tough Stonehenge stones has also attracted much speculation. Samuel Pepys wrote of 'stones of considerable bigness, most of them certainly growing out of the ground'. It is now thought that sarsen stone is formed by the cementation of coarser quartz grains in a matrix of finer grains, as a result of chemical processes which took place under tropical conditions. It seems to have developed from shallow deposits of sand and gravel overlying some sections of the English chalklands, which were converted into a hard cap rock in the Tertiary era of 40–50 million years ago when the climate was tropical. Millions of years of weathering eroded this 'orthoquartzite' capping into fragmented blocks and it is likely that the periglacial conditions of the Quaternary Ice Ages assisted the passage of the blocks to the valley floors. As the upper soil layers froze and thawed, while the lower levels remained solidly frozen, the sarsens may have come slowly gliding down the slushy slopes like stately sledges to await the Neolithic builders of a warmer era.

The Stonehenge bluestones are a different problem altogether. There is little doubt that they can only be matched with the igneous rocks of the Preseli area of Pembrokeshire, but the manner of their transport to Stonehenge has caused controversy. In 1971, in a much publicized article in *Nature*, G. A. Kellaway suggested that spreading ice sheets from the west had conveyed the bluestones to the Salisbury Plain. Here we must call upon the expertise of another '-ology', in this case, glacial geomorphology. It is clear that glacial geomorphologists do not like Kellaway's theory at all. This is not because any vested interests are at stake, but because the idea simply does not accord with the facts of British glaciation as they are generally understood. The older and much more spectacular conclusion that the bluestones were moved by water transport from Wales seems the only one possible.

In the mid-1950s, Professor Atkinson showed that 4 schoolboys and a simple raft were equal to the task of moving a two-ton bluestone by river. The largest bluestones are twice this size and the men who transported them on the heavy tides of the Bristol Channel must have had seaworthy craft, nerves of iron and a liking for the blue-grey rock which bordered on insanity.

Many questions relating to stone circles have been reviewed and few clear-cut answers have emerged. The astronomical speculations may seem to many to be the most remarkable, but the simple facts are equally amazing. These are briefly that at a time when Britain was inhabited largely by peasants who, like their masters or leaders were illiterate, ignorant of the uses of iron and with no concept of the town, there were kings so powerful or priests so inspiring that hundreds of men could be taken out of the subsistence economy to work elsewhere for hundreds of days. The monuments that they built produced not an ounce of food, nor material wellbeing, yet they attracted a social effort that is equal, relatively speaking, to any undertaking in the modern world. Within a society which was perhaps economically and technologically comparable to the Red Indian farming cultures of pre-Columbian North America, there existed the organizational capability to assemble labour in massive amounts, produce the extra food needed to feed the workforces, plan and divide tasks, synchronize different operations, anticipate engineering problems and maintain momentum.

Little could be more amazing than this. And it is not even controversial.

Arbor Low. Lies 9 miles SE of Buxton (20 miles SE of Manchester) and 5 miles SW of Bakewell in a remote location. It is the most important prehistoric monument in the Peak District. The henge, with a circular bank and ditch enclosing a stone circle, has a diameter of 250 ft. All the stones lie flat and may always have done so, since no sockets have been found which might have held the stones upright. Four stones in the centre seem to have formed a cove. A Bronze Age round barrow known as Gib Hill was later built into the S entrance of the henge.

Auchagallon Stone Circle. This remote site on the Isle of Arran lies near the centre of its west shore. A circular Bronze Age cairn lies within the ring of 15 stones, which like many in NE Scotland includes a recumbent kerbstone.

Avebury. The largest monument of its type in Europe lies around the Wiltshire village of Avebury (10 miles S of Swindon on the M4). A high bank surrounds a ditch, which in turn surrounds the Great Circle of sarsens 1400 ft in diameter. The site seems to have an entrance at each of the 4 cardinal points. Inside are the remains of 2 more circles, the Central Circle and the South Circle. It is thought that a third one was destroyed during the Middle Ages. The Great Circle and the West Kennet Avenue which leads towards it are spectacular, despite some missing sarsens. Archaeology has not yet yielded a construction date, but all are thought to be the product of a single operation lasting many years. The Sanctuary, Silbury Hill, the West Kennet long barrow and the Windmill Hill causewayed camp are all within a couple of miles of Avebury village, which is charming and contains a museum.

Cairnpapple Hill. Lies $1\frac{1}{4}$ miles ESE of Torpichen in West Lothian (3 miles N of Bathgate, 17 miles W of Edinburgh). The summit, at 1000 ft, gives fine views of the Firth of Forth. The first stage of activity, $c.$ 2700 BC, involved the erection of a trio of massive boulders close to some cremation burials. Later the area was enclosed in a circle of 24 standing stones, and a ditch was dug outside it into the rock. Inside the circle were 2 Early Bronze Age burials (one of which is reconstructed on the site). Later still a massive cairn edged with kerbstones was constructed inside it, overrunning part of the stone circle. Its diameter was later doubled to 100 ft and a new kerb erected. Two cremation burials in cinerary urns were made. A last 4 graves were dug in the flank of the cairn during the Early Iron Age.

Callanish. Isle of Lewis, on a promontory over Loch Roag, 13 miles W of Stornoway. For astro-archaeologists this circle ranks second after Stonehenge, but its location ensures that it receives only a tiny fraction of the visitors and publicity. Its outline is unusual. A chambered cairn within a stone circle formed a nucleus, with 4 avenues of standing stones leading off in different directions. Professors Hawkins and Thom believe that it was for

Silhouettes of the Callanish stones.

determining moon setting positions, with sighting lines on Mount Clisham to the S. Four other scientists (Cooke, Few, Morgan and Ruggles) disputed this in 1977. Whatever its true nature, Callanish is spectacular and unusual, and its setting is magnificent.

Castlerigg or Keswick Carles Stone Circle. High in the Cumbrian mountains above Derwentwater (1½ miles E of Keswick), the Castlerigg circle is in perhaps the most beautiful setting of all, and is easily accessible. The ring of 38 stones is flattened at one end and contains a rectangular structure of 10 stones that touches one side. Two massive stones 12 ft apart may be a north entrance.

Cerrig Duon. This is one of the largest and most impressive of Welsh stone circles. It lies in the Black Mountains in the dark Tawe valley (take the A4067 NE out of Swansea, 6 miles S of Trecastle). The circle of 20 stones is 55 ft in diameter. An avenue leads off towards the NE and a tall outlier stands to the N of the circle. Two smaller stones continue this alignment, which Thom suggests may mark the rising of Arcturus in 1950 BC.

The Devil's Arrows. One of these 3 monoliths is the second tallest in Britain (the highest stands in the churchyard at Rudston, inland from Bridlington, N of Hull, on the Humberside coast). They lie in fields beside a lane SW of the North Yorkshire village of Boroughbridge (on the A1, 22 miles N of Leeds), along a N–S axis. Their function is not known. The millstone grit was quarried at Knaresborough 6½ miles to the SW and can only have been moved with great effort and ingenuity. The strange grooves at their tops are due to weathering since the Bronze Age when they were erected.

The Hurlers Stone Circles. On Bodmin Moor, N of an unfenced road ¼ mile NW of Minions (5 miles N of

The Castlerigg circle near Keswick.

Two of the Devil's Arrows stones near Boroughbridge.

Liskeard, 15 miles NW of Plymouth). Here are the remains of 3 apparently Bronze Age circles; some stones are missing, but those which remain seem to be set in the ground so as to protrude to an equal height. The name relates to some 16th cent. or earlier ball-players who were punished for hurling their ball on the Sabbath by being turned to stone.

The Knowlton Circles. Lie 3 miles SW of Cranborne (12 miles SSW of Salisbury) in Dorset. The visitor can see the earthworks and ditches which enclosed 3 circles aligned SE–NW. Only the remains of the Central Circle are accessible. At its centre are the ruins of a Norman church with a Perpendicular tower, clearly demonstrating that the religious associations of the place survived into the historical era. To the E is the Great Barrow, about 20 ft high.

The Ring of Brodgar. This circle is the largest in Scotland, and among the most imposing. On the landbridge between Loch Stenness and Loch Harray (B9055) on the Orkney mainland 4 miles NE of Stromness. Twenty-seven of the original 60 stones remain, towering up to 15 ft high. The 6 ft deep ditch around it was crossed by causeways to the SE and NW. There are some runic and ogham inscriptions. Thom believes that the island of Hoy, to the S, was a marker for lunar sightings.

The Rollright Stones. The King's Men is one of the most attractive of English stone circles. This, together with the nearby Whispering Knights (p. 27) and the isolated monolith known as the King Stone, constitute the Rollright Stones, to be found beside the minor road between the A34 and A44 which runs through Little Rollright (5 miles NW of Chipping Norton, 20 miles NW of Oxford). The so far undated circle of 77 limestone boulders is some 100 ft in diameter. It lies on a swelling ridge, close to an evergreen wind-break which creates an atmosphere of mystery in cloudy weather; but the delightfully lichened stones sparkle in sunlight.

Stanton Drew. Includes the second most extensive stone circles after Avebury. They lie to the E of the Somerset village of Stanton Drew (6 miles S of Bristol, off the B3130). The 'Cove' – 2 uprights and 1 fallen stone near the churchyard – is aligned with the Great Circle more than 200 yds away. This is huge: 368 ft in diameter with 27 stones. Following the alignment you come to the North-East Circle, 97 ft in diameter, with all its original 8 stones. Another alignment begins at the South-West Circle (11 stones and 145 ft in diameter), passes through the centre of the Great Circle, and terminates in the fallen stone known as Hautville's Quoit $\frac{1}{4}$ mile to the NE. The circles are probably Late Neolithic. The dark-reddish tints of the stones lend an added beauty to the site. Some are of oolite from Dundry 3 miles to the NW, but most are of local conglomerate. The very size of these monuments makes their components hard to trace, but visitors should not be put off. The attractive toll-house outside the village is a good example of its kind.

Stonehenge. Clearly signposted 2 miles W of Amesbury (7 miles N of Salisbury) in Wiltshire. Visitors tend to be surprised by its height, since the various stone rings are tightly packed together and form a far loftier cluster than most photographs are able to suggest. The first constructional phase is Neolithic (*c.* 2700 BC) and includes a perimeter ditch 380 ft in diameter. The earthbank lies, unusually, within the ditch. Inside the circle are the Aubrey Holes, and there may also have been a small stone structure. The Heel Stone next to the causeway in the ditch dates from this phase. The second phase, about 200 years later, involved the importation from South Wales of at least 80 bluestones, erected in a double ring. The Avenue was set out leading towards the River Avon. In stage IIIa the bluestone circle was dismantled and the site levelled, while 80 great sarsen blocks were brought down from the Marlborough Downs near Avebury (25 miles to the N). They were erected in a circle, surrounding a horseshoe formation with lintels over the uprights to form 'trilithons'. The bluestones were reused in stage IIIb, when 20 were erected in an oval and holes dug to accommodate some of the others. But this was never completed. The final phase, in about 1800 BC, involved dismantling the existing bluestone arrangement and constructing an inner circle and a second horseshoe-like setting inside the inner 'trilithon' horseshoe of phase IIIa.

Woodhenge. One can imagine the giant timber buildings that once stood here, for modern posts mark the 6 concentric rings of wooden posts. Woodhenge lies near the A345, 2 miles NE of Stonehenge.

A re-erected trilithon at Stonehenge.

Cattle graze on the ramparts at Hambledon hillfort in Dorset.

Chapter 4

Mysteries of the British hilltops

IN THIS CHAPTER we are concerned with two enigmas of the British landscape: the causewayed camp and the hillfort. These large, often vast, certainly imposing manmade features girdle many British hilltops. The origins of the camps have always been mysterious and have never been satisfactorily explained. The hillforts, conversely, become increasingly mysterious the more we learn about them – although twenty years ago they were widely regarded as the least ambiguous monuments of the prehistoric landscape. Sometimes causewayed camps and hillforts share the same hilltop site; but the camps and the fully-fledged hillfort may be separated by more than a millennium and we do not know whether the connection between the two is any more than geographical.

Most schoolchildren have heard of hillforts and may be able to recognize their ditch and bank defences, but the causewayed camps are less well known in every sense. Though more numerous in some regions than others, there are hundreds of hillforts scattered throughout the British Isles, but we scarcely know of twenty causewayed camps (although many more doubtless await discovery) and these are mostly in Dorset, Wiltshire and Sussex.

If we do not know what a causewayed camp was for, we have a fair idea of what it looked like: it is a roughly circular enclosure, normally situated on a hilltop or plateau, surrounded by a bank beyond which are one or more concentric ditches. The enclosed areas vary in size; the majority are 3–7 acres in extent, but the largest examples, Maiden Castle and Hambledon Hill in Dorset, and Windmill Hill in Wiltshire, each cover around twenty acres. The two Dorset examples coincide with formidable hillforts and several undiscovered causewayed camps may still lie obscured and overshadowed beneath later fortifications – just as at Maiden Bower fort, near Houghton Regis in Bedfordshire, where quarrying revealed part of a causewayed camp which underlies the fort. It is vital to remember, however, that the causewayed camps could not have been defended enclosures like the hillforts, for in every case numerous gaps or causeways were left unditched, allowing easy access from several directions. Although the majority of the camps stand on hilltops or downland plateaus, there are a few which lie on lower, open ground.

The oldest known causewayed camp was discovered by air photography in 1972 and the excavations completed in 1978. It is at Briar Hill, on the south side of the River Nene valley, overlooking Northampton and within half a mile of Hunsbury Iron Age hillfort. It has yielded a date of about 4400 BC. Previously, the oldest known was Hembury Camp in Devon, of about 4200 BC, while other camps date from the next 2000 years. The camps are, therefore, a feature of Neolithic southern Britain. They are contemporaries of the Neolithic long barrow burial mounds and a little older than Stonehenge and most other great stone monuments, though the camp at Windmill Hill was still in use when the massive circle was built nearby at Avebury. The people who buried their dead in the long barrows of southern England must have been the people who built and used the causewayed camps, and there may be other links between the two types of monument. The long barrows are much more numerous, and one can guess that, whatever the uses of the causewayed camps, the barrows served smaller communities than the camps.

We may go a little further, because when we map the pattern of camps and barrows, we see that in a number of cases the camp is located within a cluster of barrows, on average around 20 in number. A knot of 18 barrows lies within a radius of 10 miles from the camp at Maiden Castle – as we move north-eastwards towards the River Avon, we find a belt of 32 long barrows forming a 25 mile zone, with the camp at Hambledon Hill at its western tip. If we go northwards to the Hampshire Downs, we find that Robin Hood's Ball causewayed camp stands within a tight cluster of 20 long barrows; while still further north, the 18 long barrows located close to the famous Avebury complex of prehistoric monuments are provided with a generous quota of 3 camps: Windmill Hill, Rybury and Knap Hill. The evidence of the contemporary long barrows alone shows that each camp lay in well-populated countryside. But before we begin to explore the central problem of the camps – their function – we should look at one example in a little detail.

The causewayed camp at Windmill Hill in Wiltshire was the first of its kind to be recognized. Soon after excavations began in 1925, the term 'Windmill Hill culture' was adopted to describe the Middle Neolithic peoples of southern England. Various excavations and investigations allow us to reconstruct some of the events at Windmill Hill. Before about 3250 BC, gangs of workers on the hill began to cut the ditches; they were not innovators inspired by a grandiose new idea, for other much older causewayed camps already existed. The area enclosed by the outermost ditch covered 21 acres; nobody was greatly concerned that the enclosure should be perfectly circular and there is no reason to suppose that astronomical guidance had any part in the plan. In all, 3 concentric rings of ditches were dug, and the material from each ditch was thrown inwards to make an internal bank running beside each ditch. The outermost ditch was the deepest, dug to a depth of 7 feet, the innermost being the shallowest at 3 feet in depth.

We do not know how many workers were involved, but it seems likely that they worked in teams, with each team engaged in digging a section of ditch. It has been estimated that Windmill Hill is the result of 120,000 man-hours of organized labour – sufficient to occupy 50 men for 300 days, or whatever interpretation of the man-hour calculations you may prefer. In addition, other members of the community must have been occupied in supporting the labour force – providing and preparing food, searching for discarded antlers for picks, and erecting shelters.

Confronted with all this organized endeavour, we ought not to forget that

A Neolithic bowl from Windmill Hill in Wiltshire.

it was the work of a Stone Age community. The whole operation does not square with a vision of isolated communities of artless and ignorant savages: this society was sufficiently cosmopolitan, with travel sufficiently developed, to allow the people who lived near Windmill Hill to import the best stone axes from Wales and Westmorland. The upper layers of the ditch-filling debris date from 2000 BC, testifying to over a thousand years of continuous use, and, in places, debris-filled ditches were occasionally recut.

A past generation of prehistorians liked to visualize the camps as great cattle pounds, but this is not confirmed by the excavated remains. I am also sure that the Neolithic herdsman would have found it easier and more convenient to drive herds into valley pens, using topography to channel their movement, rather than to drive the beasts uphill to camp enclosures. Most camp interiors remain to be excavated, but it appears on present evidence that the camps were not centres for permanent occupation, but for regular visiting. While the most obvious features of the causewayed camps are their banks and ditches, the focus of attention was probably the area within so that these outer works simply existed to define a special area inside.

Probably the best clues for the uses of this special area come from material discovered in the surrounding ditches, for these ditches were used as dumping grounds for debris, with earth being added to cover the mounting pile from time to time. Considerable quantities of both human and animal bones have been recovered from the ditches of causewayed camps. At Windmill Hill the careful burial of two children has been discovered in the outer ditch, while adult skulls and long bones are scattered among the debris; Whitehawk Camp on Brighton racecourse has more human bones, a scatter of skulls, the rough burial of a woman with a new-born child, and the remains of another woman who was callously thrown in the ditch but not buried. Human skulls were again found at Hambledon Hill camp.

These remains, it has been suggested, are the macabre relics of grotesque cannibal feasts, but this explanation does not fit the bones from Windmill Hill. The adult bones are few in type and there are no complete skeletons. In addition the bones seem to have been broken when they were already old and dry. The most likely explanation is that they were removed from neighbouring long barrows for use in some kind of prehistoric ceremony perhaps connected with ancestor worship, although the bones themselves do not seem to have been venerated, for they were not returned to the barrows but simply discarded in the ditches. Similarly, old skeletons within the barrows were often cast aside roughly to make room for new burials. With the human bones, large quantities of animal bones have been unearthed: an ox skull at White Sheet camp in Wiltshire, the bones of domestic cattle, aurochs, sheep, goats, pigs, deer, horses, cats and foxes at Windmill Hill, and more of various kinds at Hambledon Hill.

Though the camps do not yield evidence of permanent occupation, there are clear signs of feasting. This supports the claim that they were ceremonial centres, used by the surrounding communities for periodic feasts, perhaps accompanied by religious rituals in which the bones of ancestors played a prominent part. Since it is clear from the pattern of their distribution that each camp served a number of communities, represented by its long barrows, we have every right to suggest that folk from the villages and homesteads would meet at the camps from time to time, for feasts or worship. In the course of these ceremonies or celebrations, contacts would be made or bonds established which reached beyond the realm of the day-to-day world. Moreover, though the work involved in the construction of such a camp was not great when compared with the ditch-building enterprise of Avebury, no single Neolithic community would have had the surplus resources of manpower to build more than a small portion of a causewayed camp.

In a controversial reappraisal of the pyramids, the physicist Kurt Mendelssohn has suggested that the real purpose behind the phenomenal task of pyramid construction was not necessarily the building itself, but rather the creation of a cohesive social unit throughout a vast dynastic territory, with men being brought together from all corners of the empire and confronted with an objective which required their united efforts: 'These huge heaps of stone mark the place where man invented the state,' he writes. On a much smaller scale, the causewayed camps may represent a similar stage in the development of the bonds of community. Indeed, it is not too fantastic to imagine that the first camp expressed a flash of inspiration in the mind of a local chieftain who discovered a means of moulding a larger community from the clay of his dispersed and parochial peasant subjects. If this suggestion is correct, then the motives of the pyramid builders were anticipated in Britain by perhaps 1500 years.

Equally, prehistorians may never recover the evidence that will allow them to agree on an explanation for the causewayed camps. It is most unlikely that we will ever be able to reconstruct the ceremonies which took place within their banks and ditches, to know whether they involved innocent and roisterous fun-making, elaborate and awe-inspiring ceremonials or dark and terrifying ritualized murders.

With our curiosity aroused but unsatisfied, we may turn to that other more common – and visually more impressive – hilltop feature: the hillfort. The results of excavations led by the great Mortimer Wheeler in the late 1930s at Maiden Castle in Dorset created a consensus among prehistorians several decades ago that hillforts began to crown the British landscape in around 300–250 BC, as defences against a Marnian invasion from the Continent, while in around 50 BC refugees arrived in Dorset from the north-west of France with new and more sophisticated forms of hill defences from across the Channel. These 'multivallate' defences involved several generally concentric rings of banks and ditches. Their makers were thought to have fled from Caesar's suppression of the Breton tribes in 56 BC, and the additional rings of defences were seen as a response to the development of the sling, which could hurl stones well beyond the range of the older javelin.

The vision of history to which most experts then subscribed seemed rational and consistent: the hillforts were defensive refuges built during the Iron Age as the citadels of the conquerors, or in answer to Continental threats and invasions; not only could the hillfort be fairly firmly dated but so too could the stages of its development. This view reflected the common 'invasionist' way of thinking, which tended to trace any development in the British backwaters of Europe to a Continental source, and it also reflected

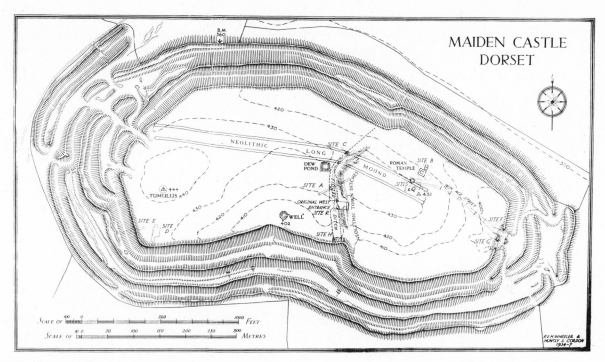

Sir Mortimer Wheeler's plan of Maiden Castle in Dorset.

Maiden Castle in Dorset, photographed in 1912.

the way in which artefacts can dominate the interpretation of history. With considerable patience and ingenuity, archaeologists can relate objects such as swords, brooches and domestic items to certain cultures, some of which (like the Celtic Hallstatt and La Tène peoples) can be traced to Continental homelands. It may then seem sensible to relate the monuments (such as hillforts) in which they were found to phases of Continental colonization.

It was not until 1969 that Euan MacKie did the logical thing: to apply radio-carbon dating to some Scottish hillfort materials. They were confidently believed to date from a little before 200 BC, but to everyone's surprise they yielded dates in the seventh century BC. The technique was then used south of the border, and some English hillforts produced astonishing dates earlier than 1000 BC. Clearly the prehistorian Rice Holmes had been essentially correct in 1907 when he said that although hillforts were widely used in the Iron Age, many had been built in the Bronze Age. Yet another manmade feature of the British landscape had been shown to be much older than was generally thought.

As the old structure of ideas began to collapse, more problems began to emerge – the more elaborate forms of defence, such as double or 'bivallate' ramparts, were found to be features of some of the older hillforts and were not always the products of later sophistication. Of greater importance are the discoveries made since attention has been directed more towards the interiors than the defences of the hillforts; in a number of forts considerable numbers of dwellings, sometimes set out neatly in a planned fashion, have been found, so that hillforts cannot simply be regarded as temporary refuges for local populations at times of trouble. Some of them, although the number is unknown, were permanent settlements of larger than village proportions, and it may be that the prominent defence works were integral to the town or village which they contained. The discoveries of the recent years have solved very little; rather, they have made from what seemed to be a straightforward type of monument a riddle of the utmost complexity. Now, for example, we are obliged to ask: 'If a community had its home in the hillfort, what kind of community was it – what set it apart from the people of the surrounding farmsteads and villages, and should the hillfort be equated with the tribal capital, the keep of a powerful baron, the market and manufacturing town, or the walled city?'

In southern Britain alone there are almost 1500 hillforts, differing widely in their form and date. The first question which we might pose concerns the reasons for the fairly sudden profusion of these vast defensive creations. Whatever their other functions, the defensive nature of the forts testifies to a troubled and turbulent society. As in 1939, when air-raid shelters mushroomed in many English gardens, the threat must have been such that people spent a considerable time in building defences. The great hillfort movement begins some time around 1000 BC, and before this date, although some weapons were carried, the picture which archaeology paints is of a generally peaceful and stable population preoccupied with agricultural pursuits. The majority of the hillforts were probably built between 1000 BC and 500 BC, after which the movement tailed off, though there were periodic upsurges in the making and the hasty reconstruction of hillforts – for example, at the time of the Roman and the Saxon invasions. The period of

Old Sarum, by Constable, 1834.

most active hillfort building coincides with a well-attested worsening of the British climate during the onset of a climatic period known as the 'sub-Atlantic'. At this time the average summer temperature fell by around 2°C (3.5°F) and it became moister as well as cooler, with the establishment of unsettled cyclonic conditions not unlike those of today. The communities farming the more marginal and exposed uplands must have borne the brunt of these changes, but even the farmers of the fertile lowlands must have been obliged to withdraw from expanding marshes and north-facing slopes. If a balance between people and farmland resources had been established during the preceding climatic optimum, it must have been severely upset: local conflicts, massacres and evictions may have taken place as men struggled to control the diminishing areas of farmland.

A second well-recorded development was the manufacture in increasing numbers of a range of effective bronze long-swords in the years following 1100 BC, which, like the machine gun and dive bomber of this century, must have brought new dimensions of awfulness to mankind's internecine struggles. Land pressure, a declining area of farmland and frightening new weapons – a combination of environmental and technological causes – may have been sufficient to drive communities into refuges on what had become blasted rain-lashed hilltops. We have no need to invoke any Continental invasion. Excavations by Professor Cunliffe at Danebury hillfort in Hampshire suggest that ritualized cannibalism may have accompanied the fiercest period of strife.

Before becoming deeply involved in the mysteries of the hillforts it is important to note that the term itself is applied to a range of defensive enclosures which vary widely in size, function, design and date. At one extreme it embraces the small and only slightly altered hilltop refuges of the thinly peopled corners of upland Britain; at the other, it might include the *oppida*, the British tribal capitals developed in the years preceding the Roman conquest of England which appear to have been defended political

81

capitals and centres for the dispersal of goods obtained from Continental trade. We have already seen that the hillfort period spans more than one and a half millennia, from the earliest British examples before 1000 BC in the Late Bronze Age, through the Iron Age and into the Dark Ages.

It is not known for certain, but the earliest British hillforts may have appeared in north Wales, or the western margins of England, with northern England and southern Scotland being at the tail end of the diffusion process. During the millennium before the Roman conquest, phases of abandonment, reoccupation and reconstruction succeeded one another. In the end, south-western hillforts, such as Maiden Castle in Dorset, were hastily refurbished to resist the westward advance of Vespasian's Second Augustan Legion during the Roman conquest of AD 43 in which, according to Suetonius, more than twenty hillforts were subdued. In some cases, such as South Cadbury, the population was resettled in Roman towns, and the hillforts left empty during the Roman occupation. In others, such as Old Sarum in Wiltshire, the population remained. The defensive value of the hillfort was not forgotten, however, and as the Saxons advanced on the abandoned Roman province, hillforts such as South Cadbury, Badbury Rings in Dorset and Cadbury Congresbury in Somerset were again occupied and defended during the fifth and sixth centuries AD. At South Cadbury in Somerset (the legendary Camelot), a further phase of Saxon occupation followed, and a mint constructed in the old hillfort was issuing coins only fifty years before the Norman conquest – by which time the hillfort was redundant in England.

In terms of size, again the range is wide; 'fortlets' which enclose less than a quarter of an acre are dismissed as too small to be dignified as hillforts, while archaeologists often make a convenient if arbitrary distinction between 'minor' hillforts covering less than 3 acres and 'major' hillforts. A few of the largest ones pass the 100 acre mark – Borough Hill near Daventry has a lower earthen bank which follows the 600 foot contour to enclose 150 acres.

An air-view of Borough Hill in Northamptonshire.

Variation is also evident in the types of defences constructed. One factor they have in common, however: whatever the techniques employed, the ramparts were generally considered secure, while their entrances were treated as weak points which attackers would try to exploit. The basic idea of hillfort defence involved accentuating the difficulties of the sloping ground which attackers would have to negotiate. In its most simple form, the defencework consisted of an outer ditch and an inner 'dump bank' which was composed of material thrown inwards from the ditch. In some cases, a palisade of stakes crowned the dump bank, adding considerably to its strength, and it seems that some hilltop rampart systems were preceded by the erection of a simple wooden palisade. In the rocky uplands of Britain, where the soil was too shallow to allow ditch digging, the bank and ditch were replaced by an encircling wall of boulders gathered from the hillsides.

Increasing sophistication in construction methods led to stonework and timber frameworks being included in the defences. While the 'Fécamp' type had a stone capping to the earth bank and a wide flat-bottomed ditch, the 'Priest' type had vertical timbers set at intervals to support the outer face of the bank, with stone revetments between the timbers. The more vertical the outer face of the bank, the greater the difficulties facing attackers. In the timber-laced forts, transverse and longitudinal timbers were incorporated in the core of the bank for extra stability. This type of construction was also used in the vitrified forts of Scotland, which are puzzling enough to merit a chapter of their own (pp. 137–41). The vertical timbers in front of the timber-framed rampart may well have originally carried a wooden breastwork which would have shielded sentries and defenders from light missiles. At Maiden Castle and at Rainsborough fort in the south of Northamptonshire a sentry walk ran along the top of the ramparts.

It was at the entrance that the defenders and attackers concentrated their efforts. In some cases the approaches to the entrance were channelled by banks and ditches so that attackers would have to expose their unshielded right sides to the sling-stones and javelins of the defenders. At Battlesbury Camp in Wiltshire the entrance is protected by a hornwork – a pair of projecting ramparts outside the gate, the ends of which curve towards each other to form a second, outer gateway. There is gruesome evidence that these defences proved inadequate on one occasion at least, for chalk quarrying outside the north-west entrance has uncovered what is probably a war cemetery, with a mother and child among the dead, while inside the defences stores of clay sling-bullets have been found.

At Danebury hillfort in Hampshire, the defences were remoulded several times between the fifth century BC and its last reoccupation against the threat of Roman invasion. At the beginning of the first century BC, the south-west entrance was deliberately blocked off and considerable ingenuity was employed in making the north-east entrance impregnable. Again the ramparts were curved outwards to guard the approaches, and blind alleys were provided to deceive and bottle up the invaders. An outpost was placed on one of the out-curving banks; from here a gallant force of defenders must have prepared to rain sling-shots upon the congested ranks of the attackers, for numerous hoards of ammunition were found there. A fighting platform capped the main gateway, and here once more the efforts of the defenders seem to have been frustrated, for the inner gateway was destroyed by fire shortly after its completion, presumably during an attack.

In a number of Irish, Scottish and Welsh forts, large boulders were set on end outside the ramparts to form a *chevaux de frise* to break a mass charge. Evidence of constant vigilance by the hillfort folk comes from the discovery of guard chambers flanking some entrances; at South Cadbury the single guardroom beside the south-west entrance during the first century AD had evidently been preceded by a period of neglect, for two centuries earlier there had been two guard chambers there. The guardroom at Rainsborough was much older and has been radio-carbon dated to around 600 BC.

Even visitors to a medium-sized hillfort can hardly leave unimpressed by the scale of the undertaking and the amount of organized effort required to produce such a stronghold. Even so, the hillforts did not take so long to construct as one might imagine. Bindon Hill is a promontory fort which guards the natural all-weather harbour at Lulworth Cove. After excavation, a 3 metre length of the timber-laced earth ramparts was reconstructed, and 6 men completed the task in 1 hour. This suggests a work rate of one half metre of defenceworks per man-hour, although an additional allowance should be made for the felling and transport of the timber, and the excavation of earth for use in the ramparts from the ditch.

One small mystery, which may turn out to be a red herring, concerns the countryside around the hillfort. Chapter 2, which speaks of the vanished wildwood, suggests that the removal of Britain's forests was well under way by the time of the hillforts. Yet if a palisade or a timber-framed rampart formed part of the plan, then the hillfort might have been expected to consume large amounts of nearby woodland. It is strange then, that the very few pollen analyses available for hillforts suggest that they in fact stood in woodland. This anomaly seems to be confirmed by an observation of Julius Caesar's: 'The Britons apply the term "strongholds" to densely wooded spots fortified with a rampart and trench, to which they retire in order to escape the attacks of invaders.' If the hillforts were wooded, this must have been by the choice of their defenders – an odd choice, for one of the advantages of hilltop positions is the view commanded, which allows for early warning of attack and for preparation to defend any threatened section of the ramparts. Wandlebury hillfort, three miles south-east of Cambridge, is surrounded by magnificent beechwoods planted in the nineteenth century. The result is instructive: although the fort is perched on a ridge of the Gogmagog hills and would command a view over miles of the low surrounding farmland, everything is completely obscured by the enclosing beechwoods. Why the occupants of hillforts neglected one of their prime advantages over surprise attack seems inexplicable. When other pollen analyses become available, we shall have more evidence with which to answer this problem.

As we have seen, prewar archaeologists tended to concentrate on hillfort ramparts and ditches rather than on their interiors. Not surprisingly, their excavations produced evidence mainly of military aspects of hillfort life, with sling-stones and even weapons being unearthed. Mortimer Wheeler's prodigious excavations exposed sling platforms and an arsenal of 54,000 sling-stones at the eastern entrance of Maiden Castle, while a mass grave at the gate testified to Vespasian's successful attack under a hail of missiles. The skeleton of one defender had a fearsome ballista bolt lodged in the spine.

The interiors of hillforts, which often cover tens of acres, present the archaeologist with a much more daunting task than the ramparts, and it is only recently that systematic excavation has extended to them. It is here that the mysteries concerning the true functions of the hillforts begin to emerge. Several seasons of excavation began at Danebury hillfort in 1969 under the direction of Professor Barry Cunliffe. Inside its complex defences both circular and rectangular houses were discovered, along with a mass of storage pits from between the fifth and the second centuries BC. The rectangular houses were not scattered in a random fashion, but were set out in streets, while some areas were set aside for refuse or food storage pits, between the rows of houses. Each house – assuming the rectangular buildings were houses rather than barns – measured about 12 feet by 10 feet, and the roof, which was presumably of thatch, stood on 6 posts.

Such planned and ordered layout implies the presence of a chieftain with the power to direct building operations and to view the project as a whole. There is also evidence that a sizeable community lived in the hillfort on a permanent basis, and excavation has uncovered plentiful domestic remains, such as grain, animal bones, pottery and weaving and smelting equipment. There was also a hoard of 21 iron bars to be used as currency.

Excavations at Crickley Hill in Gloucestershire began in 1969 under the direction of P. Dixon. A Neolithic causewayed camp discovered beneath the hillfort contained Windmill Hill-type pottery, and regularly arranged within the hillfort were both round and rectangular buildings. The round houses were about 23 feet in diameter, but although the rectangular buildings were generally quite small, one of them was vast – 81 feet long by 26 feet wide – and must clearly have had a special function.

At Croft Ambry in Herefordshire, a planned arrangement of rectangular houses appears yet again, while the powerful hillfort of 52 acres at Hod Hill in Dorset, like the hillfort at Chalbury in the same county, appears to have

The hillfort and Roman camp at Hod Hill in Dorset.

Excavation in progress at South Cadbury hillfort in Somerset.

been packed with circular huts. Although only about an eighth of the interior has been excavated, almost 50 hut circles have emerged. A scatter of ballista bolts surrounds what may have been the hut of the Hod Hill chieftain. After falling to Vespasian's legions, a large Roman infantry and cavalry fort was set up in the north-east corner. Although this Roman fort filled less than a sixth of the interior, it had accommodation for 600 legionaries and 250 horsemen – further evidence for the large population which might have lived on Hod Hill had huts completely covered the area within the defences. At Maiden Castle and South Cadbury excavations have revealed closely-packed homes from between the fourth century BC and the Roman conquest. The platforms of huts appear on air photographs of Hambledon Hill.

It becomes clear that although the small stone-walled enclosures of the remote uplands may have been no more than bolt-holes for a single family, and large forts were perhaps partly for livestock, a great many important hillforts must have housed village- or even town-sized communities. If this was so, the hillfort was less a temporary refuge than a fortified settlement. But how did the hillfort dwellers differ from their lowland neighbours; and what induced them to make their homes on windswept hilltops?

Some researchers have equated them with baronial keeps, or with fortresses of aristocratic families surrounded by retainers and maintained by tribute extracted from the surrounding peasant folk. The banked enclosures that appear to radiate from some of the hillforts could then be seen as the corrals of a cattle-owning élite. Alternatively, the hillforts could be seen as manufacturing centres, which began as local capitals, attracting traders and craftsmen until they became thriving commercial foci and centres for redistributing imported goods.

While neither of these views can be refuted, they are not on the whole supported by the findings of archaeologists. If the hillforts were the citadels of a wealthy élite, then we would expect to find goods of high quality, such as trinkets, ornamented weapons and costly brooches. But most of the objects recovered seem to indicate a population with the same standard of living as the peasants of the surrounding countryside.

We can see from ancient field boundaries that the hillforts controlled nearby farmland and pasture, which would have required most of its inhabitants to harvest grain, store the ears in pits, and grind the seeds in humble stone querns. Like the peasants outside the forts, they seem to have been subsistence farmers, with famine never far from mind. Without any doubt, these folk were also the subjects of chieftains; but whether these same chieftains were the central figures of hillfort life remains to be discovered. Given the freedom of choice which an aristocrat might enjoy, the decision to reside on a gusty hilltop would seem in itelf to require some special explanation. What aspect of their lives called for such protection? Weaving and some metal smelting were practised there, but it seems to have gone on outside the forts too. Industrial wealth would supply just the sort of reason required – but there does not seem to have been any to speak of.

Indeed, as Professor Cunliffe points out, agriculture was the primary concern of the hillfort builders around Salisbury Plain. All lie about one mile from a stream or river and are located so as to give access to good meadowland grazing for cattle, and upland sheep pasture. The clear implication is that they were located in accordance not with the needs of warfare but in the interests of the peasant farmer. Still, we must not forget that the hillfort is a very special kind of settlement, and that its construction and occupation would require the sanction of a local ruler, even if he did not always live there. Could these defences have been built to advertise the might of such a chieftain, or were they perhaps the desperate works of a frightened and threatened community?

It is probably necessary to choose a compromise between these interpretations, for it seems highly likely that each hillfort, whatever its other functions, was the capital of a surrounding territory and that rather than existing in static equilibrium, there was competition between them for the control of territory, with the victors assuming control of the lands of the vanquished. Before we look at the evidence for this hillfort Monopoly game it may be relevant to glance at the nature of warfare in the turbulent Celtic society of Britain. The bowed back of the peasant supported a martial, heroic aristocracy. At the top of the social pile was the chieftain or king, whose leading subjects included priests, elders, seers and bards, as well as young and reckless members of the warrior caste. Each important family had its following of clients, with the vast majority of society comprising the peasantry in its customary position at the bottom of the pile. Every young warrior dreamed of having his feats of arms immortalized by the bards, and

Hambledon hillfort; the air-view reveals the outlines of the ramparts, the long barrow and the depressions which mark the outlines of the Iron Age huts.

in a society in which cattle-raiding and vendettas were endemic, the opportunities were probably numerous. As M. Avery remarks: 'Classical authors tell us how the Celts were eager to join battle, seeking honour, intolerable in victory, with their head-hunting, but totally despondent and submissive in the dishonoured humiliation of defeat.' Much Iron Age fighting was ritualized and simply enabled young warriors to win the honours they sought. In such wars, the main attack may have been preceded by contests between the champions of each army; and those who survived would stalk the battlefield by chariot in search of noble opponents, whose heads would later hang from the becks of warhorses and be embalmed as trophies.

The hillfort had little part in this ritual, but once the outcome of war was decided upon the open plain, it would have been a place for peasants fleeing the scene of plunder below. Fighting at hillforts must have been especially desperate, with the screams of terrified children rising above the hubbub at the ramparts. Although the focus of heroic battle may have lain elsewhere, the hillfort might also have been a place where the chieftain and his retainers could sleep a little more securely.

Such warfare was effective, however, for it is possible to trace the fluctuations of power within a region. We are theoretically able to approximate the territory controlled by each hillfort by means of the 'Thiessen polygon'. Each fort is joined to its nearest neighbours by lines that are then bisected at their midpoints, and the bisecting lines extended at right angles to the joining lines until they meet other bisecting lines. Each polygon formed in this way has a hillfort at its centre, and includes all the locations that are nearer to this one rather than to another, and were therefore probably controlled by it. In practice, of course, this lacks precision, because we do not have a sufficiently accurate idea of which hillforts were in use at any one time. But even so, it appears that the first centuries produced a profusion of forts, which were later reduced in number by conflict and competition. For example, Professor Cunliffe suggests that by the fifth century, Danebury had absorbed the territories of the forts of Bury Hill, Balksbury, Figsbury and Quarley.

It is possible to argue that this competition between hillforts produced two highly significant end products – the town and the state. In the south-west of Britain, the Durotriges seem to have maintained their hillforts and traditional way of life right up to the Roman conquest; while in the south-east, large fortified settlements or 'oppida' (from the Latin for a walled town) had come to the fore by about 50 BC. While some oppida were protected by earthworks at many of their approaches, they were not truly hillforts. They covered large areas, often of lowland plains, and were mainly political capitals and manufacturing centres. Also – at least until Caesar's conquest of Gaul – they were engaged in international trade. The locations of many Late Iron Age oppida are not known, and some suspected sites are indicated only by earth banks which resemble oppida defences. It is quite probable that by the time of the Roman conquest, important Celtic towns existed behind the earthworks at Bagendon in Gloucestershire, Chichester Dykes, near Selsey Bill in West Sussex, and on the site of the modern towns of Colchester, Canterbury, St Albans and Silchester.

Notably most of these pre-Roman oppida went on to become towns under the Roman empire. The oppida dominated territories larger than those controlled by the hillfort chieftains. But since they almost certainly evolved from the densely occupied hillfort settlements such as Danebury or Maiden Castle, the claim that the hillfort provided an important link in the development of the British state and town is not without substance.

Though research over the last fifteen years has revealed much about the hillforts, W. Douglas Simpson is as correct today as he was in 1965 when he wrote: 'these astounding defence works, appearing so suddenly amid the "peaceful rusticity" of the native hut-circle villages, present many baffling problems'. Eleven years later, M. Avery could still write: 'The hillforts of the first millennium BC constitute a phenomenon unparalleled in the history of these islands. Perhaps never before, nor since, did such a large proportion of our population huddle in sizeable communities on relatively inaccessible hilltops and fortify itself so laboriously for the defence of these separate communities.' In Scotland, where inaccessibility was taken to extremes, communities even managed to survive on Tap o'Noth at an altitude of 1855 feet, and Bennachie at 1698 feet. How they did this is a mystery in itself.

We began this chapter with Neolithic causewayed camps and end it with the rule of Rome. A full millennium of prehistory separates the camp from even the earliest hillforts, and we may close by wondering whether there is a continuous link to be found between the camps, the forts and the emergent British towns. Some facts are unambiguous: a remarkable number of hillforts stand on causewayed camps. Others, such as Mam Tor in Derbyshire, are on the sites of early villages; those at Harting Beacon and Highdown in Sussex are on the sites of apparently rich villages. Others still occupy the sites of plateau enclosures; while in a few cases the hillfort appears to have been preceded by a defencework consisting of a wooden palisade. Much remains to be discovered – and it is only certain that the camp, the hillfort and the oppidum are all stages in the integration of people and territory around central places. It is by means of further excavation that we can hope to penetrate this link and follow each step of the way from the causewayed camp to the town.

Landslips threaten the Mam Tor hillfort in Derbyshire's Peak District.

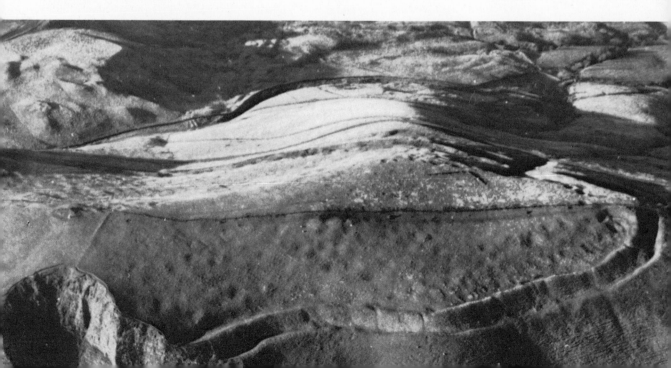

The concentric ramparts of Badbury Rings in Dorset.

Badbury Rings. Lies N of the Blandford Forum to Wimborne road, B3082 (10 miles NW of Bournemouth on the Dorset coast). This multivallate fort with 3 rings of almost circular banks and ditches has 2 easily defensible entrances. Thought to be the site of Arthur's Mount Badon victory, it may have been reoccupied during the Saxon/British wars. It awaits excavation.

Bagendon Dykes. These earthworks, close to the minor road from Perrott's Brook to Woodmancote in Gloucestershire (10 miles SE of Cheltenham), appear to be the remains of the bank and ditch defences of an oppidum, or pre-Roman British town. It was the tribal capital of the Dobunni.

Battlesbury Camp. Lies $1\frac{1}{2}$ miles NE of Warminster (15 miles SE of Bath) in Wiltshire. Almost 25 acres are enclosed by banks and ditches, partly double and partly triple. Pottery, clay sling-stones, tools and part of a chariot wheel have been found, as well as a war cemetery. At Scratchbury Camp hillfort, 1 mile to the SE (a path leads from the A36), a complex of 7 barrows lies within the enclosure.

Boddington Camp. The Iron Age hillfort lies less than 1 mile E of Wendover (5 miles SE of Aylesbury, NW of London) in Bucks., and can be reached by a track from the housing estate in the NE of the town. The 17 acre interior is wooded and parts of the ramparts have been destroyed, but there is a well-preserved stretch of ramparts along the SW and NW sides.

Borough Hill. The second largest hillfort in Britain. Best approached on foot across the golf course from the Daventry to Norton road (10 miles W of Northampton). The inner defences enclose $4\frac{1}{2}$ acres, and the lower area, perhaps for livestock, covers 150 acres.

Cadbury Congresbury. This univallate hillfort lies N of Congresbury (10 miles SW of Bristol on the A370) in Avon (formerly Somerset), and can be reached by footpath. It is one of the western hillforts refortified during the 5th cent. AD, presumably to meet the threat of Saxon invasion. Round and rectangular buildings, one of them possibly a temple, stood within it.

Carrock Fell. The largest hillfort in the Lake District, 800 ft long by 370 ft wide, perched at an astonishing 2174 ft on the summit of Carrock Fell, a northern outlier of the Skiddaw-Blencathra massif (8 miles NNE of Keswick). Perhaps a citadel of the turbulent Brigantes, and reduced by the Romans.

Croft Ambry. This hillfort in the Welsh borderlands (5 miles NW of Leominster, 25 miles W of the M5 at Worcester) is one of those in which there is evidence of a village within the ramparts. Occupation may have begun, during the 6th cent. BC, with the construction of simple dump-bank ramparts. The main enclosure covers about 7 acres, with a adjoining livestock enclosure of a further 7 acres. Stone guardchambers were added to the entrance in the 3rd or 4th cent. BC.

Danebury. On a prominent hill 3 miles NW of Stockbridge (9 miles NW of Winchester and N of Southampton) in Hampshire. It contains both circular and rectangular huts. One entrance of the 13 acre enclosure has been blocked at some stage and the other elaborately fortified. An adjoining 3 acre compound enclosed by a dump-bank was probably a stockade for livestock. The hillfort dates from the 5th cent. BC but was quite possibly built on the site of a Bronze Age shrine – a ritually interred dog was found there. The defences were improved on at least three occasions during the 2nd and 1st cents BC, and again during the 1st cent. AD, most probably in response to the Roman invasion of Britain.

Hambledon Hill. This impressive hillfort stands on a spur of Hambledon Hill in Dorset, E of Child Okeford (5 miles NW of Blandford Forum, 12 miles NW of Bournemouth). A Neolithic causewayed camp on its SE side, considerably damaged by ploughing and quarrying, has yielded human and animal bones and flint axes. The 2 main ramparts of the hillfort enclose 31 acres, following the natural contours. It is subdivided by the remains of ramparts marking stages in its expansion. The platforms of huts that housed its large population can be seen. One of a pair of Neolithic long barrows lies within the Iron Age site.

Hembury Camp and Fort. A hillfort and a causewayed camp at Hembury (15 miles NE of Exeter) in Devon, can be reached by footpath from the A373 between Honiton and Cullompton. One of the oldest known causewayed camps, dating from the 5th millennium BC. The multiple ramparts of the triangular hillfort enclose about 7 acres and intersect the ditches of the causewayed camp in a number of places.

Hod Hill. Lies 2 miles S of Iwerne Minster (6 miles N of Blandford Forum, 15 miles NW of Bournemouth) in Dorset. The 52 acres of the hillfort contained a large number of circular huts. The innermost rampart, of timber-framed defences fronted by a wooden palisade, was constructed first, and others added later. The Durotriges tribe was defeated there by Vespasian's legion before the work was complete. After the Roman conquest a large camp in the NW corner housed up to 1000 legionaries.

Maiden Bower. A hillfort and causewayed camp ($1\frac{1}{2}$ miles NW of Dunstable, on the M1 N of London) in Bedfordshire. A chalk quarry beside the 11 acre hillfort revealed the causewayed camp beneath it.

Mam Tor Hillfort. Lies 3 miles NW of the Peak District village of Castleton (on the A625, 15 miles W of Sheffield). The 16 acre hillfort is enclosed by a double bank and ditch, with 2 Bronze Age barrows in the SW corner. The road which skirts the Tor is occasionally closed owing to landslips. The road to the fort is clearly signposted from Castleton. On the way, note the abandoned ore-crushing wheel and the canyon or 'rake' of the Odin Lead mine.

Maiden Castle. Perhaps the most famous hillfort, it lies 1 mile SW of Dorchester (7 miles N of Weymouth on the Dorset coast and 25 miles W of Bournemouth). Almost 50 acres were progressively enclosed. The first fort contained 16 acres and was built *c*. 350 BC. The second and final plan was completed *c*. 250 BC. The third phase, a century later, produced a higher rampart and additional defence lines. More sophisticated defences were added to the 2 entrances *c*. 75 BC. The fort was stormed by the Romans in AD 43, but was inhabited for another 30 years, until it was replaced by Dorchester. In the last century of Roman domination a pagan temple was built. Beneath the hillfort a Neolithic causewayed camp was found, with 2 ditches enclosing about 20 acres of the eastern part of the

Hambledon hillfort viewed from the roadside below.

The defencework at Maiden Castle in Dorset.

91

hill. After its abandonment a remarkable barrow more than $\frac{1}{3}$ mile long was built across the hill.

Rainsborough Camp. A formidable hillfort S of Charlton (5 miles SE of Banbury, and 20 miles N of Oxford) in Northamptonshire, enclosing 6 acres. Begun in the 6th cent. BC, it is an early example of bivallate defences and guardchambers. Despite its sophistication the fort was conquered and burnt at the beginning of the 4th cent. and not reconstructed until 200 years later. Work was never completed.

The Rumps. A north-Cornish promontory fort in the beautiful coastal setting of Pentire Head (NE of Padstow). Three ramparts, with well protected entrances, bar the neck of the promontory. It seems to date from the first centuries BC or AD and to have housed hut dwellers.

South Cadbury. In legend this is King Arthur's Camelot, towering above South Cadbury (7 miles NE of Yeovil, S of the A303) in Somerset. Excavation by Leslie Alcock in the 1960s confirmed its occupation during the relevant period. The hill was occupied during the Neolithic, Late Bronze and Early Iron Ages, and the hillfort was begun in the 5th cent. BC. A town had grown up inside it by the 1st cent. BC, but the defences were neglected until shortly before the Roman invasion. The Romans destroyed it some 30 years after their invasion, and slaughtered 30 people at the SW entrance. The defences were renewed at the end of the 5th cent. against Saxon invasion, and a long timber hall was built. A Saxon mint operated from the hilltop at the start of the 11th cent., when the defences were finally reconstructed against the threat of Danish conquest.

Traprain Law Hill Town. A large Scottish oppidum 2 miles SW of East Linton (20 miles E of Edinburgh) in East Lothian. A stone rampart encloses 32 acres of hilltop, 500 ft above the surrounding countryside. It was occupied from the 5th cent. BC to the 5th cent. AD, and became the capital of the Votadini tribe who appear to have formed a treaty with the Romans. It seems to have been attacked by Picts in AD 197 and AD 297. A magnificent hoard of Roman silver, discovered in 1919, probably dated from the evacuation of the town under threat of Saxon invasion.

Walesland Rath. Almost half the 580 hillforts in Wales cover less than 1 acre, so Walesland Rath, near Haverfordwest (SW Wales) in Pembrokeshire, is a characteristic example. Occupation lasted from the early 1st cent. AD until the 3rd cent. AD. There are 2 entrances, one guarded by a gate tower. Excavation has revealed the traces of about 6 circular huts inside the oval enclosure.

Wandlebury. The fort stands on a hilltop within a nature reserve, 3 miles SE of Cambridge, N of the A604. It was first occupied in the 5th cent. BC, when the outer bank and ditch were built. A later, inner rampart was levelled during 'landscaping' in the 18th cent. by the Earl of Godolphin. It was probably last used by the Iceni in the early 1st cent. AD for resisting the northward advance of Belgic tribes. Building remains and storage pits have been found inside the ramparts. Magnificent beechwoods shade the circular ditch.

Whitehawk Camp. Neolithic causewayed camp between 2 small hills on Brighton Race Course (East Sussex coast, E of the town). A unique series of 4 concentric ditches encloses 12 acres. Excavation revealed human burials, scattered human and animal bones, flints, and 2 fossilized sea-urchins collected by somebody about 5000 years ago.

White Sheet Castle. This causewayed camp and hillfort lies $1\frac{1}{2}$ miles NNW of Mere (27 miles W of Salisbury, footpath from the B3095) in Wiltshire. The 4 acre causewayed camp has a single bank and ditch. A Bronze Age barrow stands across the ditch to the SE. The 15 acre hillfort stands opposite, on a spur, with further barrows inside it. Red flags warn of shooting in the nearby range.

Windmill Hill. This celebrated causewayed camp, described above (pp. 76–7), lies NW of Avebury (10 miles S of Swindon on the M4) and can be reached by taking the minor road running N from Avebury Truslow.

The Rumps, a Cornish promontory fort.

Gough's Cave, Cheddar Gorge, Somerset.

Chapter 5

The homes of ancient man

THE MOST IMPORTANT QUESTIONS in archaeology, history and geography do not concern pots, documents and distributions – they are about people. Students will spend hours peering at old implements, manuscripts and maps but the realization should dawn that these dusty relics have little value in themselves: they are useful only as bridges to link modern man with his ancestors. Few things can be more revealing about families or communities than their homes; but research on prehistoric British homes has not yet closed the enormous gaps in our understanding of ancient life. Some central questions remain unanswered, and the further back in time we go, the more sketchy the evidence becomes.

Settlement sites are by far the best source of information concerning the day-to-day lives of ordinary people. But even if such sites can be found, the challenges of dating and interpretation remain to be faced, with the help of evidence which is often fragmentary and ambiguous. Indeed, one of the most mysterious facts consists of the remarkable rarity of Neolithic and Bronze Age homes and settlements, particularly since there are plenty of stone and bronze tools and trinkets from these periods. There is also widespread evidence of forest clearance, which suggests a fairly numerous population. The rarity of even earlier dwellings, of Palaeolithic and Mesolithic Age Britain, is much less surprising since these were small communities which probably followed a partly migratory lifestyle, with homes that were either natural caves or insubstantial shelters.

The very earliest evidence for man in Britain takes us 150,000 years back, beyond two major ice ages. Beside the River Thames, some 20 miles downstream from modern London, is Barnfield Pit at Swanscombe – one of the most celebrated prehistoric sites in the world. Gravels deposited here by an ancient river included the flint tools of 'Swanscombe Man', along with the bones of the elephants, rhinoceroses and lions with which he shared his environment. Although archaeologists detect changes in human physiology between Swanscombe Man and the much later community of Wookey Hole in the Cheddar Gorge, which flourished between 25,000 and 10,000 BC, it is unlikely that there were any great changes in home making.

Man remained in Britain during the last great Ice Age. But at the height of this, between about 14,000 and 25,000 years ago, the northern parts of the British peninsula of Europe were abandoned to the frigid grip of its glaciers and ice sheets. Man remained a hunter, adjusting his diet to enormous fluctuations in flora and fauna produced by climatic variations. At Gough's Cave in the Cheddar Gorge the natural limestone formations provided a ready home and shelter, which although it was cool, was never as cold as the sleet-lashed landscape outside, where reindeer and bears roamed the birch-dotted tundra. Natural caves are quite rare and there were certainly not enough of them to go round. We must imagine small bands of Palaeolithic hunters, their womenfolk and children snuggling into fur garments, seeking sheltered hollows, and perhaps even scooping out sleeping pits and building snow houses in the winter. We will never find such places – no home leaves less trace than an igloo. Since so little is known about other Palaeolithic dwellings we can only note that Palaeolithic man had one advantage over the animals upon which he preyed – he knew the use of fire. Fuel must have been a problem in the treeless tundra landscape, so perhaps he burned animal droppings and fat.

As the glaciers receded, their cold waters flowed into rising seas; bushes and trees began to recolonize the British landscape. Gradually the Palaeolithic economy gave way to a Mesolithic way of life. The icy, open hunting ranges gave way to forest cover; fishing and the gathering of shellfish and nuts and berries became more important. Before the arrival in Britain of true farmers in the fifth millennium BC, man had probably achieved the domestication of some wild animals – dogs, deer and perhaps cattle. But our knowledge of the homes of Mesolithic people is very limited; we know of only about 25 settlements, and of these only 7 have yielded traces of actual dwelling structures. The best known of these sites is at Star Carr in north-east Yorkshire's Vale of Pickering, and is Carbon-14 dated to about 7500 BC. Here a campsite covered 250 square metres and a lake-side platform of brushwood was built among the reeds. The people of Star Carr hunted deer, wild cattle and pigs, and caught hedgehogs, beaver, hare, foxes and badgers, probably using trained hunting dogs. The evidence from the annual layers of antler remains suggests that the site may only have been used seasonally, in winter and spring.

Star Carr has yielded no traces of dwellings, but these are evident at other Mesolithic sites. At Low Clone South in Wigtownshire a boomerang-shaped hollow has been found, 13.6 metres long by 5.5 wide and a little over half a metre deep, in association with stake holes which may have been for a shelter over the pit. Other stake holes found at Morton in Fifeshire show very slender branches being used either for windbreaks or flimsy huts. There were other settlements at Blubberhouse Moor in the Yorkshire Dales, Selmeston in Sussex and Farnham and Abinger Common in Surrey – the two postholes at Abinger and the one at Farnham may show that tent-like structures covered the pit-dwellings. In contrast, at Thorpe Common in the south of Yorkshire a limestone wall served to screen a rock shelter.

It is unlikely that these primitive dwellings were permanently occupied, since a hunting and gathering economy required mobility; but larger communities may well have congregated at sheltered lowland sites in the winter, dispersing into small family bands for the summer hunting season. The Mesolithic home seems to have been an oblong pit, between 4 and 12 metres in length, which was covered by a light, tent-like structure of brushwood thatch or hide. During the colder months families would huddle together for warmth, shelling stores of nuts gathered in the summer.

A rather more sophisticated Mesolithic house was discovered in 1970, and its excavation by the retired Ordnance Surveyor Michael O'Malley

An antler head-dress from the Star Carr site in Yorkshire.

continued throughout the 1970s. It is at Broom Hill near Braishfield in Hampshire and it has features both of the Saxon sunken hut (described pp. 110–11) and of the Iron Age roundhouse. Like other Mesolithic dwellings, it has the character of a 'transit camp' to be used seasonally, rather than of a permanent home. The excavation of only a small portion of the site has so far produced more than 2600 microliths, tiny flints of the kind which Mesolithic people used to edge their hunting weapons and tools. But this site is so far unique and the typical Mesolithic home remains largely mysterious.

The birth of the Neolithic Age was marked by the introduction of farming. After the discovery and development of agriculture, families became increasingly tied to particular farming locations, although the earliest fields were probably only temporary clearings which were frequently shifted. Despite the surprising rarity of excavated dwellings of the Neolithic and Bronze Age periods, the remarkable circular timber buildings at Woodhenge, Mount Pleasant and Durrington Walls (see pp. 64–8) demonstrate considerable building skills. But since they were associated with ceremonial sites it is unlikely that they were representative of the common dwellings of the period. In order to imagine them the archaeologist relies heavily on postholes left by vertical timbers, or on foundation trenches; for these may survive long after timbers, thatch, or wattle and daub have disintegrated. But even when such remains are found there is little means of knowing how tall a building was, whether it had windows, or what the roof was made of.

Experiments have shown that the reason for which dwellings have not been found may not be because they never existed, but because they have disappeared without trace. A wooden or mud-walled building which has not disturbed the underlying earth might vanish utterly within a few centuries. Furthermore, in dealing with periods as distant as the Neolithic and Bronze Ages, natural erosion of the landsurface must be taken into account. The geomorphologists Eric H. Brown and K. J. Gregory have made observations and calculations which suggest that, over a period of a thousand years, erosion may lower a valley by between around 3 and 10 cms, while fairly level chalk may be lowered by around 10 cms, and limestone by 4 cms. While these areas are being eroded, others accumulate the deposits. Soil appears to gather at the boundaries of enclosed fields at a rate of 0.6 cm every thousand years. The Neolithic period being 4000 years behind us, posts sunk to a depth of half a metre might by now have been completely obliterated if erosion was active. However, the survival of the far earlier Mesolithic dwellings shows that areas exist in which erosion and deposition are in balance, and where traces of Neolithic postholes would survive, if there had ever been any. Simple erosion cannot account for the lack of evidence for early homes.

There are several types of building which could vanish without leaving a trace. One of them is the log cabin. The European settlers in Canada soon discovered that the log cabin is a sound and serviceable home, that can be built with far less effort than a timber-framed house of English type, or even than an Iron Age hut constructed around earthfast posts. Canadian pioneers

A reconstructed hut from Lough Gur in Ireland.

proved that a log cabin measuring 6 metres by 4 metres could be constructed in no more than 4 days. John Coles, in his book on experimental archaeology, compares this economy of time and effort with the 150 man-days required to construct a replica of the Neolithic daub and wattle house discovered at Allerslev, near Zealand in Denmark. Most importantly, no foundation trench needs be dug for a log cabin, and an archaeologist would need luck as well as skill to discover the small stakes sometimes used to prevent log slip.

The argument in favour of the Neolithic log cabin was therefore based on the paradoxical fact that scant traces had been found of any contemporary constructions. On the other hand, there is little doubt that Neolithic people had the necessary skills to build such dwellings, for they incorporated log-built mortuary chambers inside some of their earthen burial mounds. The most serious argument against the widespread use of log cabins in Britain revolves around the requirement for straight coniferous timbers which could be stacked vertically without leaving large gaps. Most of England at this time was dominated by broadleaf timber. It should not be forgotten, however, that struggling for light in the forest, the oak, elm or lime will produce a longer and straighter trunk than the hedgerow examples with which we are familiar.

Another type of dwelling which could vanish without trace would be one built of stacked turf, or with the footings of walls in turf. Again, American pioneers showed that the 'sod shanty' was a practical if not a luxurious home. A few British sites are known, however, which contained dwellings of a less ephemeral type. In addition to the Danish daub and wattle example mentioned earlier, a group of houses was excavated at Lough Gur in Co. Limerick by S. P. Ó Ríordáin between 1939 and 1955, and one of them was subsequently reconstructed. The houses had stone settings and were supported by earthfast posts, and one example, sited on a slope, measured 10 by 6 metres and was clearly quite spacious.

Stone furniture in Skara Brae in Orkney.

But it was precisely the lack of good timber in the bare windswept landscape of the Orkneys which ensured the survival of the magnificently preserved Neolithic villages of Skara Brae and Rinyo. In 1850 a storm stripped away part of a sand-dune in the bay of Skaill at Skara Brae to reveal a Late Neolithic village of 8 roughly rectangular huts, built of the local stone and connected by crazy-paved alleys. Each hut had walls 5 to 8 feet thick, which oversail inwards above waist height and enclose a circle about 15 feet across. The doors were set well back in the walls. The roofs have long disappeared but may well have been of sod or thatch laid on whalebone rafters. But the most charming features of the village are the complete suites of stone furniture made from the excellent local flagstones – stone beds which were probably packed with fleece, bracken or heather; stone dressers; and clay-lined stone basins set in the floors, perhaps for storing shellfish.

A little of the charm fades at the thought that the discarded shells and household refuse of the community were stacked against the outside walls of the huts until the village all but sank beneath the insulating midden. The Scottish historian W. Douglas Simpson points out that with its tunnel entrances and the smoke of fires rising from chimney holes above the midden, Skara Brae must have looked like an anthill: 'needless to add that the settlement must have stank to high heaven'. In fine weather, the villagers probably sat on top of the refuse mounds to work, and scattered bones suggest that they ate their meals in bed. One hut had no bed or dresser, but the floor was covered with the debris of flint-knapping and lumps of clay for pot-making, so this hut probably served as a workshop. Among the finds were stone axe-heads, odd carved stone balls (perhaps for a game), necklaces of sheep bones and whale teeth, poor pottery, and little stone and whale-bone pots containing paints – maybe used for decorating the body on important occasions.

Skara Brae has some secrets that it has so far refused to yield – why was it deserted in such a great hurry? A scatter of beads found in one passage

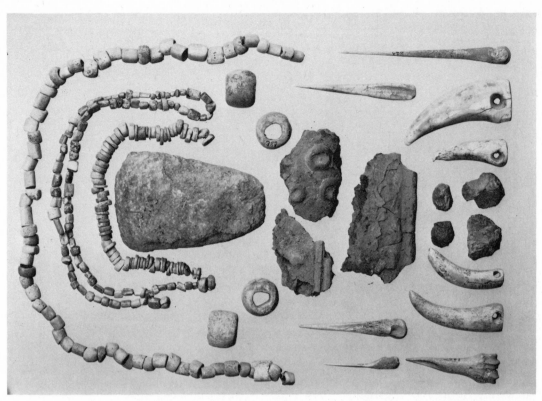

Some of the archaeological finds from Skara Brae.

suggests that somebody left in too much haste to collect them for rethreading. Later the village was engulfed in a sand dune, but it is most doubtful that a sandstorm was sufficient cause for the inhabitants to flee without taking or storing their possessions. The huts, half-filled with sand, were then reoccupied, but not by the original villagers, for these people ate deer and shellfish rather than domestic animals as did their predecessors. Skara Brae is usually presented as the home of farmers and fishermen; however, a recent excavation of two untouched areas of kitchen midden has produced evidence of burnt grain, implying that farming also took place. It is seen as a translation into stone of the more commonly found timber buildings and furnishings.

Euan MacKie, however, sees the village as the home of a special community of seers or magicians. The argument is based on the relative sophistication of the stone built huts, suggestions that the remains of joints of meat may represent tribute, the fact that one of the huts has an arrangement for barring the door from the outside rather than the inside, and could be a prison or place of vigil, and the fact that we know of only two other comparable settlements in Orkney – Rinyo and Knap of Howar – although the Neolithic population of the islands may have numbered thousands. The initial settlement at Skara Brae may date from 3100 BC, making it contemporary with many of the great ceremonial sites in England. Similarities have been noted between its pottery and the Neolithic East-Anglian pottery known as Clacton ware, but contact between these widely separated regions has not yet been proved.

A further remarkable discovery, made in 1978, throws vital new light on the nature of the Neolithic house, and hints that other types may indeed have been discovered, but wrongly identified. Nicholas Reynolds of the Inspectorate of Ancient Monuments, and Ian Ralston, a geographer at Aberdeen University, were excavating the remains of what was thought to be a Dark Age hall, the home of a powerful local personage, at Balbridie on the banks of the Dee near Banchory. However, the C-14 dates that were obtained from excavated materials proved not to belong to the Dark Ages, but to the middle of the Neolithic period, averaging around 3700 BC. On the very day that Reynolds collected the laboratory results in Edinburgh, his companions at Balbridie were recovering Neolithic pottery from one of the post holes. The Balbridie dwelling is a very large rectangular building measuring 26 by 13 metres, and is the widest Neolithic house known in Europe. The implications of the discovery are still to be evaluated, but meanwhile we must wonder whether some of the other 'Dark Age' rectangular halls which have been discovered might also prove to be Neolithic.

For the Bronze Age, as for the Neolithic, the small number of known settlements does not match the large size of the population suggested by the number of tombs. Again, the explanation may lie in the use of sill-beams rather than earthfast posts in house construction, but erosion and settlement drift probably also play a part. Archaeologists of the Near East are fortunate that building sites were used again and again, for the most recent house will simply be perched on top of a beautifully stratified mound or 'tell', composed of the remains of all the previous houses. In Britain, each settlement tends to drift round a site, both in prehistoric times and the Dark Ages. Not only does this drift produce less obvious remains, but when the archaeologist discovers a group of huts he is unlikely to be able to know whether he is seeing six huts which were all occupied at the same time, or one, two or three dwellings which have gradually been reconstructed and relocated within the same general area.

The Bronze Age is rendered even less clear by cultural movements. During the early part of the second millennium BC there was a gradual but steady movement into Britain of newcomers from the Rhineland. They must have brought some new ideas about home-making with them, and also have adopted some of the techniques of the indigenous peoples. It is not possible to describe a 'typical' Bronze Age home, partly because of the paucity of the evidence, and partly because several different styles are represented. It is dangerous to attempt to identify and label a people solely by reference to the type of pots, pins or dwellings which they made, and this point is underlined by the evidence from the Bronze Age settlement site at Belle Tout in Sussex. Homes were found there of Early Bronze Age immigrants known as Beaker Folk, because of their ritual of burying a drinking vessel with their dead. Three were circular and three rectangular, showing that one social group may build in a variety of styles.

By the Middle Bronze Age, settlements must have become a little more permanent, for small fields are sometimes found in association with them. At Itford Hill and Plumpton Plain in Sussex, and Shearplace Hill in Dorset,

The entrance to the Grimspound Bronze Age village and enclosure on Dartmoor.

little rectangular fields were farmed by small groups of peasants living in circular huts within a defensive compound. The settlement at Thorny Down in Wiltshire covered about $\frac{1}{2}$ acre and contained 9 circular huts, with saddle-querns for grinding grain and the weights from a loom, all dating from about 1100 BC. A defensive bank and ditch guarded its north-west side. There were at least 13 huts at Itford Hill, 20 at Stannon Down in Cornwall, and Plumpton Plain had 4 rectangular enclosures containing huts, while 3 more huts were unenclosed. But without knowing the degree of settlement drift we cannot deduce how many huts were occupied at any one time; and still more confusing is the possibility that the houses found are untypical, and that others have left no trace at all. One of the most impressive prehistoric settlement sites is Grimspound on Dartmoor, where several circular stone walled huts nestle within an encircling enclosure wall. Rings of stones which preserve the outlines of prehistoric huts are scattered on Dartmoor and a small group can be seen on the eastern side of the road less than a quarter of a mile to the north of Grimspound. Like Grimspound itself, they have not been precisely dated, but presumably belong to the Bronze Age.

Other problematical Bronze Age sites are Mam Tor in Derbyshire, Grimthorpe in east Yorkshire, Norton Fitzwarren in Somerset, and several others in Scotland, such as at Muirkirk in Ayrshire. Here, the foundations consist of circular or oval rings of mixed stones and earth, surviving to heights of 2 or 3 feet. They enclose areas of between 20 and 35 feet in diameter, and are about 3 feet thick. It is assumed that these supported wattle and daub walls and a thatched conical roof. Though huts of this type recur at several periods and may even have continued into the Christian era, the hut circles at Muirkirk in Ayrshire are thought to be datable to the Early Bronze Age by the finds made there: pottery, flint knives and scrapers, a saddle-quern, a jet armlet and a 'pot boiler' – a large stone which was heated and dropped into the pot to heat its contents. At Jarlshof on the mainland island of Shetland, Late Bronze Age houses form part of an amazing sequence of settlement from the Neolithic to the late medieval periods. Similarly extraordinary are those at Stanydale, also on the Shetland mainland, where there are 2 groups of 5 and of 4 houses. The best preserved is oval in outline with walls 9 feet thick, enclosing an area 30 feet along its axis. The walls swing outwards from the doorway to flank the entrance with a porch probably designed to shield the inmates from the piercing winds. The spacious interior has a stone wall-bench and central hearth and is partitioned into recesses along the eastern wall. There is a small near-circular inner room.

We cannot leave Stanydale without mentioning the building known as 'the temple', which is probably contemporary with these houses. A wall of rough slabs, 12 feet thick, encloses a 40 by 20 feet area, which is oval except for the south-western end where the wall becomes concave to contain the entrance. Inside there are 6 carefully constructed recesses in the walls. The sockets for 2 massive posts in the floor contained fragments of timber found on analysis to be spruce. The pottery showed it to belong to the very Late

A reconstruction of a roundhouse based on evidence from Maiden Castle at the Butser Ancient Farm Project Trust in Hampshire with a roof of interwoven hazel rods.

Neolithic or Early Bronze periods, yet spruce was not introduced to Scotland until 1548. We must either believe that huge driftwood logs had found their way to Shetland from North America, or that the prehistoric builders engaged in timber trade with Scandinavia requiring massive boats and great skills in seamanship. It cannot be proved that the building served as a temple, but it is large and distinct in style from the surrounding houses, and happens to resemble the temples of Malta. The houses and fields grouped around the temple at Stanydale form a unique and mysterious village unit.

Iron came to replace bronze in many tools and weapons in about 700 BC, and the process was accompanied by drifts and surges of Celtic immigration which continued until the Roman conquest. The typical Iron Age house was a large circular hut, 12 or more feet in diameter, with a conical thatched roof supported by circles of vertical posts. Of various reconstructed examples one of the best is the farm project at Butser Hill in Hampshire, containing 2 circular huts with thatched roofs and walls of wattle and daub, and a third of turf. Huts such as these were widespread during the Iron Age, built singly or in groups, and often within thorn-fenced or ditched and banked enclosures.

An interesting example is at Little Woodbury in Wiltshire, where a roundhouse some 45 feet in diameter stood within a banked enclosure 4 acres in extent; a structure of such impressive dimensions may have been the home of the local chieftain. At Glastonbury in Somerset, where a village of the second and first centuries BC has been extensively excavated, there are signs that the first occupants, between 150 and 60 BC, covered the marshy site with stout rectangular timber houses on piles above the mud. The village site was recolonized after 60 BC – apparently without a struggle – by

Mortised beams excavated at the
Glastonbury Lake Village.

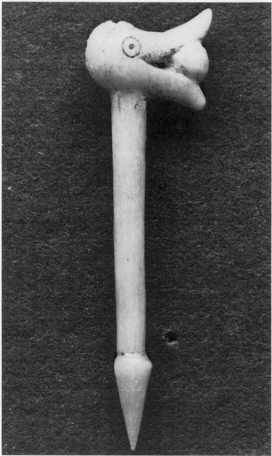

A bone pin discovered at the
Glastonbury Lake Village.

immigrants who tore down the rectangular huts and built quite different dwellings inside a palisade. Brushwood provided firm foundations for the floors of clay. The completed huts were circular, with wattle and daub walls. The remains of almost a hundred such huts have been discovered, although only 10 or 20 may have been occupied at any one time.

In 1966 one of the circular Glastonbury huts was reconstructed as part of an experiment. Posts and roofing poles formed a centrally supported tripod 13 feet in diameter. Withies were woven round the wallposts and made weathertight with plaster made of clay and chopped straw. The hut took 175 man-hours to complete, but was burned down by vandals before studies were complete. Similar studies have shown that the greatest threat to mud-plastered houses came from rising damp and frost damage. They would need to be reconstructed completely every 15 or 20 years. Excavations at Wharram Percy show that the medieval peasant huts had lifespans of less than 30 years.

Differences in constructional techniques and building materials depend on diverse factors. At Ewe Close in the Lake District building stone was abundant and a walled village based on a square groundplan was built in Roman or pre-Roman times (the Roman road between Lancaster and Carlisle was diverted to pass near it). In the middle of the village a circular stone hut some 50 feet in diameter is surrounded by 10 lesser stone huts. A single rectangular house reminds one that homes may be of contrasting design. There is also a well, some stone-walled cattle pens, and drystone walling surrounding the fields beyond.

With unsolved mysteries never far away, we should now consider Carn Euny in Cornwall. On top of Neolithic and Bronze Age remains, two Iron Age villages were erected. The first was of timber, dating from the second century BC, and the second, begun in the first century BC, was occupied during the Roman period. One of the houses of the later period contained the entrance to a peculiar underground passage: strongly built, lined with stones, and curving for a length of 66 feet. At one end a short alley leads into a circular chamber. At the other end, a short lateral passage branches off. Such passages associated with Iron Age houses are known in Cornwall as 'fogous' and in Eastern Scotland as 'earth-houses' or 'souterrains'. They were built by the native Celtic population during the centuries of the Roman occupation; Roman coins and pottery of the first and second centuries AD have been found in several examples, while those at Newstead in Roxburghshire and Crichton in Midlothian include stones removed from Roman buildings.

They typically consist of long curving underground galleries walled with drystone masonry, which is corbelled until the roofspace is sufficiently narrow to be bridged by lintels. At Tealing and Ardestie in Angus, in particular, they have quite elaborate systems of branching lateral galleries. Their function is mysterious, and W. Douglas Simpson has quoted the remarks of a visiting French archaeologist who said that it 'passed his understanding how a people clever enough to build such structures were not also clever enough to remain outside them once they were were built'. It has been suggested that they were for storing food, but some contained the remains of hearths and food refuse, showing that at certain times they were

The Carn Euny Fogou, Cornwall.

The entrance to the Culsh
Souterrain in Aberdeenshire.

This detail of a map of *c.* 1603 depicts an attack on an Irish crannog and reveals the long history of these lake dwellings.

lived in. It is difficult to believe that they were hideaways, because they were always adjuncts to huts which will have betrayed the presence of a settlement; so anyone who bolted down one of the underground passages would be completely trapped and defenceless. The occasional construction of drains, such as at Culsh near Aboyne in Aberdeenshire, may point to the souterrains being used as cattle pounds, but the problem still awaits its final solution.

The souterrain is of help, however, in providing a link between Roman Scotland and Ireland, for similar underground passages have been discovered at some of the Irish defended farmsteads known as 'raths'. Almost 40,000 Irish raths are known and the existence of many more are implied by place names. Some were built during the three centuries before Christ, but the great majority seem to be from between the fifth and eleventh centuries AD. The tradition was amazingly long-lived, for raths were still being built during the seventeenth century and perhaps even later. They seem to have been the homes of cattle farmers, and they consist usually of a circular earthen bank within which a round or occasionally rectangular thatched wooden farmstead stood, often sited near the western bank to gain shelter from the wind. Small raths less than 50 feet in diameter may have been merely cattle compounds, but most of the enclosures which contain dwellings are 100 to 150 feet in diameter. Those up to 300 feet in diameter could be the homes of chieftains. Several concentric rings of banks and ditches are sometimes found, perhaps to enhance the status of the occupant. The ditch is usually in the defensive position, on the outer side of the bank, but ditches are also found within the earthbank – perhaps to provide water for the enclosed cattle. Although the earthbanks were sometimes faced in drystone masonry, they will have been insufficient to exclude any sizeable force, and the rath is best interpreted as the stockaded farmstead of a family engaged in livestock farming. In the evening the cattle were probably penned within the stockade, out of reach of wolves and small bands of cattle rustlers. Cattle raiding was certainly widespread in Ireland until well into the historical period.

Occasionally, souterrains occur beneath the floor of the rath homestead. Some contain traps for unwelcome intruders, although others have chimneys and chambers to make human occupation possible. But the problem is similar to that posed by fogous and Scottish souterrains – it is unlikely that anyone would live in the dank, inky blackness of a souterrain without good reason. The strangely polished surfaces of the sides of some rath souterrains may be the result of prolonged rubbing by cattle – perhaps showing that they were used for livestock in times of danger.

Another distinctive homestead found both in Scotland and in Ireland is the 'crannog', or lake dwelling. Although natural islands were sometimes used, the crannog dwellers more often went to enormous trouble to build their own islands on which to construct their homes. This would be an understandable, if extreme, response to the threat of marauders, had there not been many other families and communities living in undefended huts or behind simple earthbanks or flimsy palisades.

The little research work which has been done on the Scottish crannogs shows them to belong to the second half of the first millennium BC and to end in the first century AD. In Ireland on the other hand they are part of an astounding defensive tradition which appears to begin in the Late Bronze Age and continues until after the Middle Ages. Attacks on crannogs are recorded in the sixteenth century and a map of 1603 is decorated with a drawing of a spirited defence of a crannog in which two houses are surrounded by a rectangular wickerwork palisade.

One of the few Scottish crannogs to have been thoroughly explored is at Milton Loch in Kirkcudbrightshire, where 2 crannogs were exposed when the water level was reduced in 1953. The north-western house stood on piles and was linked to the shore by a 100 foot causeway. There was also a small boat-pen. The hut was circular and had a central clay hearth which stood on stone slabs to protect the floor timbers. The house timbers produced a Carbon-14 date of 460–500 BC, as did a unique example of an Early Iron Age 'ard' type of wooden plough. An enamelled dress fastener of the second century AD prompted Professor Stuart Piggott to write: 'What more natural than to find some Roman or native using the little decayed and grass-grown crannog as a suitable position from which to fish, some six hundred years or so after the original occupants of the site had died'.

The buildings which stood on the manmade platforms of Scotland and Ireland were trivial compared with the platform itself. Various techniques of construction were employed – some were on timber piles, others just massive accumulations. The building of a crannog, particularly when we consider the efforts needed to hold down timbers beneath the lake surface, must have been equivalent, relatively speaking, to that involved in building a small stone fort. In the north and west of the central plain of Ireland, crannogs are relatively common during the Late Iron Age. The watertable was higher than it is today and lakes therefore more numerous. In Scotland fewer are known, and are mostly in the south-west of the country.

We must wonder whether such specialized homesteads belonged to a particular class or sub-nation, or whether they were the homes of natives whose insecurity and energies were great enough for them to wish to build an island. But many more lake dwellings must be excavated before we have an answer to this question.

Air-view of a crannog site by Lough Gara in Co. Sligo.

Lastly in the Iron Age there is the wheelhouse – perhaps the ultimate in drystone huts. This is a circular building, 30 to 40 feet in diameter, with a roof of stone slabs about 10 feet above the floor. It is distinctive for the spoke like partitions which radiate from the open centre of the house containing the hearth, and which divide the interior into a series of compartments. Only a few are known, all in northern and western Scotland, where they seem to have spread from Shetland to the Hebrides, with a handful in Orkney. The Shetland sites give us the chronology of the wheelhouse, for they clearly follow the abandonment of the broch in the cases of Jarlshof, Clickhimin, Mousa and Clumland. When brochs became obsolete, in the early second century AD, their walls were quarried to provide stone wheelhouses. Since there are relatively few of these massive and sophisticated structures, we may suppose that they belonged to an élite rather than the common people.

Although the modern English family probably has more Celts than Saxons amongst its forbears, the Anglo-Saxons have usually been regarded as the ancestral English. This helps to account for the interest in Saxon villages, although research has produced much controversy concerning the sort of people they were, as well as a number of red herrings. When E. T. Leeds excavated the late fifth-century Saxon village at Sutton Courtenay (Berkshire) after the First World War, the Saxons got a very bad press. Their small huts were described as squalid hovels, and traces of other Saxon huts have been found. The bones of a dog in one of the huts inspired horror at the thought that Saxons were either so shamefully un-British as to eat dogs, or that they were prepared to share their living quarters with a decomposing animal. Fortunately other explanations for the presence of the dog are far sounder – the animal may have crawled there to die. But more recent excavations cast doubts on the initial interpretation of Sutton Courtenay – for example, it is now thought that many of the buildings interpreted as homes may have been no more than sheds and outbuildings.

Discussion still continues round the function of Saxon sunken-floored dwellings. There are 35 examples at Sutton Courtenay – roughly rectangular pits about 12 feet long, 9 feet wide and 2 feet deep. Similar

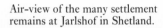
Air-view of the many settlement remains at Jarlshof in Shetland.

examples on the Continent of Europe date from the time of Saxon migration to England. At Wijster in Holland there are 80 sunken huts, in close association with 86 quite different long-houses, and it has been suggested that the sunken huts were their outbuildings. About 50 settlements with sunken huts are known between the Elbe and the Rhine, as against about 25 in England. But what sort of buildings stood over the shallow hollows? What was the relationship between the sunken huts and the more elaborate rectangular houses so frequently found in the same village complex?

It is hardly surprising that descriptions based on the simple scooped out hollows and the 2 or 3 posts which supported a tent-like roof should emphasize the squalidness of these buildings. But experimental archaeologists near the Early Saxon village of West Stow, in Suffolk, reconstructed such huts and found them to be sound, snug and serviceable. As for who used them, the 112 huts at the Early Saxon village at Mucking in Essex were thought by M. U. Jones to be part of a fluctuating settlement, linked either to summer pasturing or to Saxon mercenaries in the pay of the Romans. He asks whether it would be too fanciful:

to regard the sunken huts of the Mucking landscape as the Nissen huts of the Migration world; as low cost, easily erected shelters, useful for soldiers, refugees, immigrants, stores, camp followers, camp traders, as need arose? Perhaps Mucking developed into a sort of transit camp for sudden influxes of homeless people, a first landfall after a North Sea crossing, with most of their wealth on their bodies, on their way to resume their farming role, and found anglicized Saxon villages in their new country.

Not all such structures are of the same type, however, and several designs often occur on the same site. A Saxon hall stands among the huts at Mucking; at Chalton in Hampshire the main building was rectangular and measured 14 by 7 metres and had 3 entrances. It was surrounded by a cluster of smaller rectangular structures, perhaps outbuildings, lying in a fenced enclosure which could only be reached via the main farmstead. The 68 sunken-floored huts at West Stow seemed to be arranged round larger and taller 'halls', with walls of vertical oak planks and roofs of straw or sedge laid on a woven hazel framework. The excavators saw the halls as domestic foci and the sunken huts as workshops and storage places, perhaps only sometimes to be used as living quarters.

So if we are not sure whether the Saxon sunken hut was the outbuilding of a farmstead or the temporary shelter of people in transit, we must still ask what was the purpose of the sunken floor itself? Those who emphasize the temporary nature of the hut see it as an easy way of obtaining the maximum height of walls from the minimum of building materials. Whatever the reason, the experiment at West Stow shows that, in order to be comfortable, the floors would need to be covered with boarding, for without it the earth would be uneven and the floor damp. Space would be left beneath the floorboards for drainage or storage or, more ingeniously, to be packed with grass and straw which would create warmth while fermenting – an early form of central heating. The West Stow workers conclude by proposing a redefinition of the Saxon home: 'It no longer seems possible to suggest that they were everywhere living in murky shelters consisting of holes in the ground covered by tents'.

The Norman interior at Hemingford Manor showing the upper hall.

Although the home of the peasant family remained crude throughout most of the Middle Ages, houses of timber, wattle and thatch were employed during the Saxon era, perhaps using cruck and box framing, which are displayed in more elaborate styles in over a thousand surviving medieval houses. Crucks are constructed around two pairs of timber blades, joined at the tips and widely separated at their bases, to form the A-shaped frames visible at either end of the typical cruck-framed building. The origins of this method of timber building are obscure; some experts believe that it spread from Wessex early in the medieval period, but others point to the absence of cruck buildings in the eastern counties, and suggest that it was the standard vernacular style of Roman Britain. It may, therefore, have been displaced from the east by other building techniques introduced by the Saxon settlers.

The oldest-known and still inhabited home is a much modified Norman hall discovered under later accretions during renovations in the 1940s at Hemingford Grey in Huntingdonshire. However, the work of C. Hewett on carpentry techniques has added a new dimension to the dating of buildings, and a Carbon-14 date taken from the privately owned timber manor barn at Belchamp St Paul in Essex vindicated his predictions by producing the astounding date of 1026. If a barn can survive from Saxon times it is reasonable to expect the eventual discovery of a number of Saxon homes, probably incorporated in later houses where they now lie unsuspected.

The roots of excavated dwellings seem dead and soulless; the discovery of the more durable of the possessions of their occupants breathes a little life into the scene. Reconstructions impart new colour and reveal many of the constructional problems encountered, and the possible human responses. As we have seen, if the remains of dwellings are to help us bridge the time gap with peoples of the past, generous quantities of lively imagination are essential. Such imagination, combined with archaeological effort and expertise, has already helped raise some folds of the shrouds of mystery from over the homes of ancient Britain.

Butser Hill. Signposted W of the A3, SW of Petersfield (10 miles N of Portsmouth) in Hampshire. There are Bronze Age barrows and fields, and incomplete Iron Age earthworks. The most significant feature is the Butser Ancient Farm Project, where a reconstructed Iron Age farm is run with livestock, crops and farming methods characteristic of about 300 BC. A group of circular huts, based on examples excavated nearby as well as in Dorset, stands on a high spur. There is a fine view from above the farm. It is open to visitors, and guided tours can be provided on prior arrangement.

Carn Euny Village and Fogou. Site ½ mile NNW of Brane in Cornwall (leave the A30 at Drift, 2 miles W of Penzance). Car-park in the village. The earliest wooden huts have completely disappeared, and the foundations of several stone examples belong to the second phase of construction, in the 1st cent. BC. Far more impressive is the fogou, the function of which is unknown. Its sinuous passage is 66 ft long. The boulder walls arch upwards under stone roof-slabs. There is a lateral passage and circular chamber. Open to the public.

Chysauster Village. Signposted from the B3311, N of Penzance and 10 miles E of Land's End. A small village of oval huts, with rooms set into the thickness of their massive outer walls. Garden plots adjoin the houses and the old field boundaries can be traced on the surrounding slopes. The settlement was occupied from a little before 100 BC until around AD 200.

Clea Lakes Crannog. This Irish crannog lies 2 miles NE of Killyleagh (20 miles SE of Belfast, on Strangford L.) in Co. Down. The circular 'island' is 200 yds from the shore of the eastern lakes. A partial excavation in 1956 showed how boulders were laid on the boulder-clay bottom of the shallow lake as a foundation, and rock chips, earth and refuse heaped around them. The crannog has seen prolonged occupion, although most of the pottery, beads and iron slag found were from the Early Christian period.

Cockley Cley. A reconstructed Iceni village is part of an open-air museum which also contains an abandoned Norman church and a medieval forge cottage. Experts may dispute details of the reconstruction, but the village defences and the gateway convey accurately the fears and dangers of ancient British life. Cockley Cley lies on the Swaffham to Stoke Ferry road, about 30 miles W of Norwich in Norfolk.

Culsh Souterrain. Lies 1 mile NE of the village of Tarland (5 miles NW of Aboyne, 30 miles W of Aberdeen). The curving underground passage is complete with roof, so a torch is needed.

Ewe Close. Eight Romano-British settlements lie within a 1½ mile radius of Crosby Ravensworth (3 miles E of the M6, 5 miles S of Penrith, E of Keswick) in the Lake District. Ewe Close is the only one to have been excavated. Lies at a height of 850 ft. It is the most impressive of all. The rectangular, walled village covers 1¼ acres and contains the remains of 10 hut circles, an oblong

Air-view of the stone huts at Chysauster Village in Cornwall.

The gate defences at the reconstructed Iceni village at Cockley Cley in Norfolk.

dwelling, cattle pens and a well, all in stone. The 50 or so inhabitants were probably farmers who raised sheep and cattle and grew a little grain. The traces of fields can be seen nearby.

Glastonbury Lake Village. Lies 12 miles E of the M5 at Bridgwater in Somerset. Successive Iron Age and Romano-British villages stood in the water meadows near this historic town but no structures remain. The finds recovered from the peat bog and models of the settlement are in the museums of Glastonbury and Taunton (near the M5, S of Bridgwater).

Gough's Cave. Caves in the Cheddar Gorge (15 miles SSW of Bristol) were occupied in the Late Palaeolithic period. Gough's Cave (off the B3135 just N of Cheddar) contained flint tools, human and animal remains and the nearly complete skeleton of 'Cheddar Man', all on display at the site. The skeleton is probably slightly later, from the Mesolithic period.

Grimspound. A walled enclosure containing stock pens and 16 circular stone huts, apparently dating from the Bronze Age. A footpath to Grimspound on Dartmoor leaves the minor road which links Widecombe and the B3212 (18 miles NE of Plymouth).

Itford Hill. Partly obscured by cornfields in the summer, this important Bronze Age settlement is reached on foot E of Itford Farm on the B2109, $2\frac{1}{2}$ miles N of Newhaven (10 miles E of Brighton) in East Sussex.

Jarlshof. On the southern tip of Shetland, S of Sumburgh airport. Jarlshof contains an amazing range of homes from different periods. The earliest resemble those of Neolithic Skara Brae, yet there are also Late Bronze Age dwellings, circular Iron Age houses some of which have souterrains, a broch, an aisled roundhouse, a superb wheelhouse, and lastly a Viking and

medieval farmstead, to link this remarkable series with historical times. An excellent Official Guide is available. The stone house appears in 'The Pirate' by Walter Scott.

Lisnagade Rath. Thought to be the largest rath in Ireland. Lies in Co. Down close to the Dark Age earthwork known as Dane's Cast (SW of Newry). Ten others lie within a $\frac{1}{2}$ mile radius, making this a spectacular concentration. The trivallate rath is 370 ft in diameter. The outermost line is extended to enclose a secondary rath almost 400 yds away, containing the remains of a square house, and maybe also of a square barn. The deep ditch visible today is the second on this site.

Lough Gur. This is the only lake in Co. Limerick (SW Ireland). It lies among limestone hills in an area of almost incomparable archaeological richness. A lowering of the level of the lake has revealed the remains of several crannogs; stone axes made in the area were exported as far as southern England, and the largest stone circle in Ireland is at Grange, between the western shore of the lake and the Kilmallock to Limerick road (S of Limerick).

Lochrutton Crannog. In Kirkcudbrightshire, 5 miles W of Dumfries and just S of Lochfoot. Lies in the middle of Lochrutton Loch and S of the natural island of Dutton's Cairn. Excavations at the start of this century showed it to consist of an earth mound 30 yds in diameter resting on a structure of logs. Medieval remains were recovered, but they represent a later use of the Iron Age platform.

Milton Loch Crannog. Lies 1 mile S of Crocketford (9 miles W of Dumfries, on the A75). Two crannogs were found in 1953 when the loch was partly drained. One of them, described on p. 109, resembles a low stony island.

Rinyo Neolithic Village. This lesser-known twin of Skara Brae is on Rousay in the Orkneys, 3 miles N of Brinyan Pier. Partly excavated in 1938; huts, pottery and many flint tools were found. The site was infilled, so there is less to see than at Skara Brae.

Skara Brae. This remarkable and almost perfectly preserved Late Neolithic village is described on pp. 99–100. It lies beside a sweeping bay 6 miles N of Stromness on mainland Orkney.

Stanydale Village and Temple. The dwellings and the problematical temple are described on pp. 103–4. They stand on a by-road a little over 1 mile SE of Bridge of Walls on mainland Shetland.

Star Carr. This was the richest Mesolithic site in Britain. Although it is marked on 1 in. maps (1 mile NNE of the A64 and A1039 junction, 5 miles S of Scarborough), there is next to nothing to see on the site. The finds are at Scarborough and Cambridge.

Thorny Down. Little can now be seen of this important Bronze Age settlement, but it is conveniently close to the Iron Age hillfort of Figsbury Rings which lies 1 mile to the W. A track leads N from the A30, 4 miles NE of Salisbury (opposite the turning S to Winterslow). The excavations of 1937–9 uncovered remains of 9 circular houses on a rectangular, ½ acre site, which contained a bracelet and a spearhead of bronze, some pottery, a saddle-quern and loom weights.

West Stow. Early Saxon dwellings have been reconstructed among the Breckland forest and heath to the W of the modern village, which lies off the A1101, 4 miles NE of Bury St Edmunds in Suffolk. Great care has been taken over their authenticity. Both sunken huts and larger halls can be seen. The original site, lying nearby, was deserted early in the 7th cent. AD and entombed in sand. It was excavated in 1965 and 1972.

Reconstructed Early Saxon huts at West Stow in Suffolk. The most distant example is of a type not found at this village site.

Chapter 6

Engraving in the landscape

THIS CHAPTER concerns some of the most striking and puzzling of the works of man in Britain. Hill figures, especially in the summer sun when they blaze white against the green and blue backdrop of pasture and sky, make a lasting visual impact. A smaller scale of engraving occurs in Pictish symbol stones, and there is little in prehistory more tantalizing than what their symbolism means. In both cases – the chalk-cut giants and the smaller, elaborate Pictish carvings – they must surely have conveyed a message which was widely understood when the images were made, however elusive these meanings may now prove to be. But there remain other mysterious carvings of a less obvious nature which still arouse debate – the Neolithic cup-and-ring carvings in the stones of many desolate hillsides. There are also, as we shall see, secret messages in the landscape which have no existence outside the imaginations of their discoverers.

The cup-and-ring marks are perhaps too small to be dignified as landscape features, so their treatment here will be brief. They commonly appear as depressions, each surrounded by one or more concentric circles. Some, perhaps the oldest, seem to be enlargements of natural depressions, while others are completely artificial. They occur in many highland areas, frequently associated with standing stones and tombs, as at the West Kennet Avenue at Avebury, on the 'Long Meg' monolith in the oval known as 'Long Meg and her Daughters' near Penrith, and in the chambered cairn tomb of Barclodiad-y-Gawres near Port Trecastell. Others date from the Early Bronze Age and these are also found widely on the Continent of Europe. They are quite small, just inches across, and large numbers have been measured by Professor Thom, who thought that the measured series contained a basic unit of length of 0.816 inches – equal to one fortieth of his Megalithic Yard. But some of the experts who were prepared to give consideration to the proposed Megalithic Yard are far more reluctant to commit themselves on a Megalithic Inch.

These carvings are numerous, widespread and standardized, so they cannot be dismissed as random and meaningless. Many efforts have been made to decode the symbols, some have produced answers which are possible, others are entertaining, but none have obtained the consensus which might token the cracking of the code. They have at various times been said to represent religious or fertility symbols, mirrors, ore prospectors' marks, systems of counting and even pointers to the distant homelands of the people who carved them. Most of these explanations will not stand up to rigorous examination. One such version was recalled by Howard Kilbride-Jones in *Current Archaeology*:

The Westbury White Horse of 1778 with the ramparts of the Iron Age hillfort above.

Cup-and-ring marks, Routing Linn, Northumberland.

Ludovic Mann maintained that . . . cup-and-ring marks . . . were in fact observatories. He went to enormous lengths to measure them up and to plot them on huge sheets of paper, rather like graph paper with vertical and horizontal lines marked thereon, which he claimed to be representative of a prehistoric linear scale. Dammit, but didn't all those squares fit beautifully over those cup-and-rings, each square being the square of the prehistoric unit in the manner of a square foot or square metre. This grid fitted into each and all of the markings plotted, and who is to say that he didn't hit on something. He wrote a paper on the subject and sent it to Callander, who was editing PSAS (*Proceedings of the Society of Antiquaries of Scotland*) at the time, and poor Callander nearly had to be revived, for his blood pressure reached dangerous levels. After that, I had to deal with Ludovic Mann, and everywhere we went with that wretched grid, it fitted! What's the matter with them all? asked Ludovic. But who would dare even now to agree.

Symbolism on a completely different scale is displayed in the chalk-cut figures of the English hillsides. Only a small handful of them are or may be prehistoric, but the carvings of these figures is one of our longest standing traditions which has continued into this century. Most of the white horses date from the late eighteenth and early nineteenth century, a period when landowners were fascinated by the aesthetic possibilities of landscape creation. Wiltshire, with its thinly turfed chalk, possesses a small

herd of these horses: Cherhill (1780), Marlborough (1804), Pewsey (1812), Hackpen Hill (1838) and Broad Town (1863). A few strays lie outside the Wiltshire paddock, including the Kilburn Horse in the north of Yorkshire (1857), the Osmington horse in Dorset (1815), and near the village of Strichen in Aberdeenshire is a horse of white quartz dated to 1775 but which may be still later and an imitation of the English horses. The lion cut in the chalk scarp at Whipsnade Zoo carries the tradition into the modern era; and a medieval example is the Whiteleaf Cross in the Chilterns overlooking the Vale of Aylesbury and the Icknield Way, which is perhaps a version of the wayside cross.

Providing that the local geology is chalk (or some other rock of a brilliant hue), the hill figure presents those with a taste for graffiti on the grand scale with an opportunity to make the maximum impact with the minimum of effort – it is for this reason that no efforts should be undertaken without the approval of local conservational bodies. One simply marks out the figure, perhaps with the help of a signaller on a distant vantage point, and then removes the turf and shallow subsoil from the chosen outline. Chalk seldom supports a thick soil cover and the dazzling fresh rock surface is easily exposed. The snag is however that if nature is allowed to take its course, the

(Above left) The Marlborough White Horse of 1804.

The Whiteleaf Cross on the Chiltern scarp is thought to be medieval.

119

Symbolic horses appear on a
variety of British coins: here, a
gold stater of the Atrebates tribe.

exposed figure will quite rapidly be recolonized by vegetation and a scouring
will be necessary about every 10 years. In view of this, the survival of any
Iron Age examples at all is remarkable, and several are known to have
become overgrown and lost.

From an archaeological point of view, the figures are frustrating because
they incorporate no datable materials and dating must depend on chance
documentary references or on drawings. The oldest survivor is probably the
White Horse of Uffington, for several strands of evidence support its
antiquity. The horse is cut into a steep 30° slope which overlooks a dry chalk
valley on the northern margin of the Berkshire Downs. The first thing that
the visitor will note is that the figure is most unlike a conventional horse.
The beaky head is dominated by an enormous green eye of turf, unnatural
curves represent the prancing legs, the neck arches while the long tail merely
droops.

There are clues which allow us to trace the horse back through various
periods. It must predate the Normans because a twelfth-century document
of Abingdon Abbey reveals that the horse had already provided the Vale of
the White Horse with its name by the time of the Conqueror. There is good
reason, therefore, to suppose that it is of Iron Age origin. As with some other
ancient hill figures, such as the Cerne Abbas Giant and the mysterious
Wandlebury figure, the horse shares its upland with a nearby hillfort. The
peculiarly stylized outline of the horse is also characteristic of representations of horses on Celtic metalwork. The beast lies in the territory of
the British Atrebates tribe, who had their capital by Silchester, and horses
not unlike the Uffington beast are represented on the reverse of their gold
stater coinage. Although on one surviving example the horse has nobbly
legs, hoofs and a three-stranded tail, generally the outline is reminiscent of
the Uffington horse. The similar circular head and narrow beak seem to be
too close to the Uffington parallel for coincidence. The occupants of
Uffington hillfort may simply have filled some slack period by cutting the
horse on the nearby slope, displaying the fantastic beast which was perhaps
their tribal totem. But this may not be the whole story. Were they inspired
by aesthetic motives similar to those of the Georgian Wiltshire landowners?
Maybe the beast signified a ritual centre? Or perhaps, indeed, was a gigantic
statement and warning of territorial control.

Another dazzling chalk horse, far more life-like but less dynamic in its
pose, can be seen above Westbury in Wiltshire. Again there is a close
juxtaposition of horse and hillfort, but much less reason to suggest that the
two are contemporaneous. Here we have a horse which can be dated to 1778,
when an appropriately named Mr Gee had it cut. T. C. Lethbridge believed
that the remains of an older beaked horse lay beside the modern one, and
that its outlines could be traced on air photographs made before the area was
overgrown by scrub. People who have tried it know that scrutinizing air
photographs can produce visions to rival the Martian canals, but one should
be far more respectful of the local legend which relates that a horse was cut at
Westbury to commemorate Alfred's victory of Ethandun over the Danes in
878. Mr Lethbridge also wrote of the hill figure of the Cerne Abbas Giant
that 'the cloak dangling from his extended left arm is clear enough and it
surprises me that no attempt has been made to expose it'. I have the air

photograph of Cerne Abbas before me as I write, but peer as I may, the missing cloak quite refuses to emerge.

The Uffington White Horse, seen from the air.

Hill figures have particularly exercised the wits of those 'archaeologists' whom the professionals prefer to regard as the 'lunatic fringe'. Janet and Colin Bord, for example, have managed to date the Uffington Horse to the Neolithic Age although they do not have a scrap of evidence, and even to relate it to some peculiar 'dragon power that flows through the leys'. But having imagined these into existence the writers continue: 'Could it be, as some have suggested, that it was intended to be seen from above, a signal from Neolithic man to his gods in their airborne craft who would then land on Dragon Hill?' A hill figure cut with the intention of visibility from the maximum height would be dug on a flat chalk plateau and not on a slope. These sites were chosen to maximize their visibility from below. Most slopes appear deceptively steep to the eye, and those with angles of more than 40° are uncommon and precipitous, yet anyone who has clambered to the top of the Uffington slope will appreciate that the hill is so steep that the diggers must have had difficulty in keeping their footing on the one-in-three gradient. This horse is to be seen from below – not by some disorientated airborne deity.

A coin of Constantius Gallus of AD 351–5. The figure bears Christian standards.

The Wilmington hill figure Sussex (*right*).

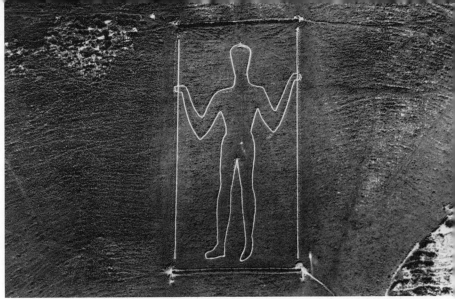

A warrior with spears and a horned helmet on an Anglo-Saxon bronze buckle from Finglesham in Kent.

Two other surviving hill figures seem to be of considerable antiquity: the Cerne Abbas Giant and the Long Man of Wilmington. The naked giant who stands 180 feet tall on the Dorset chalk slope brandishes a fearsome club in his right hand. A small, possibly Iron Age enclosure known as 'The Temple' lies above the giant, and was used in medieval times and later as a site for May Day ceremonies. These may hark back to pagan fertility rites, and their proximity to the giant can scarcely be coincidental. There is little evidence with which to date the giant. A local tradition relates it to a sixth-century visit by St Augustine and there is a possible connection with the Roman Emperor Commodus (AD 180–92), who was at the centre of a Hercules cult. According to another local tradition the figure was carved around the body of a decapitated Danish giant as a warning to other invaders. The similarities between the Herculean posture and engravings on Roman altars and pottery indicate a Roman connection, but this is as yet unproven.

The Long Man of Wilmington, outlined in the turf of Windover Hill in East Sussex, is more spidery in form and appears to be holding a thin staff in each hand. The only internal features are the turf mounds which crudley delimit facial features. Again we have no positive date for the figure, nor can we say what he is doing. He may have been altered by recutting in the nineteenth century, although similar figures found elsewhere suggest a far earlier date. He could well be Romano-British, since he resembles the figure of a soldier bearing standards topped with *chi-rho* Christian monograms on some Roman coins of the fourth century AD. Similarly, finds at the Anglo-Saxon cemetery at Finglesham in Kent included a buckle decorated with a figure presumed to represent Wodin. He wears a helmet with serpent-headed horns and holds a spear in each hand. The side-on orientation of the feet of the Wilmington man is characteristic of Dark Age art. There is also the possibility that the Long Man is a sun god, and that he is not bearing staffs but is opening the doors of heaven. The clever foreshortening of the figure shows that it was not intended for viewing from nearby (or from heavenly chariots), but from away in the Weald. Although the Long Man's origins are unknown he is almost certainly older than the Middle Saxon period. In 1979 an article in *Folklore* by Jacqueline Simpson drew attention to an engraving of 1851 and to vague oral traditions suggesting that the Long Man formerly had some headgear. Indeed, the name of the old division or hundred containing the figure can be translated as 'Tree of the Helmeted Waendel'. The Waendel name is particularly interesting because it may provide a link between the Long Man and a chalk-cut giant which once graced the Gogmagog Hills at Wandlebury ('Waendel's fort') near Cambridge.

One of the most unusual tales of British historical research, that of the Gog Magog figures, or the Buried Gods of Wandlebury, has been told and retold – mainly in order to sensationalize the British past. But their full story is still more fascinating and has not yet been completely recounted. The leading figure was T. C. Lethbridge, one of the most colourful characters in British archaeology, an area hardly devoid of such figures. Between the wars Lethbridge was employed by the University of Cambridge and worked under the great archaeologist Sir Cyril Fox, whom he subsequently succeeded. During this time he won a reputation as an intelligent and advanced excavator. But Lethbridge's vivid powers of imagination blossomed and expanded after the war, and displaced much of the rigour and technical expertise for which he had been admired. Today he is most widely known for his book *Gogmagog, The Buried Gods*, in which he describes the rediscovery of an elaborate tableau of hill figures lying on the southern slopes of the Gogmagog Hills near Wandlebury, south-east of Cambridge. Thereafter, Lethbridge trod the dubious paths of the occult and the UFO, almost anticipating the sensationalism of Von Daniken and his *Chariots of the Gods*, and misleading many of those who had grown to respect him.

In *Gogmagog* Lethbridge began by drawing attention to the highly probable former existence of a hill figure on the slopes of Wandlebury, the evidence for which is preserved in a tangle of folklore and mythology. In 1605 Bishop Joseph Hall used the *nom de plume* Mercurius Britannicus to publish a Latin work in which he mentioned a figure that Cambridge scholars had cut in a neighbouring hill. An English translation of the book appeared in 1609 with the site given as Gogmagog, and mentioning a giant called All Paunch who was 'not like him whose Picture the Schollers of Cambridge goe to see at Hogmagog Hills. . . .' Later, in about 1640, a Cambridge antiquarian, John Layer, wrote that he could not understand how the Gogmagog Hills got their name, 'unless it were from a high and mighty portraiture of a giant wch the schollars of Cambridge cut upon the turf or superficies of earth within the said trench, and not unlikely might call it Gogmagog, which I have seen but it is now of late discontinued.' The cleric, eccentric and antiquarian William Cole quoted this and added that when he was a boy, in about 1724, he had travelled from Babraham village to Cambridge along a hillside track. His parents 'always used to stop and show me and my Brothers and Sisters the figure of the giant carved on the Turf; concerning whom there were then many traditions now worn away.'

Lethbridge's next important source was Sammy Cowels, a laboratory assistant at the University, who as a child had known an old man, who had said that when *he* was a child, the hill figure of a giant was still visible from Sawston, some 2 miles from the possible location of the giant. No dates were given, but this would seem to take us back to the middle of the last century. Similar recollections of old men were reported by Mr G. Maynard, curator of the Saffron Walden museum. But such memories are at best unreliable, and may be the last flickerings of the same stories that reached the earlier antiquaries. The strongest argument against their accuracy is that amateur antiquarians abounded in the last century and it is hard to imagine how they could have missed the figure – if it was there.

Much of the evidence which Lethbridge assembled was based on the name of the Gogmagog Hills. In the Bible, it is the prophet Ezekiel who mentions prince Gog and the land of Magog. The names were united in the twelfth-century writings of Geoffrey of Monmouth, a notorious embroiderer of history, as Goëmagot, one of the mythical giants who fought a battle with the Britons. His companions were slain and he was hurled from a cliff by Corineus, a Trojan general. All these characters were invented by Monmouth, or culled from legend.

Similarly significant was a tale from *Otai Imperialia* by the roguish clerk Gervase of Tilbury in about 1211. He writes of a place near Cambridge called 'Wandlebiria', and describes the hillfort there. He proceeds to quote what was probably a folktale then current in the area, that a warrior entering the enclosure at night could summon a ghostly knight. The tale was then put to the test by Baron Osbert, who unhorsed the ghost but was wounded in the thigh. The ghost's horse escaped, but Osbert survived to become a Crusader, and his wound opened on each anniversary of the ghastly contest. Lethbridge assumed a connection between the ghost knight and the white hill figure, and felt it proved the antiquity of the Wandlebury giant. But if anything, Gervase's tale suggests that the figure did not exist in the late twelfth century, for since the hillfort itself is described one would expect so vital a detail as a hill figure also to appear. Gervase relays the legend correctly, but perhaps it is related not to a hill figure but to the 'Harwood' of childrens' games – perhaps a memorial of the Fenland hero Hereward the Wake, who resisted the Normans and survived in the childrens' songs of Cambridgeshire almost to this day.

The exposure of part of the supposed Gogmagog hill figure at Wandlebury near Cambridge.

Another reason for doubt lies in the attitude taken by the investigator. Witnesses report that Lethbridge arrived at Wandlebury determined to discover a hill figure, and was undaunted by the apparent impossibility of discovering one in an area covered by woodland for almost a century. He employed a probe – a stainless steel bar $\frac{5}{8}$ inch thick and 5 feet 9 inches long. He thrust it into the turf, and wherever the bar penetrated deeper than usual he assumed he had located the buried trenches of the hill figure. He probed like this thirty thousand times, until his wrists were swollen and aching. This helps to explain his fury when experts wandered along to voice their doubts. He plotted his findings and defined on paper an extraordinary complex of figures that bore no resemblance to any other known hill figures. From left to right there was a winged sun god, then a goddess with horse and chariot, and lastly a warrior brandishing a sword. A small portion was excavated in 1955 and the photograph of the upper part of the 'goddess' – the only area of any substance to be cleared of turf – has been uncritically reproduced in a host of publications.

Archaeologists observed the excavations with scepticism, and the digger records that 'I began to notice from the faces of other archaeologists, that they were seriously disturbed by my interpretation of the excavation. It was clear that they neither believed in the outlines, nor understood what they were to expect'. Their incredulity was hardly surprising, since Lethbridge explained to them that ploughing had removed the actual trenches which formed the figures, and that 'all that remained was the mud and rot at the bottom, in the chalk rock which was too hard for the plough to break up and turn into humus'. Sceptics believed that all that was emerging was a naturally weathered chalk surface – and subsequent examinations have proved them right.

The *Gogmagog* narrative itself makes some conflicting claims. He writes that: 'there were ceremonies at Wandlebury in the days of the Tudors [and] it seems reasonably clear that the three figures had not been filled in at that time.' In the Notes, however, Lethbridge writes that the track crossing the goddess figure 'tends to confirm that the goddess had vanished before Tudor times'. Why then did Lethbridge concentrate on the goddess – the longest-lost figure – instead of one of the male figures which could still be seen from a couple of miles away only a century before? Surely one of the giants would be far more freshly preserved, having survived for so much longer?

Then there is the question of ploughing. There was no doubt that the land had been ploughed; but when was it done? If the figure of the giant seen in 1724 was still visible in the middle of the nineteenth century, then it must have been set in pasture and could certainly not have been ploughed before then. We know that the land around Wandlebury was acquired in the eighteenth century by Lord Godolphin. Later it was planted with beechwood to provide cover for game; it can be seen today and dates from between 1810 and 1840. So the ploughmarks which Lethbridge found must have predated the creation of parkland in the first half of the nineteenth century. A committee, appointed by the Council for British Archaeology in 1957 to report independently on the hill figures, criticized the crude archaeological techniques employed and agreed that the only evidence for human interference was the plough scars. The soil analyst was emphatic that the exposed sections were otherwise entirely natural and typical. More recent still, in the winter of 1978–9, the Warden of Wandlebury organized independent tests with a magnetometer and a receptivity meter to measure soil disturbance, while the Warden himself traversed the site with metal dowsing rods. All the participants picked up the remains of an Iron Age burial to the east, and an area to the west where there may be a fragment of ironstone, but absolutely nothing was registered in relation to the figures themselves.

It is most unlikely that the real Wandlebury giant will ever be found. He was certainly there in the sixteenth century, probably before, and was last recorded in 1724. His exact location is unknown; he might have lain on the flat ground inside the ring, or he could have been on a nearby spur since devastated by chalk quarrying. He might equally have been lost in 1840 when a small cricket pitch was laid near Lethbridge's site; but it is certain that all trace would have been destroyed by the spreading roots of beech woods and elm thickets.

The Lethbridge saga has many peculiarities. I do not think that Lethbridge was attempting a hoax, although he was an expert practical joker as a boy. Even so, his behaviour was strange; a rare postcard exists showing an air photograph of the site taken just after the excavation of the mother goddess, and it shows that the site was much more wooded than it now is two decades later. The discovery of the goddess, sitting neatly within a small triangle of open ground, is fortuitous to say the very least. As the tableau unfolded, Lethbridge was claiming to discover the additional figures by probing ground which was clearly an impenetrable tangle of elm roots. The stumps of these young trees can be seen today and they are four, five and six inches across. A mature elm can send out its roots over 100 yards, and it is impossible to imagine that accurate probing could have been undertaken.

One may only hazard the guess that having set himself the task of rediscovering the figures the doubts expressed by experts intensified his resolve to the point of no return. There were heated discussions, recriminations and upset friendships, but it is perhaps a tribute to his powers that he hoodwinked so many, including himself. It is only sad that Lethbridge may be remembered for the Gogmagog fiasco rather than for the important contribution he made to Anglo-Saxon archaeology as a younger man.

Wandlebury has continued to attract its share of outlandish claims. A retired oil executive has 'revealed' that the Iron Age fort is in fact a prehistoric observatory, with particular importance attached to the gaps in the ring (which were in fact cut to admit Lord Godolphin's muck cart). Alignments intersect at a crucial stone set in the lawn. Having examined this stone I can affirm that either it is of eighteenth- or nineteenth-century brick and mortar, or that the very numerous whitish brick houses and terraces of Cambridgeshire are not, as was thought, the product of the last couple of centuries, but are in fact prehistoric!

The outlines which Lethbridge cut in the Wandlebury turf twenty years ago are now half overgrown and will possibly soon disappear. Other losses have been more serious – a giant on Shotover Hill near Oxford, the Red

Horse of Tysoe near Banbury in Warwickshire, and possibly a giant at Plymouth Hoe, all mentioned in reliable records. It is, in fact, far more surprising that examples such as the Uffington, Cerne Abbas and Wilmington figures have survived for as long as they have. Their preservation was at least partly due to their use in local festivals. The Uffington horse was scoured by villagers every seventh year, accompanied by a fair, fun and games and a cheese-rolling sport. Maypole celebrations took place for centuries in the enclosure above the Cerne Abbas Giant, and, most probably, seventeenth-century Cambridge scholars were up to something similar at Wandlebury.

As though Wandlebury were not enough, let us follow another extraordinarily rich vein in archaeological fiction. An often resurrected claim – one of the least credible of them all – concerns the 'Glastonbury Zodiac'. In 1929, Katherine Maltwood, after deep immersion in Arthurian mythology, the fantasies of the sixteenth-century mystic John Dee, and those of the bizarre nineteenth-century astro-archaeologist 'Mr Waltire', convinced herself, and some of her readers, that she had discovered an enormous zodiac circle marked out on the landscape around Glastonbury in Somerset. Dr Dee had said no less in the 1580s, but the credit for mapping and publicizing the idea must go to Mrs Maltwood. The credulity of people when confronted with unfamiliar aspects of the landscape and a suggestive narrative is quite amazing – when I look at Mrs Maltwood's map of the symbols, my first thought is how little most of them resemble the signs they are supposed to portray.

The outlines were produced by joining features of the natural and manmade landscape. Lanes, canalized rivers, and some enclosure hedges which are clearly more recent than Dr Dee, all form links in this chain of nonsense. The ever imaginative Janet and Colin Bord feel constrained to ask how this was originally done: 'was it sculpted by intention, or formed by unknown psychic forces moulding the thoughts and actions of the local populace?' This seems preposterous, to say the least.

Any landscape historian could demolish the Glastonbury Zodiac by showing that the features which compose the 'symbols' were built at different times for sensible and practical reasons. More amusingly, one might demonstrate that landscapes can be shown to contain virtually any pattern one chooses. The same Somerset landscape that provided Mrs Maltwood with her 'Zodiac' gave me, for example, Mickey Mouse and Goofy in under ten minutes, and Winnie the Pooh soon after. Small fortunes have been made at this game of linking coincidences to create spectacular symbolic chains, and – not wishing to be left out of the goldrush – I shall make my contribution here:

The sensational discovery of the Glastonbury Bear has forged the missing link in the chain of earth-discovery. The nose of the Bear is formed by Glastonbury Tor – where the tomb of King Arthur was discovered during the rebuilding of the Abbey in 1184. The recovery of the Bear confirms that King Arthur was the central figure of a pagan cult – the name 'Arthur' is a Celtic pun on the word for 'Bear'; and Gildas, who knew Arthur well (and who as a Christian Celtic monk had good reason to fear the Bear Cult), wrote: 'Why have you been rolling in the filth of your past wickedness ever since your youth, you bear, rider of many and driver of the chariot of the Bear's Stronghold, despiser of God and oppressor of his lot. . . .' (Gildas, *De Excidio Britonum*, 32.1).

It is now proven that when Arthur, our once and future king, fell, and his slumbering body was buried by the Tor, his followers provided a key to his resting place, manipulating the landscape – perhaps by forgotten psychic powers – to produce the gigantic bear symbol, invisible to the earthbound eye. Who then did this mighty signpost serve?

The answer to this question is clear from Gildas' reference to the despisers of the Christian God, who drove the chariots of the Bear's Stronghold. So the Bear is a signal to the riders of the UFO chariots of the gods.

Glastonbury is well known to lie on a magnificent leyline which connects the occult centres of Land's End, Avebury and Wandlebury. The UFO astronauts, flying along the ley and drawing power from its earth-forces would see the Bear Symbol clearly displayed on the landscape below and be drawn to the resting place of their leader.

But where do the UFO missionaries come from?

The answer is clearly written in the mystical landscape of Somerset: from the ancient bear constellation of Ursa Major – The Great Bear.

Now, at the dawn of the Age of Aquarius, King Arthur of Britain lies amidst the other zodiacal symbols discovered by the remarkable Mrs Maltwood just half a century ago. He waits his second coming while the Bear Symbol, his gigantic tombstone, signals his resting place to the UFO charioteers. How long can the blind and sterile world of so-called science continue to deny the unshakable proofs of occult lore? . . .

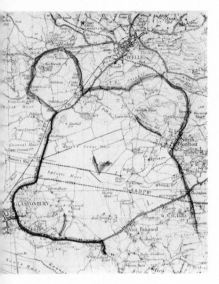

The 'Glastonbury Bear'.

The bite of this satirical exercise is made sharper by the accuracy of the facts on which my fantasy was hung: the name 'Arthur' may well be based on a Celtic 'bear' pun; Gildas is quoted correctly and his relationship with Arthur may well have been hostile; a lead plaque engraved with the Latin words, 'Here lies the renowned King Arthur in the Isle of Avalon', was indeed unearthed at Glastonbury. The inscription is generally regarded as an attempt to boost the medieval pilgrimage trade, or as a political stratagem to prove the death of Arthur and to forestall an Arthurian revival in Celtic lands. Lastly, by pure coincidence, Glastonbury does lie on a line which connects the points mentioned and is about as straight as most other such 'leys'.

It is time now for a real mystery. It concerns a series of engraved symbols for which no meaning has yet been found – the Pictish symbol stones. The ancestors of all the British were immigrants, with the influx of new cultures periodically revitalizing the local population. Of all the varied ethnic strands in the British ancestry, no people is more mysterious than the Picts. They are not a dim and distant Stone Age tribe, but a nation that lived in Scotland at the dawn of the historical period, when England and Ireland were developing their literatures. The Picts and their forbears were known to the Romans. Their princesses married Saxons and they received missionaries from the Celtic west. We know a little of what they looked like from contemporary carvings; the surviving literary descriptions of them come from various non-Pictish sources and some peculiar aspects of their culture are implied. All trace of them was swamped during a ninth-century

Three Pictish warriors armed with spears and shields on a slab found at Brough of Birsay, Orkney.

colonization of northern and eastern Scotland by Scots, Christian Irish Gaels who dispersed across Pictland from their Scottish foothold kingdom of Dalriada in the west. The Pictish language was replaced by the Celtic dialect of the Scots or Gaels, and the people who had spoken it shifted from the realms of reality to those of mystery. Their independent political existence terminated in the middle of the ninth century when the throne passed to the Scot Kenneth McAlpin, and the Picts apparently evaporated from the historical record.

They did not die out, for in a sense they survive in each Scot, as part of a blend of Pictish, Scottish, Saxon and Norse blood – sometimes spiced with a little from an Armada-shipwreck survivor. It is unlikely that the Picts were massacred in the transfer of power to a Scottish king, but the extent of the extinction of their culture would be no less complete. Even the problem of Pictish origins is unsolved, but it is clear that the suggestions of Eskimos or a lost tribe of Israel are not to be taken seriously. Early historians are not helpful. Gildas, writing of the barbaric races who plundered Britain, bracketed them with the Scots as being like 'dark throngs of worms who wriggle out of narrow fissures', and as people 'readier to cover their villainous faces with hair than their private parts and neighbouring regions with clothes'. Bede repeats the legend that they had come from Scythia (perhaps he meant Scandinavia), were not allowed to settle in Ireland but took wives from among the Scots they met there and followed Scottish advice to settle empty lands in the north of mainland Britain. But more probably there was never a purely Pictish invasion or colonization of Scotland, for they were simply an amalgam of the people who had lived in Scotland from the earliest times – descendants of the burly Bronze Age

Double disc and Z-rod, comb and mirror case and a 'flower' symbol on the Pictish stone from Dunnichen, Angus.

The Newton Pictish stone.

settlers – and Iron Age Celtic immigrants from the south. The foundations of Pictish culture probably lie in the various peoples of northern Scotland in the centuries when Romans occupied the lands to the south.

We lack even the most obvious clue to their identity: knowledge of their language. It may have been a Celtic dialect, but was not the 'Q' Celtic of the Scots. It could easily have been heavily influenced by the unknown tongue of the old Bronze Age population. Although we know next to nothing about the homes and settlements of the Picts, a hint as to their distribution is provided by 'Pit' place names. Names which contain this 'Pit' element, like Pitlochry and Pittodrie, are plainly concentrated in the old Pictish territory of north-east Scotland, and are not found in non-Pictish areas. We do not know for certain what the Picts called themselves – their name may derive from the Latin 'Picti', to describe a painted or tattooed folk, but it may have been the Picts self-name.

There seems to have been something distinctly odd about the social basis of Pictish life. Outsiders like Bede referred to Pictish promiscuity, while Irish monks confined themselves to listing kings and their descendants. These lineages, however, reflect a strange matrilineal succession not characteristic of Celts, but normally associated with more primitive societies, where fatherhood of a child may be uncertain. Bede also refers to the matrilinear succession of the Picts, but he thought the system may have been imposed on them as a condition, when they wished to take Scottish wives.

By about AD 300 the Picts seem to have become a fairly coherent nation. In 367 they played a leading role in the concerted barbarian invasion of Roman England, and in 685 they inflicted a defeat on the Saxons at Nechtansmere (probably Dunnichen in Angus). But by the ninth century they had become an embattled people, beset on all sides. Perhaps it was the immediacy of the Viking threat from the northern seas which led them to overlook the Scottish threat from the west.

This is most of what we know of the Picts – and it is not much of a light in the darkness. Not a single phrase of the Pictish tongue survives, but a thoroughly tantalizing and baffling range of symbolic engravings remain dotted throughout Pictland, which would probably serve as a key to many of the secrets of their makers – could we but understand them. These are known as Pictish symbol stones. They are unique, vertical stone slabs decorated with remarkable displays of carved symbols. In the words of W. Douglas Simpson: 'Nothing like these monuments is known anywhere else in the whole world; and, despite much study, the meaning of "Pictish symbolism" remains the grand unsolved problem of Scottish archaeology.'

No great breakthroughs in understanding have been made since the beginning of this century when J. Romilly Allen realized that the carved stones could be grouped in three successive classes. The Class I stones are the oldest, and consist of roughly dressed stones with the symbols confidently incised. Class II stones are well-dressed slabs with the Christian cross on one face in a lively interlace style, and usually Pictish symbols on the other. The relief carving seems to become higher as the style progressed. The Class III stones bear the cross alone, generally in bold and intricate relief carving.

The Glamis manse Pictish stone.

The stones seem to span the period of Pictish paganism and conversion. The combination of cross and symbols on Class II stones perhaps reflects the state of affairs in the transitional period. Authorities are divided on the exact dating of the classes; there is some agreement that Class II belongs to the eighth century, since they sometimes carry small undeciphered inscriptions in the eighth-century Ogam alphabet. Class III stones take over in the ninth century, and by the twelfth century Anglo-Norman influences swamped the indigenous artistic style. As the sequences progressed, Pictish symbols appear to become little more than decorative space-fillers. Enquiry into the meaning of the symbols should therefore focus on Class I stones. These have been attributed to the seventh century but may have begun a century before or even earlier.

The symbols appeared on the stones unheralded, with masterful confidence. There is no apparent experimentation in design, so the symbols must have been perfected in other media before they were transferred to stone – perhaps in wood, metal, fabric or even body tattoos. The symbols, which have also been found in silverwork at Norrie's Law (Fife), apparently of the sixth century, are clearly not intended as abstract decoration. They are uniquely Pictish, perfectly standardized and without any question intelligible to the people who made them. One common group shows lively but uniform portraits of superb fluency – bulls, stags, boars, grouse, serpents and salmon.

131

Secondly, there are the symbols, which come in a number of frequently recurring and precisely executed forms. One closely resembles a mirror case of a type introduced by later Celtic settlers. A pair of tongs occasionally occurs. Then there is the 'Pictish beast', a fantastic animal which is always shown with a porpoise-like snout, back-curving horns, feet and a curling tail. The other images are even less recognizable: the crescent V-rod, the serpent and Z-rod, double disc and Z-rod, notched rectangle and Z-rod – and several more besides.

If one cannot hope to understand the signs on the stones, one can at least enquire as to their function. Should they be compared with the signposts, hoardings and boundary markers of today? They do not seem to be simple tombstones, for few are associated with burials (although many have been moved from their original locations). Do they equate with the stacked symbolism of Red Indian totem poles and do their messages advertise the attributes or lineage of their carvers, chieftains, or clans? Do they describe territory? Do they inform, boast or warn? We do not even know whether the symbols are connected with the Pictish religion. Isobel Henderson doubts this because they seem to coexist happily with the cross on Class II stones – but then we sometimes find sheila-na-gigs (see pp. 172–3) on medieval Christian churches. A wide variety of interpretations have been offered – ranging from Roman triumphal standards viewed from unusual angles, to stylized versions of Celtic military impedimenta; heraldic emblems which denote the status or profession of individuals commemorated by the stones; clan badges, or evolved copies of Roman tombstones. In 1963 A. C. Thomas concluded that animal symbols represented clan badges while the others were symbols of personal rank; but in 1971, Isobel Henderson suggested that the stones themselves were boundary markers bearing symbols of ownership, while stones with crosses delimited the boundaries of church lands.

Confirmation that each symbol had a meaning and that the proper assemblage of symbols was essential in Class I stones, comes from one now at Logie Elphinstone near Inverurie in Aberdeenshire. A double disc and Z-rod symbol was largely erased, to be replaced by a crescent and V-rod together with a recut double disc and Z-rod. This would only have been done were the order vital. But the Pictish symbols await the skill of a great cryptographer, and until then they must remain a closed book. But who can tell what might emerge from a simple study of the context of each of these mysterious signs, by a thorough and committed amateur?

Pictish art has its own individual qualities, but it also embraces influences which occur elsewhere in Dark Age art. The mid-seventh century purse cover from the Sutton Hoo ship burial is decorated with stylized animals which echo the Pictish beast; the seventh-century illuminations in the Book of Durrow have a stiffness which may suggest metal prototypes, while the internal decorations of some Pictish symbols, like the crescent, also have parallels in decorative metalwork and jewellery. The V- and Z-rod symbols, for example, are reinforced at their angles with what appear to be metal angle brackets. The Pictish boar has points of similarity with a first-century boar relief from Euffigneix in Haute Marne, while Northumbrian relief sculptures may have influenced the Class II crosses. Some believe that the

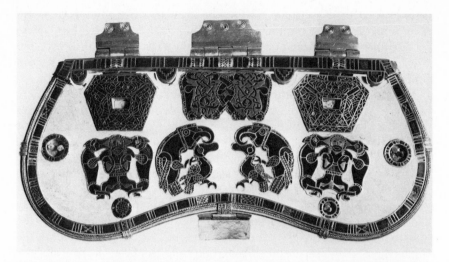

(*top*) Outlandish animal figures decorate this purse from the Dark Age ship burial at Sutton Hoo.

The figures are carved in whalebone in this panel from the Northumbrian Franks Casket of about AD 700.

Symbolic decoration from the seventh-century Book of Durrow.

The Papil Stone from Shetland, dated to the early ninth century.

The Drosten Stone in St Vigean's Museum.

Picts learned their art from Northumbrian manuscript illuminators, and there is no doubt that the Picts and Northumbrian Saxons were indeed in contact during the seventh century. But if the Picts learned their art from Northumbrians, why did they not also adopt the economical Roman alphabet to articulate their messages?

The intricate Pictish symbols must have been perfected before they were transferred to the stones. I can offer only the wildest guess at how this was done: the Picts in battle were described as naked painted savages, and it is possible that the symbols began as tatoos. A warrior with a double disc and Z-rod emblazoned on his chest would have been a fearsome sight. Whether the symbols denoted social rank, or accomplishments and clan totems, one simply does not know.

The Picts provided their own unique cultural epitaph in a durable display of national artwork whose messages – quite fittingly – are as enigmatic as the Picts themselves. When the nation was extinguished as a political force, the key to the Pictish symbols died too. The code has been probed, but the carved stones still stand as if in mocking defiance.

Although we have not sought to include the macabre in this book, one recent discovery is completely mysterious and endowed with the potential for a spine-chilling horror story. Dunstable in Bedfordshire offers a wealth of archaeological interest and contains important remains of the prehistoric, Roman, Saxon and medieval periods. In the late 1960s excavations intended to locate a Dominican friary made a spectacular start with the discovery of the Dunstable swan jewel, in gold and enamel, dating from around 1400. Although the monastic excavations proved unexciting, large numbers of Roman sherds and coins emerged. Finally an earth-cut cross was discovered, measuring 10 feet from arm tip to arm tip, and dug to about 2 feet in depth. More and more crosses were then identified, 72 in all, arranged in 6 rows of 12 crosses. Then a second and a third group of crosses were found, the edges of which lay inaccessible in nearby gardens. The crosses have proved difficult to date, being mixed up with the remains of a Roman cemetery. Their proximity to the cemetery could be deliberate, and might indicate a Dark Age date, when the position of the Roman burial place might still have been apparent. Alternatively, the crosses could be associated with the medieval monastery.

Their meaning still puzzles the experts, who reject the suggestions that they represent the foundation trenches of a timber hall, or that they were bedding trenches for trees. It has been proposed that the site witnessed an event of such a grotesque and evil nature that the crosses were dug in an attempt to excorcize it. Those who favour this interpretation can point to the discovery in the late 1970s of a series of decapitated skeletons in the adjacent Roman cemetery. In some cases the skulls were placed at the knees or feet of the corpses. But nobody has yet been able to provide a convincing explanation for the mystery of the Dunstable crosses.

The Cerne Abbas Giant.

The Logie Elphinstone Pictish Stone, Aberdeenshire.

Cerne Abbas. The giant stands N of the ancient village (6 miles N of Dorchester on the A352) in Dorset. The path to the Giant runs through the churchyard and past a ruined abbey.

Dyce Symbol Stones. The ruined church at Dyce (5 miles NW of Aberdeen) has 2 symbol stones of different classes. The Class I stone bears a Pictish beast and a double disc and Z-rod symbol. The Class II stone next to it has a floriated cross and shaft, and a set of undeciphered symbols in relief.

Fowlis Wester Symbol Stone. The 10 ft tall Class II stone stands 5 miles ENE of Crieff (16 miles W of Perth, 20 miles SW of Dundee). It has the usual cross on one side, while the other has representations of Pictish horsemen and a cowherd, as well as a number of symbols.

Logie Elphinstone Symbol Stone. Near Logie Elphinstone, 5 miles NW of Inverurie (14 miles NW of Aberdeen on the A96). Its symbols are described on p. 132. It also has a 'wheel Ogam' – a circle with characters from the Ogam alphabet around its circumference.

Meigle Symbol Stones. Meigle, 12 miles NW of Dundee on the A927, has a museum containing 25 stones, bearing a wide range of symbolic art.

St Vigean's Symbol Stones. A collection of symbol stones $1\frac{1}{2}$ miles N of Arbroath (17 miles NE of Dundee on the A92). They include the 'Drosten Stone', which bears an inscription in Hiberno-Saxon as well as numerous symbols and representations of animals and men.

Uffington White Horse. Visible from Uffington (17 miles SW of Oxford). It can be reached from the Ridgeway above, or the road below. Visitors should not walk on the fragile turf surrounding the figure. To the SE is the 8 acre hillfort of Uffington Castle, with counterscarp bank defences in addition to a ditch and bank. The Neolithic burial of Wayland's Smithy can be reached along the Ridgeway.

Wandlebury. The conservation area car-park is signposted N of the A604, 2 miles SE of Cambridge. It is an island of woodland in an arable landscape. The fading outlines of Lethbridge's excavation are just S of the pond near the hillfort entrance. It has been suggested that the 'goddess' should be preserved as a curio. There is no admission charge but a collection box at the reserve entrance should not be overlooked.

Westbury White Horse. The horse is a wonderful spectacle from the road below. It was cut in 1778, perhaps over a much older one. Clearly signposted from Westbury (12 miles SE of Bath and SE of Bristol) in Wiltshire. To the E is Bratton Castle, a 25 acre hillfort.

Wilmington Hill Figure. The Long Man stands on the hillside above the priory at Wilmington, on the A27, 6 miles NW of Eastbourne (20 miles E of Brighton) on the East Sussex coast.

Chapter 7

The strange fortresses of Scotland

AN AIR OF BROODING MYSTERY seems to linger over most ancient fortresses. Although ancient documents may record the granting of licenses to erect castles and to crenellate manors, and excavations reveal the layout of defence works, Scotland possesses large numbers of two distinctive types of impressive prehistoric strongholds about which many questions remain baffling. These are the broch and vitrified fort.

The broch is a defensive round tower of sophisticated and cunning design of which many were built between 100 BC and AD 100; but by whom, and for what reason, we do not know. The vitrified fort is still more mysterious. It resembles in most respects an English or Welsh hillfort, built with timber-laced stone ramparts. It differs in that the ramparts have been at some time so heavily burnt that their stonework has been turned to glass, and their boulders have reddened and fused with the heat. How this came about, and why, we have yet to discover.

The brochs in the main are closely tied to coastal sites, studding the rocky seaboards of the Northern Isles, the Western Isles and the western coast of Scotland. The vitrified forts, on the other hand, tend to crown the summits of central southern and north-eastern Scotland. While brochs are not commonly found south of a line from Mallaig to the Dornoch Firth, vitrified forts are rare to the north of this line. The interlocking patterns of distribution led some members of the last generation of Scottish prehistorians to visualize a Scotland fiercely divided between 'fort people' and 'broch people', each occupying different environments and securing themselves in opposed strongholds of completely different design. It was the broch people, they argued, who wrought the flaming devastation on the hilltop citadels of the fort dwellers. However, the tidy geographical hints were misleading, for the brochs of the early days of Roman rule cannot have been pitted against their scorched neighbours – recent datings of vitrified forts oblige us to place them in a far earlier and more distant period.

Let us then give precedence to age and begin with the riddle of the vitrified forts. We know a good deal about vitrification and the temperatures required to melt stone into glass; we can even reconstruct the form of the ramparts before they were burned. We know almost everything in fact, except for the really important questions of how and why the ramparts became vitrified. Since excavation provides us in this case with our best evidence, let us glance at the case of Craig Phadrig fort in Inverness-shire.

At some time around the year 350 BC a party of workers arrived on the conical hill overlooking the entrance to the Beauly Firth, opposite the Ord of Kessock hillfort on the southern shore. On the flat summit of Craig Phadrig,

Interior of Mousa Broch, Shetland.

Vitrified stones from the ramparts of Knockfarrel fort.

more than 500 feet above the Firth, the workers began shifting a mass of rocks and boulders weighing 25,000 tons, and cutting timbers almost 2 miles in length, and hauling them to the summit. The result of these endeavours, sufficient to occupy 100 labourers for 3 months, was a rampart nearly 20 feet thick and over 25 feet high, enclosing a rectangular area of about 2250 square yards. Then, or a little later, a second rampart was added to encircle the first. The ramparts were built of a mixture of hard rocks and of conglomerate boulders (a plum pudding-like stone), and the construction was made more stable by incorporating wooden beams between the courses of stone.

Then, a few years or perhaps decades after the work was complete, a great fire raged along the ramparts. Draughts swept the flames to the beams within the stonework, and as these turned to charcoal, the temperature inside the ramparts soared to more than 1200°C. The conglomerate blocks cracked and melted; the quartz in the rock reverted to the molten state from which the granites and basalts had been formed millions of years before, and cascades of molten rock showered from the slumping ramparts. Even those boulders which escaped the worst of the heat blast were reddened by the blaze, and many were welded together as the streams of glass solidified. Large areas of the ramparts had now collapsed and in place of the neatly coursed timber-laced wall there were just heaps of glass-bound slag, some preserving the impressions of disintegrated beams.

But although ruined, the defences were not worthless, for a community continued to live in Craig Phadrig. At one stage they gathered heat-reddened boulders from the wreckage of the inner rampart to raise the outer defences, and built huts in the shelter of the walls. Occupation within the broken ramparts continued during the Dark Ages, and Craig Phadrig has speculatively been identified as the stronghold of Brude, a Pictish king of the sixth century AD who was visited by St Columba. The saint's biographer, Adomnan, tells how the missionary climbed to meet the king in his stronghold. The gates were barred, but Columba traced the sign of the cross on them, and they miraculously flew open. Brude was so impressed that he agreed to be baptized, opening the way for the conversion of his subjects. But although he may have lived in the area, it seems unlikely that the king would have made his home in an ancient, broken citadel.

In the centuries which followed, the deserted fortress passed into local legend as 'the Giant's Castle'. From the end of the eighteenth century it was visited by a variety of antiquarians, some of whom paused to dig among the rubble. As early as 1777 the vitrification of the ramparts was noted, though there were others who interpreted the fortress ruins as a dormant volcano. It was only in 1971–2 that a modern excavation, led by Alan Small and Barry Cottam of the Department of Geography at Dundee University, told us much of what we now know of the site.

Forts of this kind are virtually unique in Europe, but dotted about the Scottish summits there are no less than 70 of them, ranging in size from modest defence works 50 feet across, to vast hillforts hundreds of feet in length. The largest, Ord of Kessock in Easter Ross, encloses 17,000 square yards. From this it appears that the vitrified forts are not to be seen as a special class of fort, but are in fact simple timber-laced stone hillforts which have been vitrified. Other Scottish forts of similar construction have escaped vitrification, but such a large number of them have not, that it is a major problem to be able to say why this should be.

Chemists have shown that different types of rock crystal will melt at different temperatures, so an analysis of the constitution of a mass of vitrified stone will reveal the temperature reached. A few constituents become liquid at only 800°C; while most of them melt out at 1000°C, and even basalt becomes liquid at 1200°C. Since the best way to learn things is usually to try them, it is not surprising that many mysteries of archaeology have yielded to experimental replication.

As early as 1906 the antiquarian A. B. M'Hardy tried, but failed, to repeat the process of vitrification, simply by building fires on top of heaps of rubble. An enormous amount of heat was clearly required, and it was only at the end of the Middle Ages that blast furnaces were developed which could melt rock. It was felt that rock might have been reduced to a molten state in crucibles, which were then emptied over the rocky ramparts to fuse its stonework. But this was clearly not the technique involved, as excavation showed. The imprints of beams in the vitrified slag and the presence of vitrified masses deep in the core of the ramparts showed that the lacing timbers played an important part in incineration.

It was in the late 1930s that Gordon Childe, the doyen of prehistory, and his partner Thorneycroft, made another attempt to reproduce vitrification. At Plean colliery in Stirlingshire a replica of a modest timber-laced rampart was built. It was 4 metres long, 2 metres wide and 2 metres in height; and the basalt rubble forming the body of the rampart was laced with timber. A facing of stone slabs and fireclay bricks was provided. No less than 4 tonnes of brushwood were heaped around, and during a 20 mph snowstorm the mass burned fiercely for half an hour. After 3 hours, both faces of the wall collapsed; and after 5 hours, as the timber lacings seared the stonework, the rubble became red hot. It smouldered for a day. After allowing it to cool, the archaeologists groped among the wreckage and discovered the successful vitrification of the interior rubble. Like the slag in genuine vitrified ramparts, it bore the casts of lacing timbers.

They had proven what had previously only been guessed – that vitrification required a rampart built with lacing timbers. But they had also shown that a vast amount of additional brushwood was required to start the conflagration, and that a strong wind was a major help.

Great controversy has raged over the important matter of whether vitrification was a constructional technique employed by the fort builders, or whether it was the result of deliberate or accidental destruction. There can be no other monument which allows for doubt as to whether it is the work of an architect or a vandal (some modern sculptures perhaps excepted). Until quite recently, adherents of the 'creative vitrification' viewpoint thought that the deliberate vitrification of a rampart might leave the defender with a superior wall of massive welded rubble. But the detailed archaeological study of such ramparts reveals that vitrification could hardly have been intended by men who were capable of building perfectly sound and serviceable stone and timber defences. Among the strong arguments for this point of view are the facts that molten glass fell on top of buildings standing inside the defences; that it is often only a portion of the ramparts, usually near the gate, which underwent vitrification; and that the resultant fused mass never stood more than shoulder high.

But since timber-laced forts were quite common throughout Late Bronze and Iron Age Europe, why were those in Scotland singled out for conflagration? The building technique was probably continental in origin, but who were the destroyers of the forts? Were they neighbours; invaders from the south; or from overseas? There was not a sudden wave of assaults on the Scottish forts, for they cover a wide span of dates. The strongly defended and fiercely vitrified great fortress at Finavon near Forfar may have been destroyed as early as 790 BC. Dun Lagaidh, situated across Loch Broom from Ullapool fell about two centuries later, and Craig Phadrig may not have been begun until more than four centuries after the fall of Finavon. The timber-laced fort at Craigmarloch Wood near Kilmacolm (west of Glasgow) may not have been built before the first century BC. The large number of forts certainly suggests that during these centuries many Scottish communities had good reason to feel insecure, but it is not known whether the cause was invasion, domestic unrest, the consequences of a worsening climate, or a combination of these causes.

But how were the fires started? Some at least of the vitrified forts contained lean-to dwellings 2 or even 3 storeys high, bound to the inner face of the ramparts by timbers slotted into the stone wall. Many had wooden gate towers glowering over their vulnerable entrances. It could be argued that the accidental burning of these timber structures would generate sufficient heat to ignite the timber lacings of the ramparts. More simply, the periodic burning off of the surrounding moorland might accidentally have started a rampart fire. But one would expect accidental ruination of a handful of forts to be grounds for better precautions to be introduced by the chieftains, who would hardly have viewed with equanimity the conflagration of ramparts which had occupied their best manpower for weeks.

The second possibility is that vitrification was carried out during or after the capture of a hillfort. The desired effect was certainly the destruction of the defences, but it would have been so much easier to use beams to lever out stonework and roll it down the hill, than to reduce the ramparts by fire. Gordon Childe's 4 tonnes of brushwood vitrified 4 metres of small-scale rampart, the merest fraction of the wood required at Finavon, where he found heavily vitrified ramparts more than 3 times as thick and almost 3 times as high, about 500 feet long and 120 feet wide. Perhaps 2500 tonnes of brushwood would have been needed there. If the destruction of the ramparts was the aim, the gathering of so much brushwood would seem to be poorly judged and extravagant. In addition, the defenders could hardly be expected to look on while the attackers painstakingly heaped brushwood around their ramparts.

Some experts are content with the explanation that the vitrification of the Scottish hillforts was the result of simple accidents or deliberate destruction. For myself, the vitrified forts are a major unsolved mystery, about which I can advance only one suggestion. I would propose that the purging of a conquered hillfort by fire was a ritual widely practised by Celtic tribes of Scotland. This would explain the use of such an arduous, tedious, and altogether spectacular method of reducing the ramparts.

A last problem concerning these forts is why their inhabitants persisted for several centuries in building what appear to have been ineffective or perhaps accident-prone defences. If the lacing timbers were essential to the vitrification of the stonework, then in each case the conflagration must have occurred while the timber lacings were still unrotted. It is difficult to imagine that unseasoned timbers would have survived many years in the dank interior of a rampart on a rain-lashed Scottish summit, and experimental archaeology suggests that the life of a post-built timber hut in Europe can have been little more than twenty years. So a fiery end must have come to the Scottish ramparts while they were still freshly built.

Concerning the second group of mysterious structures, the brochs, at least we have some dates. In addition, their defensive function is hardly in doubt, and their ingenious construction is easy to follow. But what remains mysterious is the arrival of the broch – it seems to have appeared out of the blue, fully developed, and to have gone through no transformations. It was designed and built by an unidentified people to meet a threat that has not been defined. Euan MacKie points out that the brochs are among the most striking prehistoric monuments in Europe, and that apart from Stonehenge they are the only advanced architectural creation that took place entirely within prehistoric or early historical Britain. W. Douglas Simpson claims they are unique: 'Their evolution, the circumstances which gave them origin, and the purposes that they were designed to serve, alike remain obscure – despite much careful excavation and a great deal of earnest thought and vigorous debate'.

Despite the great skills required to build the drystone brochs, they appear to have been remarkably numerous, and the first centuries BC and AD in northern Scotland must have seen an epidemic of broch building: more than 500 are known in the Highlands and Islands. Many are little more than provisionally identified, from the earliest times of their disuse they were dismantled stone by stone to build humbler dwellings. Several brochs have been excavated and numerous finds made, including weaving equipment, iron tools, dice, querns, whetstones, bronze and silver brooches, Roman coins, and vessels and lamps of whalebone and pottery, some of them Roman. All these show that the broch bonanza began in the first century BC and lasted two or three hundred years. During this brief period, brochs erupted mainly in Orkney but also in Caithness, where there are 35 known brochs and 114 suspected ones.

The broch was a remarkably advanced, standardized and individual building, consisting of a round, slightly tapering tower which sometimes rose to 45 feet. Like the Norman keep, it was sometimes guarded by outer defences, but the focus of attention was the tower itself. Its massive walls account for between 48 and 64 per cent of the total diameter of the tower. Above the solid base the walls were hollow, making the tower light enough to soar upwards beyond the reach of attackers. With walls up to 16 ft thick at the base, the broch could not be breached except by a force of engineers, while above the usual height of a battering ram the wall was hollow and tapered. It contained a series of roofed galleries, the lowest of which might have been used for storage. All this is remarkably well planned for 'artless savages', who thereby economized on stone and made it possible for each gallery roof to be used as a platform for the next, enabling considerable heights to be reached.

The ingenuity did not end here, for the weakest point in the broch, as in all forts, was known to be the entrance. So brochs were given only one opening, and this was in the form of a cramped tunnel, usually under 5 feet high and little more than 2 feet wide. A massive door, closed by a wooden drawbar in a socket, protected the interior. A guardchamber was often built into the wall beside it. Over the entrance passage was a chamber which diverted the weight of masonry away from the passage, and in which defenders could stand to thrust spears down at the single file of crouching invaders. Inside the broch, between 5 and 10 feet above the paved floor, ran a scarcement supporting a wooden verandah. There was sometimes a second one higher up the wall. The stairway to the verandah was to the left of the entrance, obliging any invader who had forced the door to expose his unshielded side to missiles rained down as he turned towards the stairway.

Only one broch – Mousa in Shetland – still rises to its original height of 43 feet, so we do not know how high brochs tended to be in general, or what

The ruins of Dun Dornadilla
Broch in Strathmore, Sutherland.

their roofs or upper defences were like. But it is logical to suppose that each broch was capped by a timber frame supporting a roof of turf or thatch, with a hole in it to light the gloomy interior. There would also have been an upper sentry walk from which missiles could be hurled down on invaders. But besides these unknown aspects, the brochs show some slight variants which may be revealing. Perhaps the most important of these is between the solid-based broch, in which the lower part of the wall is of solid stonework, and the ground-galleried broch, in which the galleries begin at ground level. Since the solid-based broch, such as that at Mousa, would be the most secure, it could be argued that this design represents a culmination of broch design; but it could equally be argued that later brochs degenerated from a superior prototype.

In spite of differences in detail, the broch appeared and spread in such a standardized form that it is hard to understand how it could have evolved gradually through various stages, or have developed independently in different places. But one possible forerunner of the broch is the dun, a small Scottish fort or fortified dwelling place. These come in many shapes and sizes, but one type, known as the galleried dun, contains passages and galleries in its immensely thick walls, and might have provided the inspiration for the broch. Even so, the broch appeared in such a complete form that one suspects the work of an original and gifted designer. Whatever the truth about its origins, while Caesar was looking wolfishly at southern England, no Scottish mason can have gone short of work.

There has been no lack of speculation as to who built it, and why. To T. C. Lethbridge it was: 'a double-walled hut which has become too big to be roofed in the ordinary manner.' Gordon Childe thought the broch

143

builders were the Veneti tribesmen from north-west France; while others have identified them with the ring-fort builders of Cornwall, or with southern Scots. At present there are two main contenders for the place of origin of the broch: one is the Northern Isles, and the other the Hebrides. If the broch degenerated as it spread, then it may have had its origins in Orkney or Shetland – although the best entrance defences are found on the northern mainland. If, on the other hand, it was improved during its diffusion, then it may have developed on the Atlantic coast of Scotland where D-shaped forts on cliff-top sites already had hollow walls perhaps a little earlier than the first brochs. The craftsmanship of the broch suggests that professional builders were employed. A scatter of finds, including dice and spiral finger rings, suggests they may have come from southern England. The real truth of the matter is that the origins of the broch are as unknown as its emergence was sudden.

Lethbridge argued that they were the strongholds of an invading aristocracy: 'Like the Normans, the broch builders probably had to build castles for defence from the people amongst whom they lived and, like the Normans, in the end they became gradually absorbed in the population'. But he was probably wrong, for they look less like the fortress homes of domineering intruders than the temporary bolt-holes of small, mainly peasant communities. There could be few more secure forts in which to sit out a siege, and few more gloomy, claustrophobic homes for an élite, than the windowless broch. The querns, carding combs and spindle whorls found there are hardly the paraphernalia of a warrior aristocracy, and it looks as though the brochs were refuges for the indigenous people of the north of Scotland in times of crisis. The broch dwellers would have been that amalgam of Bronze Age farmers and Celtic settlers later known as the Picts. Their location suggests that each broch community worked a nearby pocket of farmland and lived off fish and seals. In addition, it was from the sea that the threat probably came.

Since brochs are so thickly concentrated in Orkney, one may be excused for speculating that it was there that they were developed and defined, and Orkney perhaps became a significant power focus. The Saxon cleric Bede twice mentions the annexation by Claudius, the conqueror of England, of the Orkney Isles. The classical writer Orosius also records the submission of the Orkney chieftains to Claudius, in a manner followed by Celtic client chiefs of the imperial margins. All this implies that Orkney somehow differed from other Atlantic backwaters, such as the Western Isles. Were the Romans seeking to ferment a bad-neighbour policy between the Orcadians of the north, and the more southerly Scottish tribes; or were the chieftains of Orkney too powerful and important to be ignored in the political geography of Britain? We do not know. One broch at least was destroyed by the Romans. It lay far from the main flock of brochs in the north – Torwoodlee overlooks Gala Water, 2 miles from Galashiels. It contained Roman glassware and a silver denarius of Titus (AD 79–81), all of which may have been looted from the fort at Newstead. The broch was probably destroyed by the returning Romans.

The brochs may have originated in Orkney and spread as part of an Orcadian expansion, but it is doubtful that they housed an intrusive and victorious Orcadian elite – mainly because they are as common in Orkney as elsewhere in the north. If we accept the thesis that brochs were simply widespread communal refuges from seaborne attack, then we must next ask against whom more than 500 towers were built. Not the Vikings, for they arrived to terrorize the north over seven centuries after the first broch was built. Only their very last recorded use seems to have been against the Vikings, for the *Orkneyinga Saga* mentions a siege of Mousa broch. Though long obsolete, the old tower was well equal to the task, and the sieging party had finally to negotiate.

The Romans too are a slim possibility, for the first brochs predate Caesar's interest in Britain. The geographer Ptolemy, in the second century AD, could draw a perfectly recognizable map of Scotland – except that he orientated it east-west rather than north-south. Later in the same century, however, Agricola sent a team led by Demetrius of Tarsus to explore the western seaboard of Scotland. Had Roman slavers been operating along the Scottish coast such exploration might have been unnecessary. Slave raiding, which would particularly have threatened coastal and seafaring communities, could well have been the foe. A mutinous cohort of German Usipii escaped their masters and sailed around the north of Scotland, where they fought the natives and were eventually captured by Suevi and Frisii tribesmen and sold into slavery. So even if the fear of Roman slavers did not launch the people of northern Scotland on a frenzy of broch building, the Roman slave market was eager to accept the human cargoes of foreign raiders.

Other factors included the Celtic tribes from Belgium who in about 75 BC began to colonize the area south of the Thames, displacing the established Celtic inhabitants. The shock waves from this movement, as well as from the Roman raids on England soon after, and the displaced people moving north after the Claudian conquest in AD 43, may well have reached Orkney. Since the environment of northern Scotland is not particularly fruitful, there may not have been the resources to support both the indigenous and the displaced populations. So the brochs could have been built to defend the meagre pockets of farmland against the dispossessed southerners. Indeed, given the scant resources, the curse of slavery and the Celtic taste for warfare, the broch people might simply have been defending themselves against each other.

Violence abated in the third century AD, and the northern Scots could mow their hay meadows, herd their cattle, and fish the girdling ocean in relative peace, until the sails of Norse pirates appeared like vultures from over the north-eastern skyline. During the centuries of peace the brochs had not been needed and their sturdy walls were pillaged for stones to build more homely dwellings. At Jarlshof on the southern tip of Shetland in about AD 200, the stone of the abandoned broch was used to build a cluster of wheelhouses (see p. 110), one of which stood like a symbol of peaceful times within the derelict tower.

Far from our modern cities, the folk of the forts and brochs may seem to be timeless. Their battered citadels remain to tell us of a way of life which, like the grey seas that wash our northern shores, could turn dark, violent and treacherous.

Interior furnishing in stone added to the Broch of Gurness in Orkney.

Dunnideer vitrified fort, Aberdeenshire. The medieval tower is built of stone gathered from the ramparts.

Dun Troddan ruined broch.

Broch of Gurness. A farm track leads to the broch from the B9057. It lies on mainland Orkney about 14 miles NE of Stromness. The sea has removed some of the outworks of the broch, which was once surrounded by concentric rock-cut ditches. When it was in decay a series of stone huts were built in the space between the broch's walls and ditches.

Craigmarloch Wood Fort. Vitrified fort in Renfrewshire, 2 miles NW of Kilmacolm (15 miles W of Glasgow, on the A761). A 10 ft thick stone wall encloses an oval area 160 ft long. Excavation suggests that it lies over a wooden palisade of the 8th cent. BC. The fort entrance, flanked by vitrified rock, lies to the W.

Craig Phadrig Fort. Lies 1½ miles W of Inverness, off the A9, guarding the entrance to the Beauly Firth, from its flat-topped hill. A Forestry Commission forest trail leads up from the car-park below. The vitrified inner rampart encircles an area roughly 250 ft long and 90 ft wide. A unique hanging bowl from about the 7th cent. AD was found during excavations, but the fort is a thousand years earlier.

Dun Carloway Broch. On the Isle of Lewis, 15 miles NW of Stornoway, near a minor road W of the A858. Standing in a courtyard 25 ft in diameter, the tower is still 22 ft high. Its walls are 11 ft thick, and much robbed for stone. The plan of the broch, with stairs leading to the galleries, has survived intact.

Dun Dornadilla Broch. On a moor road, 9 miles NW of Altnaharra (15 miles S of Tongue in the centre of the Northern Highlands) in Sutherland.

Part of the wall stands 22 ft high, making it one of the best preserved brochs. The wall is 14 ft thick and encloses an area 27 ft in diameter.

Dun Lagaidh Fort and Broch. Two for the price of one. They stand opposite Ullapool, S of Loch Broom in the Western Highlands (Ross and Cromarty). The ramparts of the fort are 12 ft thick and enclose an area 300 ft long and 120 ft wide, containing vitrified rubble. It seems to date from the 7th cent. BC, but was reused in the Middle Ages. The poorly preserved broch has similarly thick walls and stands in the E of the enclosure.

Dun Mor Vaul Broch. Lies 3 miles N of Scarinish on the Isle of Tiree. The excavations led by Dr Euan MacKie in 1962–4 enable us to reconstruct its past. A mainly timber building of the 6th cent. BC was replaced by others in stone. The broch seems initially to have been used as a communal refuge from attack. One of the wall galleries was used as a temporary toilet, and pots and animal bones were left among the hearths on the floor. About 200 years later the broch was converted into a home and the walls reduced to 6 ft in height.

Dunnideer Fort. Lies 1 mile W of Insch (25 miles NW of Aberdeen). Although the hill of Dunnideer is only 876 ft high, it commands the coastal lowlands of Aberdeenshire. The heavily vitrified fort is 220 ft long. Below it on the hillside are traces of attempts to build an outer line of defences. The medieval tower that crowns the hill is built of rubble taken from the ramparts.

Dun Telve Broch. Dun Telve and its neighbour, Dun Troddan, are among the best preserved of all brochs. They are accessible by car, near the mainland coast E of the Isle of Skye, 1½ miles SE of the remote village of Glenelg. Dun Telve is 33 ft high, while an additional 7 ft are said to have been pillaged for building material in the early 18th cent. Like the nearby Dun Troddan, which is

25 ft high, the walls are over 13 ft thick. Both have wall-cells, entrances and stairs.

Finavon Fort. One of the largest and most heavily vitrified of the Scottish forts. It stands 4 miles NE of Forfar (12 miles N of Dundee). Appears to have been built in about the 7th cent. BC, with ramparts 20 ft thick enclosing an area 500 ft long and 120 ft wide.

Inverfarigaig Fort. Visually one of the most striking places in Scotland, the fort is perched on a pinnacle over Loch Ness at the mouth of the river Farigaig. It lies 8 miles SW of Dores (7 miles SW of Inverness), down a minor road which leaves the A862 4 miles to the SW. The 15 ft high rampart encloses an area only 80 ft across, containing vitrified material. The view alone, over the loch and the highlands, is worth the walk.

Jarlshof Broch. Jarlshof ($\frac{1}{2}$ mile S of Sumburgh airport in S Shetland) was inhabited by a succession of prehistoric communities, and the broch was the work of just one of them. The complex as a whole is unique. First came Neolithic and Bronze Age villages, then a cluster of wheelhouses, and finally a Norse settlement. The broch has been damaged by stone-robbing and the sea has washed away half the tower and its oval courtyard.

Knock Farril Fort. Lies 3 miles E of Strathpeffer (15 miles NW of Inverness) overlooking Loch Ussie. The rectangular, 425 ft by 124 ft enclosure and its complex rampart are heavily vitrified.

Mousa Broch. On Mousa, 11 miles S of Lerwick, E of mainland Shetland. The best preserved and most impressive of all brochs. At 43 ft, it is also the highest. Readily available flags assisted the construction of particularly tall and massive walls. They cover two-thirds of the 50 ft wide base and they taper upwards. The broch was still able to shield a community many centuries

later during a Viking raid, when all other brochs had been abandoned.

Ord of Kessock Fort. Opposite Craig Phadrig, on the N of Beauly Firth, 2 miles N of Inverness. Accessible only from the N. The summit of the 633 ft high hill is 900 ft across, and enclosed in a rampart. Masses of vitrified rock in the walls can be traced through the woods.

Rahoy Dun. The fortified dwellings known as 'duns' may provide the missing link between the vitrified fort and the broch. This one overlooks Loch Teacuis from the N, 8 miles N of Lochaline (on the mainland, NE of Mull). Some duns, such as the galleried dun at Kildonan Bay (6 miles NE of Campbeltown on the Kintyre coast), have walls resembling those of the broch and were maybe their prototype. The Rahoy Dun is so heavily vitrified that dynamite was used in its excavation. Some of the duns clearly met the same fate as the Scottish forts. The small interior was partly paved. A bronze brooch and an iron axe found there indicate an Early Iron Age date.

Tap o' Noth Fort. This remarkable hillfort, the second highest in Scotland, stands at 1850 ft on a pinnacle overlooking the Water of Bogie, $1\frac{1}{2}$ miles NW of Rhynie (35 miles NW of Aberdeen). The summit, 330 ft by 105 ft, is encircled by a heavily vitrified wall 20 ft thick. Traces of outer defences can be seen on the N of the hill.

Torwoodlee Broch and Fort. One of about 10 brochs isolated in the south, built among the rubble of a bivallate fort 2 miles NW of Galashiels (30 miles SE of Edinburgh, on the A7). The fort seems to have been destroyed during a Roman advance in AD 80. The broch was built when they withdrew, and its inhabitants acquired coins and glassware probably by looting the Roman fort at Newstead. The Romans returned in AD 140, when they must have destroyed the broch and killed the woman whose skeleton was found in the ruins.

Finavon vitrified fort.

Interior of the Jarlshof Broch.

Chapter 8

Boundaries and barriers

MAN IS A GREAT DIVIDER of the landscape. The map of Britain is overlaid with a spider's web of boundaries, old and new: the field boundaries which compartmentalize the tasks of the farmer, ecclesiastical and administrative boundaries, and the relics of the old frontiers of political confrontation. Unable to realize the rational and unifying concept of the 'family of man', bygone societies marked out their failure on the landscape. There can be little doubt that increases in mobility and in awareness of the potential of the environment, must have resulted in larger territories with more powerful lords during the transition from the clan territories of the Mesolithic period, through the period of closely guarded tribal territories in the Iron Age, to the creation of a unified English kingdom under the Saxon kings. Each phase of political integration faced the countervailing forces of local separatism; even today, as parts of Europe head falteringly towards unity within the EEC, each component country faces the forces of irredentism which loom large in, for example, the Basque lands, Brittany and Scotland. Many of the frontier works and marchlands of the divided landscapes of the past seem to have disappeared without trace, but others, such as Hadrian's Wall, Offa's Dyke, and Devil's Dyke in Cambridgeshire, remain imposing.

It is not the multiplicity of boundaries in our compartmentalized landscape which is impressive, but the remarkable durability of so many ancient divisions. The better that we get to know this fascinating landscape, the more emphatically this point is made to us.

Parishes are an excellent example. It has been generally assumed that these land units were superimposed on a blank canvas from the tenth century AD onwards, as secular and ecclesiastical lords replaced the older system of small minster churches (see pp. 173–5) with a series of parish churches, each of which served a particular estate and its communities. If the parish churches were introduced to serve the populations of estates, however, the territorial 'package' which comprises the parish must be older than the ecclesiastical parish and as old as the estate. So how old is the estate? This is a very difficult question to answer, for it seems clear that the origins of some parish land cells extend back beyond the age of written history. Many show an uncanny resemblance to estates which are known to have been farmed by Roman villas and it is likely that a large proportion of these units for organized commercial farming were superimposed upon pre-existing Iron Age estate and village farming territories. I would not be at all surprised if a large number of parishes, in some form or other of unified landholding, had their origins in the Bronze Age – or perhaps even beyond. We have already remarked on the survival of the Neolithic communal

Air-view of Devil's Dyke near Newmarket.

centres known as causewayed camps in the form of locations for Late Bronze and Iron Age hillforts; now the study of boundaries serves to underline once more the importance of continuity in the British countryside.

The oldest surviving detailed descriptions of estate boundaries come from Saxon land grants, where features forming and identifying the bounds are often listed. Despite all subsequent landscape transformations, many of these landmarks can still be followed – although the shortsighted and destructive modern farming tendency to grub out hedgerows and to obliterate other ancient boundary marks will make life difficult for future generations of boundary hunters. In attempting to trace land boundaries before the Saxon period we tread with much less certainty, relying on the subtleties of archaeological evidence. Nevertheless, strong hints of continuity have been found. Frances Brown and Christopher Taylor have made a detailed comparison between Iron Age and medieval landscapes in Northamptonshire; they summarize the links as 'mobility of settlements and changes of landuse within a basic system of land units which are relatively stable'. They go on to ask: 'But if the links can be traced to the Iron Age how much further back can we go? To the Bronze Age or even earlier? The origins of the English landscape must now be seen as very ancient indeed.' They speculate interestingly that Rainsborough hillfort, built in the fifth century BC on an older occupation site, might have been the headquarters of an Iron Age estate whose component parts were arranged in similar ways to those of later Roman, Saxon and medieval landholdings.

Professor W. G. Hoskins has quoted the case of Ditchley in Oxfordshire as an example of a parish which clearly derives from a Roman villa estate: the villa worked an estate of 875 acres; it was bounded by ancient woodland and the earthwork known as Grim's Dyke, which was thrown up about the time of the Roman invasion and suggests a pre-Roman land unit. In this case, the villa boundaries can be reconstructed with some certainty and it can be seen that they were adopted almost in their entirety as the limits of a Late Saxon parish.

When the makers of landscape features were long forgotten their works were often attributed to the devil or pagan deities. Thus we have several Devil's Dykes, Wansdyke (Woden's Dyke) and Grim's Dyke. A second Grim's Dyke, this time pursuing an erratic 9 mile course along the ridge between the Wylye and Nadder valleys in Wiltshire, has been studied by D. J. Bonney and is interpreted by him as a boundary marker, being too low to be used for defence. Bonney is another student of the landscape who is tempted to see the origins of some boundaries as lying not in the Saxon era, but in the Bronze Age. A Roman road from Old Sarum to the Mendips cuts the dyke in a number of places and, since the ditch was filled to ease the passage of the road, the dyke must be older than the road. There is no more convenient peg upon which to hang a boundary than a road and it is very interesting that the parish boundaries in the area follow not the obvious line of the road, but that of the dyke. The implication is clear – that the land units which survived to become ecclesiastical parishes existed before the Roman road was built during the first century AD. The earthwork known as Wansdyke, on the other hand, is later, belonging to the fifth or sixth centuries AD, but the boundaries of parishes in this part of Wiltshire largely ignore the dyke, which strongly suggests that they already existed in some form before the dyke was built.

The phase of pioneer farming and colonization in the Neolithic Period must have come to an end in many places by the Bronze Age; during the latter period formidable bronze weapons were employed and, towards its close, hillforts crowned many summits. As one farming community pressed up against the margins of lands worked by its neighbours, boundaries must have become established, guarded and enforced. We can never know what proportion of our parish boundaries have prehistoric origins, but we can be certain – from the evidence of Saxon land grants and ecclesiastical documents – that many manors and estates have survived with little change to their boundaries from the time when parishes were instituted a thousand or more years ago. It is by no means outlandish to suggest that in a variety of English regions large landowners are today working estates which were first marked out three or four thousand years ago.

This continuity of boundaries is also evident on a larger scale. It is generally known that a number of English counties can be traced back to the age of the Saxon Heptarchy when the country was divided between a number of frequently unstable and warlike kingdoms – Kent, Sussex and Essex, for example – though larger kingdoms of the same period have little or no recognized political or administrative significance today, such as East Anglia, and the completely defunct Mercia. Those who believe that continuity remained the key even during the transition from Celtic to Saxon control can make a telling point by comparing the territories of Iron Age tribes with those of the later Saxon kingdoms. The boundaries of the British tribal territories are difficult to plot with certainty, while those of the Saxon kingdoms must have swayed back and forth with the rough and tumble of Dark Age warfare, but it is hard to believe that the following similarities between the territories of Celtic tribes and Saxon kingdoms are coincidental: the Coritani and Mercia; the Catuvellauni and Mid Anglia; the Trinovantes and Essex; the Regni and Sussex; the Iceni and East Anglia; and the Cantii and Kent. To what extent these boundaries represent transitions in political control, however, and to what extent they reflect the assertion of geographical factors within the environment itself (the latter suggesting the suitability of natural regions for the organization of human affairs) is very hard to discover.

Continuity in the political landscape is by no means a purely English affair. A decade ago, while I was working for my Ph.D, a Royal Commission was studying proposals for the reorganization of adminis-trative areas in Scotland, England and Wales. I studied both the past and future of political areas in Scotland, and this revealed to me the remarkable permanence of territories. At the time of the Roman invasion of England, the population of Scotland was composed of the descendants of distant Bronze Age immigrants and of more recent Celtic population. North of the Forth and Clyde were the proto-Picts and to the south, Britons. These communities were divided between a number of tribes. A map of tribal distributions was compiled by the geographer Ptolemy in the second century AD, though it lacks the detail which would allow us to designate tribal boundaries. A brief Roman occupation covered the last twenty years of the first century, but after AD 100 the legions were withdrawn to relieve pressure on the Danubian frontier of the Empire and consolidation took place further south with the construction of Hadrian's Wall in AD 128.

Eleven years later the Romans pushed north to establish the Antonine Wall along a line of forts across the Forth-Clyde isthmus which had been established by Agricola during the first Roman invasion. Various forays and reprisal raids took the Romans far north of the Antonine Wall into the areas of the Picts – a prehistoric people in the sense that they have left no written history. The earliest mention of the Picts by name does not come until AD 297, when Eumenius recorded them as being among the peoples who raided the Empire. It was probably during the immediately following centuries that a pattern of political divisions was established which survived in one form or another until the adoption of new local government areas in 1974.

There are various fragmentary and ambiguous Classical references to a basic north and south division of Pictland, resulting from the combination of tribal territories north and south of the Mounth, the spur of the Highlands which juts eastwards across the coastal plain south of Aberdeen. The various arguments for and against this division are labyrinthine; of clearer significance is a well-authenticated sevenfold division, in a twelfth-century manuscript known as *De Situ Albanie*, in which Andrew, Bishop of Caithness from about 1150 to 1184, described the division of territory in Pictland prior to the absorption of the kingdom under the Scot Kenneth McAlpin in the middle of the ninth century. In an Irish text, the *Pictish Chronicle*, written late in the life of independent Pictland, an older myth is quoted in which the seven sons of 'Cruithne' appear as eponyms for seven provinces:

> Seven children of Cruithne
> Divided Alba into seven districts
> Cait, Ce, Circinn, a warlike clan
> Fib, Fidach, Fotla (and) Fortrenn.

While philologists have claimed that links can be forged between the provinces in the *Pictish Chronicle* and the modern names of Scottish regions, a much clearer link exists between these names and the list provided by the Bishop of Caithness in *De Situ Albanie*:

De Situ Albanie	*Modern Name*
Enegus cum Moerne	Angus and Mearns
Adtheodle et Goerin	Atholl and Gowrie
Stradeern cum Meneted	Strath Earn and Menteith
Fif cum Fothreue	Fife and Kinross
Marr cum Buchen	Mar and Buchan
Muref et Ross	Moray and Ross
Cathanesia	Caithness and Sutherland

It is indeed remarkable that (with the exception of 'Fothreue') not only are the provinces of Dark Age Scotland the geographical regions of today, but they have also retained their names. The seven provinces seem to have been part of a peculiarly intricate division of territory, for it can be seen that, with the exception of Cathanesia, each consists of two components. It was

stated in *De Situ Albanie* that each lesser component (Buchan was the lesser component of Mar and Buchan, Mearns the lesser of Angus and Mearns) was ruled by a subsidiary chieftain, while all the greater and lesser rulers were under a single High King; 'those seven aforesaid were held as seven kings having under them seven petty kings'.

Although the *Pictish Chronicle* lists Pictish kings reigning up to AD 850, the kingdom seems to have fallen under the sway of Scottish insurgents from the west under Kenneth McAlpin in about 843, after which Scottish immigration intensified and the Pictish language completely disappeared, remaining to this day a mystery. The seven provinces, however, were more durable, though the early Christian kingdom was beset by Norse raids and isolated by Viking settlement round its borders. About the beginning of the tenth century, provincial rulers known as 'mormaers' begin to appear in the annals. The word is ambiguous and could mean 'sea-Stewards' – which would reflect the importance of coastal defence in Viking times – or 'great Stewards'. The mormaers were provincial sub-rulers of the Scottish king, and there is little doubt that they ruled over the provinces which had been established in Pictish times (or before).

The Scottish king Malcolm Canmore (reign 1057–93) married a Saxon princess and during his reign Saxon feudalism was superimposed upon the

Hadrian's Wall, looking east from Hotbank Crags.

153

older Celtic social fabric. The title of mormaer was replaced with the Saxon dignity 'Comes' or Earl, but again the seven provinces survived the merger of titles. Although new earldoms were created, the original seven Earls attended several important medieval occasions, such as the coronation of Alexander II in 1214, the settlement between Scotland and England in 1237, the renewal of the treaty in 1244, and the raid on England in 1297. The seven Earls, perhaps symbolizing a mystical number of elements comprising the nation, may have had some symbolic association with the old components of Pictland.

The full infeudation of Scotland involved the diffusion of Norman influences and was accompanied by the institution of sheriffs and the division of the country into sheriffdoms – roughly the Scottish equivalent of English sheriffs and counties. The earliest mention of a Scottish sheriff comes in 1119 or 1120 and their spread gained momentum in the reign of David I (1124–53). By the early thirteenth century the whole of Scotland, apart from the Highland interior and islands, was divided into sheriffdoms reflecting the imposition of feudal kingly control upon the turbulent Celtic regions. The feudal sheriffdoms, however, did not wipe out the old provinces, which may by this time have been a thousand or more years old; Buchan and Mar re-emerged in the sheriffdom of Aberdeen; Mearns became a sheriffdom later better known as Kincardineshire; and Angus, too, was preserved in a sheriffdom centred on Forfar. Moray, on the other hand, which had spawned the traitorous assassin Macbeth and may have continued to be a focus for Celtic unrest, seems firstly to have been included in a sheriffdom centred on Inverness and it was then deliverately carved up between sheriffdoms centred on Banff, Elgin, Nairn and Forres.

It was widely held that sheriffdoms were artificial creations, and that the area effectively controlled scarcely extended beyond the gates of the castle-guarded *caput* or county capital. When the medieval kings of Scotland made grants of land, the charter concerned usually stated the sheriffdom in which the lands lay; by the tedious process of plotting the dates and charter attributions of lands which lay towards the margins of sheriffdoms and by plotting information from seventeenth-century valuation rolls, I was able to show that the sheriffdom boundaries which were established in medieval times were preserved into the late nineteenth century.

Administrative reforms in 1870 and 1889 cleared up some of the small-scale anomalies in the county maps, removing the numerous tiny enclaves of one county in another that feudal wheeling and dealing had created, but before the sweeping changes of 1974 – which created juggernaut administrative regions – the political map of Scotland contained several prehistoric features. In the case of Kincardineshire in particular, the territorial continuity from Pictish province through Scottish mormaership, Anglo-Scottish Earldom, Scottish-Norman sheriffdom, to administrative county is clearly evident. The old Pictish province of Mearns managed to remain whole, for the small and impoverished authority spent £3000 of its slender funds on a campaign to resist its proposed division between Aberdeen and Dundee-centred regions. The Pictish provinces, therefore, can certainly be traced back to about the eighth century AD, but given the lack of a Pictish literary tradition and the fragmentary nature of classical and

English sources, one would not expect to be able to trace them back any further. The precise ages of Buchan, Mar, Moray and the rest of the provinces are likely to remain a mystery.

During the prehistoric period and the Dark Ages, boundaries were often marked out by banks and ditches. In some cases these earthworks served simply as statements of the position of boundaries, but in others they are clearly of defensive proportions and testify to ancient territorial struggles in a divided landscape. The linear earthworks of Britain embody a puzzling collection of features, with a variety of origins. The Chichester Dykes, with Devil's Ditch as the outermost of a series of defensive lines, lie in the west of Sussex and seem to be the defences of an undiscovered tribal capital of the Atrebates tribe. The Bokerley Dyke, in the Cranborne Chase in Dorset, appears to be a Late Roman defencework built to control movement along the Roman road between Old Sarum and Badbury Rings, while lesser works, like the Black Ditches of Norfolk, may be no more than estate boundaries.

The best-known and the best-authenticated of the numerous British linear earthworks (with the possible exception of the Antonine Wall) is Offa's Dyke. While so many dykes have been attributed to the devil or to pagan deities, there is little reason to doubt that King Offa of Mercia (757–96) had the dyke built along a boundary between his kingdom and those of the Welsh kings. Within a century of Offa's death, the cleric Asser

Silver penny of King Offa of Mercia.

cerctonef. Tunc populo in iciunuf rotoib; Ilea igitur ut dirimus ajanifeftiuf in

A fourteenth-century drawing of Offa digging for the remains of St Alban.

of St David's recorded how the king caused the dyke to be built from sea to sea. It was surveyed in detail by Sir Cyril Fox, who speculated that Offa might have been acting out the deeds of a legendary namesake from northern Germany, who (according to a sixth-century saga) did 'deeds of valour with his single sword; he drew the boundary against the Myrgingas at Fifeldor (in Slesvig)'. There are reasons to believe that the boundary and its associated earthwork were negotiated rather than imposed upon the Welsh kings, for anchorages on both sides of the lower course of the River Wye were left free for use by Welsh sailors. In the words of Fox:

Offa's Dyke marked a boundary, a frontier: it was not a military barrier. But its designer was a man imbued with a military tradition; his frontier was in general a sound piece of work from the point of view of the lowlanders whom he represented, for it gave visual control over foreign territory for the greater part of its length, and it includes tactically strong positions, such as the tremendous bastion of Herrock Hill, Herefordshire, or Selattyn Hill, Shropshire.

A few mysteries concerning Offa's Dyke remain; for example, we do not know whether it was made more formidable by the addition of a wooden palisade or wall, and its northern line as described by Fox and its chronological relationship with the nearby Wat's Dyke have been questioned by recent researchers. Much more mysterious, however, are the Cambridgeshire Dykes. A section of the largest of these – Devil's Dyke – is familiar to all visitors to Newmarket races, for it dominates the ground beside the course, making a natural grandstand.

When I arrived in the flat and unfamiliar Cambridgeshire landscape via the universities at Aberdeen and Dublin, one of the first beauty spots I stumbled upon was Fleam Dyke, a lesser brother of Devil's Dyke and a shrub-grown refuge for wildlife in the intensely farmed surroundings. I wondered what on earth the dyke could be: not a causeway, for the surrounding fields could never have been swamp, and the bank and ditch echoed the profile of hillfort defences. The standard interpretation was that the Cambridgeshire Dykes were built during the years of the Saxon Heptarchy as East Anglian defences against infantry attack from the aggressive neighbouring kingdom of Mercia. I was never quite convinced by this, and in the early summer of 1979, with a group of jaded political geography students who needed relief from the burden of imminent finals examinations, I embarked on fieldwork at the dykes.

Four dykes make up the Cambridgeshire sequence. To the north is the massive Devil's Dyke, which runs south-eastwards for $7\frac{1}{2}$ miles from its junction with a Roman canal at the village of Reach. Travelling south-west from Devil's Dyke one comes first to the imposing Fleam Dyke, then to the perhaps incomplete Brent Dyke and finally to Heydon Dyke. The latter two are largely ploughed out, but the exposure of their roots during construction work has shown that they were once quite formidable: the ditch at Heydon was 8 feet deep and 22 feet wide. All the dykes lie north-west to south-east, and 17 miles separate Devil's Dyke from Heydon Dyke.

It was thought that they barred movement across an area of open heathland and were anchored at either end by impassable terrain – the fens to the north and the 'Forest of Essex' to the south. However, it is difficult to imagine that the parts of Essex concerned were clothed in impenetrable forest during the Dark Ages, since they supported the farms of numerous villas during the Roman period and were lightly wooded in the Domesday Book. More significant is the prehistoric route known as the 'Icknield Way' which, from Neolithic times onwards, carried travellers from north Norfolk across the chalklands into Wessex. The dykes stand right across this road and, with no throughways discovered, they must have closed the branching tracks which made it up to all wheeled traffic.

The key to the riddle of the dykes lies in the problem of dating; the dykes can be bracketed in time between the late Roman period and the end of the Saxon era, by which time their original function had been forgotten and they were becoming mere components in later ecclesiastical boundaries. Within these time limits we have a period of great turbulence, migration and warfare and various combinations of adversaries are possible; since the dykes all face south-west we can at least assume that the threat came from this direction. But from where, and against whom? Since Saxon immigrants who probably came to England as mercenaries settled and intermarried with the Romano-British population of Cambridge before the Roman withdrawal in AD 410, the dykes could have been built by Romans forced into East Anglia by a (hypothetical) Saxon revolt. They could have been built by Saxons pressing down from northern Norfolk after the Roman departure, as defences against the mixed population of Cambridgeshire; they could have been built by retreating Saxons following their rout by the Arthurian forces at Mount Badon in the west around AD 500 or 517. Equally, the traditional interpretation that these are the frontier works of the Saxon East Anglian kingdom could be correct.

Partly because of their proximity to Cambridge University, the dykes have attracted the attention of some of the most gifted excavators since the Great War: Sir Cyril Fox, T. C. Lethbridge, and most recently, Professor

Air-view of Fleam Dyke.

Devil's Dyke, a view across the
ditch towards the bank.

Brian Hope-Taylor. A Saxon date for the dykes was suggested when the two
former excavators uncovered the remains of more than 60 Saxon men,
women and children, many with mutilated skeletons. Were these the bodies
of murdered prisoners captured when Mercians overran Heydon Dyke?
The remains have recently been speculatively reinterpreted as a Saxon
cwealmstow or execution site, where suicides and unbaptized children would
also be buried. Such a site could be considerably later than the defensive
earthwork. Another skeleton discovered not far away had a Late Romano-
British pot broken and placed round the skull in a Roman manner,
suggesting a pre-Saxon origin for the dyke. All these remains and the
numerous finds of Saxon weapons in other dyke locations come from
uncertain archaeological contexts, and the only truly reliable data has been
found beneath the base of the banks, pre-dating their construction. Three of
the dykes have yielded fourth-century Roman pottery from such locations,
while Professor Hope-Taylor discovered a Roman coin of about AD 350 in
1973, during a hasty excavation in advance of the construction of the
Newmarket bypass. This provides a lower limit on the age of the dykes.

Perhaps more mysterious than the age of the dykes is the function they
were intended to serve. It has been assumed that the dykes were defensible
barriers against infantry attack, but study of their military potential suggests
otherwise. Where the crest of Devil's Dyke is well preserved, there is space
for just 2 ranks of soldiers. We have said that the dyke is over 7 miles in
length, so to man it with only 1 rank of defenders, allowing each soldier a

yard of space and freedom to wield his weapons, would require a force of 13,000. Dark Age warfare was practised by small but highly mobile armies, composed largely of the members of the warrior aristocracies of Celtic and Germanic societies. The entire Roman field army in Britain around AD 400 numbered only 6000, and in AD 786 a mere 85 supporters of the claimant Cyneheard was almost sufficient to capture the rich kingdom of Wessex. East Anglia would have been fortunate to raise an army of 1000, and such a force, if ranged along the top of Devil's Dyke, could easily have been pulled out of position by feinting manoeuvres (even assuming that the defenders had correctly anticipated the point of attack); the invaders, charging in a column, would have overrun the dyke with ease. Despite the formidable appearance of the dyke, our tests showed that a fit young man could run from the outer edge of the ditch over the crest in less than half a minute. One possibly relevant feature emerged from javelin tests: the very best throw of a series by two gifted exponents succeeded in reaching the crest of Devil's Dyke, and this only at toe height. The lower Fleam Dyke, however, gave no such protection.

In terms of infantry warfare, the dykes could only offer an advantage to their defenders in a highly fortuitous situation in which the attackers were prepared to fight at a location of the defenders' choosing, and without resort to feinting or flanking manoeuvres – hardly providing the insurance that would justify the enormous efforts involved in their construction. The dykes take on a completely different significance if they are studied as cavalry defences; they would utterly break a cavalry charge, with the riders and their mounts being precipitated into the ditches where they could be picked off by spears and stones hurled from above. They would also have provided a measure of protection against raids by irregular cavalry, which could have caused untold havoc in the open landscape of heathland and farmland, villages and estates of Dark Age Cambridgeshire, and have greatly delayed the escape of plunder-laden invaders.

The cavalry explanation has not been pressed before, presumably because of the assumed Saxon date of the dykes and the belief that Saxons only used horses to convey themselves to battlefields. The great renewal of interest in Arthur, his rehabilitation as a historical figure, the speculation that he might have commanded a force of heavy cavalry – these have all turned attention towards the role of cavalry in Dark Age warfare. Armed riders are frequently depicted on Pictish stones; there are Welsh references to British cavalry in the Arthurian period (though such cavalry could be quite undisciplined); and there is an isolated reference to a Saxon cavalry victory over the Picts by the Northumbrian ruler Ecgfrith in the late seventh century. The evidence remains inconclusive, leaving the question open.

It would be wrong to imagine that the Dark Ages were simply a period of warfare; for while aristocratic youngbloods hacked at each other, the work of the peasant farmer must have gone on. Even so, it is hard to stand in the shadow of Devil's Dyke and not feel that it is the frantic response to some awful threat from the south. Agricultural life for miles around must have been disrupted in order to provide the labour required. We attempted to calculate the magnitude of this demand. Data from the experimental earthwork at Overton Down in Wiltshire provided the information that a

A Roman standard bearer rides over a Briton.

man armed with a pick and shovel could move 750 kg of solid moist chalk in one hour. A precise survey of a cross section of Devil's Dyke and the calculation of the position of the original landsurface, using information from a former excavation, allowed a calculation to be made. According to our figures, the entire earthwork weighs 1,360,090,000 kgs, so it would appear that Devil's Dyke is the result of 1,813,453 man hours of labour, or 181,345 ten-hour man days. When an allowance is made for the loss of original bank materials as ditch silts, the adjusted figure suggests that the construction fully occupied 500 labourers for 400 days (or 1000 labourers for 200 days and so on). Excavation has shown that the work began with the construction of a low marker bank of topsoil, and that some sort of earthmoving equipment was used, for tip lines, between soil dumps, as well as spade marks are evident in the fabric. In addition to the labourers whose man hours we have calculated, other workers would have been involved in quartering and feeding the workforce, and in surveying and supervising. Small breaks in the alignment suggest that quite primitive surveying techniques were involved, and that the dyke was built in sections, perhaps with each village and estate along the length being responsible for a contribution.

It is obvious that strong central control was necessary to mobilize the workforce and that it was a major undertaking which must have considerably drained and diverted the efforts of a society seldom embarrassed by agricultural surplus. We worked on the assumption that the dykes represented a rational response to a problem, but, of course, human beings are not always rational. Conceivably, the dykes represented an enormous and empty display of kingly power: the construction of monumental and impressive frontier works to dignify the approaches to an East Anglian kingdom. Although they are sometimes interpreted as defences against cattle rustling rather than military invasion, I think that a series of village corrals would have provided a cheaper solution to this problem.

We will only begin to solve the riddle when archaeologists are able to provide a date for the dykes. Even then we are unlikely to be able to establish the sequence of building. Devil's Dyke may be the earliest, and the three southern dykes would represent stages in an advance from Devil's Dyke which petered out at Heydon Dyke. Equally, Devil's Dyke – as the grandest of the series – may represent a final and desperate 'last ditch' attempt to resist the forces that had overrun the earlier defences. It certainly seems unlikely that all the dykes were in use at one time.

No discussion of boundaries would be complete without a mention of the recent technique of hedgerow dating. The theory, simply stated, suggests that the count of the major tree and shrub species which can be found in a thirty-yard length of hedgerow represents the age of the hedge in centuries. Thus a hedge with 3 species will be around 300 years old, and one with 7 species will have existed for 7 centuries. The discovery and testing of the theory arose out of a productive partnership between Max Hooper, a botanist working for the Nature Conservancy whose idea it was, and Professor W. G. Hoskins, the economic and landscape historian, who provided examples of hedges of known date against which the notion could be tested. The idea produces good results for the majority of hedges and seems to be little affected by the underlying geology of the hedge or hedgerow management. It appears that each hedge tends to gain an additional species of tree or shrub every century, but why this should be so is a complete mystery; complex ecological considerations must be involved. Useful as a general guide to the age of hedgerow boundaries in a region, the theory will give misleading results in cases where farmers have planted a hedge of several species, or where gardeners have planted a tapestry hedge including half a dozen or more shrubs of different hue.

Some of our hedgerow boundaries are more than a thousand years old, as both shrub counts and the boundary descriptions in Saxon land grants show, and a few can be dated back as far as the seventh century AD, when they provided estate boundaries. A great wave of hedgerow planting, mainly using the fast-growing hawthorn, took place at the time of the enclosure of village commons and open fields during the eighteenth and nineteenth centuries, when the landscape took on a pattern of straight geometrical hedgerow boundaries, interspersed with spinneys to harbour game. However, a large proportion of our hedges are medieval in origin and mark enclosures made by agreement between village proprietors, or the taking-in of new fields or 'assarts' from the forest. While the area around Conington in Huntingdonshire lies in a landscape which was greatly affected by the later parliamentary enclosures, Dr Hooper has shown that more than sixty per cent of the hedgerows date from before 1595. As one of the most simple techniques of archaeological fieldwork, hedgerow-dating can be attempted – with caution – by anyone who can distinguish different leaf types and pace out thirty yards. Hedgerow-dating is like the motorcar engine is for most of us – we do not know how it works, but the important thing is that it generally does.

Two factors emerge in this chapter as they do throughout the book. Firstly, familiar aspects of the landscape are far older than was thought, and secondly, supposedly primitive people were capable of phenomenal feats of construction, for purposes which often remain unclear.

The Antonine Wall at Watling Lodge.

Another Devil's Dyke near Wheathampstead, thought to be the outer defences of a British oppidum.

The Antonine Wall. Doubling the natural defences provided by the Rivers Carron and Kelvin, the wall runs 37 miles along an escarpment crossing the Central Valley of Scotland, between Bridgeness on the Forth (near Bo'ness, W of Edinburgh), and Old Kirkpatrick on the Clyde, W of Glasgow. Only small sections are well preserved, but there are fine views all along it. Built in AD 139 by the Roman governor of Britain, Quintus Lollius Urbicus, on the orders of Emperor Antoninus Pius. It has a 14 ft-wide stone base on which turves were laid, and it narrowed to a 6 ft-wide wooden walkway at a height of 10 ft. In front of the wall was a 20-100 ft-wide berm, and a ditch 40 ft wide and 12 ft deep. Thirteen garrisons or *castella* have been identified, apparently placed at 2 mile intervals. Thousands of men would have been stationed there, either to launch reprisal raids northwards or to block assaults on the rich farmlands to the south. Some of the best preserved sections of the wall are at Rough Castle near Bonnybridge (30 miles W of Edinburgh, near the M80, signposted from the B816), and at Watling Lodge (25 miles W of Edinburgh, 1 mile W of Falkirk, off the B816).

Black Pig's Dyke. Two stretches of dyke in Northern Ireland – Black Pig's Dyke, also known as Worm Ditch, which lies near Enniskillen, linked to the Dorsey earthworks and Dane's Cast, which lie near Newry, appear to be frontier relics of the ancient Kingdom of Ulster and are not far from the present border. It was claimed that Black Pig's Dyke ran 130 miles from Bundoran on Donegal Bay in the W, to near Carlingford Lough SSW of Belfast in the E; but it is more probably a series of separate defence works. Parts consist of a 12 ft ditch backed by a 10 ft-high bank and were perhaps built against cattle raiders after the fall of the northern kingdom in the 5th cent. AD. Linked to Black Pig's Dyke, the Dorsey earthworks may be the remains of a 300 acre cattle enclosure built against raiders from the south. Dane's Cast, in Down and Armagh may date from the 4th cent. AD

Bokerley Dyke. Lies S of A354 near Woodyates, 11 miles SW of Salisbury, in Dorset. A massive NE-facing bank and ditch in the Cranborne Chase, it today divides the parishes of Pentridge and Cranborne in Dorset, from that of Martin in Hampshire. Perhaps built by the Romans to control movement between Old Sarum (N of Salisbury) and Badbury Rings (10 miles NW of Bournemouth).

Cambridgeshire Dykes. Described pp. 156-60. Fleam Dyke crosses the A11 just N of the road to Fulbourn (7 miles SE of Cambridge). It is topped by a footpath. Devil's Dyke, also with a public footpath, lies near the A1304 at the roundabout S of Newmarket (12 miles E of Cambridge). Its N end joins a Roman canal at the village of Reach, 4 miles WNW of Newmarket, where a medieval green was cut into the Dyke. A well preserved and less overgrown section lies between the villages of Burwell and Swaffham Prior (W and NW of Newmarket).

Coombs Ditch. This imposing barrier runs along the summit of the downs between the Stour and the North Winterborne rivers, NW of Bournemouth, in Dorset. It faces NE and seems to have been enlarged by the Romans from a Late Iron Age boundary earthwork.

Gryme's Dyke. One of several dykes, including Sheepen Dyke, the Shrub End Triple Dykes and Lexden Dykes, that probably defended the Late Iron Age Belgic oppidum of Camulodunum, by modern Colchester, in Essex. They enclose an area of 12 sq. miles, joining the Colne and Roman Rivers to N and S. Gryme's Dyke forms the boundary to the King George V playing fields accessible from Clairmont Road.

Hadrian's Wall. The wall was built for Emperor Hadrian who visited Britain in AD 122. Six years later it breasted hill, crag and valley for over 73 miles, from Wallsend (in Newcastle-upon-Tyne) in the E, to Bowness (12 miles NW of Carlisle) in the W. Sixteen forts lay along it, with 2 'milecastles' between each. Supply lines were covered by forts and garrisons. The massive fortifications were abandoned in AD 139, when the Antonine Wall became the forward line, and were reoccupied in about AD 159. It was overrun in AD 197, but retaken and partly repaired in AD 296. A little Celtic temple stands at Benwell (2 miles W of Newcastle) where there was once a fort; another fort lies at Corbridge (17 miles W of Newcastle, on the A69) and a cavalry fort is at Chesters (4 miles NW of Hexham on the A69). A 5 acre infantry fort at Housesteads (35 miles W of Newcastle, on the B6318) is deservedly the most important tourist attraction on the Wall.

Offa's Dyke. It ran with short breaks from sea to sea. Some gaps are original, but others are due to later destruction. A well-preserved 7 mile section can be explored, beginning at the information centre at Knighton village on the A4113, 16 miles W of Ludlow. Wat's Dyke runs parallel to the northern section of Offa's Dyke, and may date from the reign of Aethelbald of Mercia (AD 716–57), anticipating Offa's Dyke. At Llandysilio-yn-Ial (10 miles SW of Wrexham, near Valle Crucis Abbey and the Dyke) an inscribed stone commemorates Offa's rival, Eliseg, king of Powys. Eliseg's Pillar was erected before AD 854 by his great-grandson.

Wansdyke. Once thought to be a single earthwork, it is more probably two. West Wansdyke runs from Maes Knoll (4½ miles S of Bristol, 1¼ miles SW of Whitchurch on the A37) in Avon, to Horscombe (2 miles S of Bath). East Wansdyke traverses the Wiltshire chalk downlands N of the Vale of Pewsey. The best sections of East Wansdyke to walk along are where it crosses the A361, 3 miles NE of Devizes, or where it crosses the A345 2 miles SW of Marlborough. It is 12 miles long, measuring in places 90 ft across the rampart and ditch. In low-lying wooded country, unsuited to open warfare, it is little more than a boundary-marker. It appears to date from the 5th or 6th cent. AD and to be either British or Saxon.

West Wansdyke also faces N, is similar in design, and can be dated with no more accuracy. Built either in the late 6th cent. to defend Britons from the Saxons, or during the early 7th cent. as the northern boundary of the West Saxons. It may, however, date from the 5th cent.

East Wansdyke, crossing St Anne's Hill, 1821.

Chapter 9

Christians in a pagan land

IN OUR EXPLORATION of the mistier realms of British landscape history, scraps of evidence have kept appearing which oblige us to revise our views on dating. The general conclusion is that things are far older than we thought they were – and this study of the Church and church buildings will serve to reinforce the lesson. However, it is certainly worth reminding oneself to beware of thinking that the older something is the better it is, for such shallow antiquarianism may even lead to comic excesses. I know of at least one undistinguished cottage, erected no doubt with little expense or effort in around 1820, which has become a cherished period residence since a cunning owner inscribed an eighteenth-century date over the door!

The traumas and turmoils of the Dark Ages, and the lighter days of the Saxon kingdom, may indeed be the most fascinating period in a heritage of incomparable richness. We certainly find problems and mystery in plenty as we trace the dark recesses of the transition from paganism to Christianity. For those who believe in 'leys' there are hosts of medieval churches which they claim were sited on older pagan sites by crypto-pagans, although how this could have taken place as recently as the Middle Ages without being recorded in a single document is difficult to understand. Increasingly too, sad little groups of bored souls seek spiritual excitement through the formation of pagan sects organized around fanciful reconstructions of the 'Old Religion'. This sometimes involves little more than senseless cavorting, but from time to time it affronts local communities by the calculated desecration of churches and churchyards. It is difficult to imagine how the paraphernalia of ley-hunting or paganism can add anything to our understanding of early Britain, for the fragmentary story which we already possess is itself sufficiently extraordinary to satisfy the most imaginative of tastes.

It is significant that while only thirteen per cent of the British population are regular churchgoers, the position of the parish church in the hearts of rural communities seems little diminished by the decline in observance. In August 1979 a fire raged in the Cam valley church at Ickleton, and members of the small village community braved the flames to form a human chain of rescuers, while others carted church treasures to safety in their wheelbarrows. We may not know how many of them were Anglican believers, but they all cared greatly for the ancient church. Afterwards, the Bishop of Huntingdon remarked that the brave villagers saving church property for a future reconstruction were a symbol of the resurrection.

Monasterboice, Louth. Detail of the Cross of Muiredach.

The Chief Druid. A 1773 copy of a drawing, believed to be of a Druid. It was made in 1676 from a verbal description of a statue found in Germany.

The pre-Christian religions of Britain – there were probably several – are little understood, and there are no written records by the worshippers concerned. Druidism as practised today belongs to the popular romance and sentimentality of a post-medieval period when, in ignorance of the most basic archaeological methods, most antiquities were attributed to the Druids, Romans, or both. In the mid-eighteenth century the colourful antiquarian William Stukeley contributed to the creation of a Druidic cult and used to bestow oak leaves on his fellow self-appointed Druids. Most of what we know about the real Druids – and it amounts to very little indeed – derives from contemporary Roman writers. Their criticism of the Druids may in part be politically motivated, for the Romans were generally flexible in religious matters, and ready to accommodate alien deities within the ample folds of their own religion. In this way they covered themselves against the possibility of excluding and offending a newly encountered god who might conceivably have had some influence; nor did they wish to alienate his followers from the cosmopolitan amalgam of peoples who composed the empire.

According to Julius Caesar's description, the Druids were official sorcerers who operated as astrologers, teachers, judges and guardians of the theology, their doctrines passed from initiate to initiate in verbal form. Since they performed these roles within what were probably the most bloodthirsty and frightening societies ever to inhabit these islands, the Druids can have borne little resemblance to the genteel, white-robed people who perform annually for early-rising visitors at Stonehenge. The Roman invasions of Britain were partly a response to the disruptive nature of the British influence on the Continental Celtic provinces of the Empire. Tacitus and Strabo may not have exaggerated in their descriptions of the sacrificial atrocities practised by the Druids – these would not have been out of character in the head-hunting Celtic society. But how widespread the Druids were, and to what extent they were held in esteem in Iron Age Britain is likely to remain a mystery for some time to come.

Leaving some of its bloodier rites aside, the 'old religion' seems to have been related to nature, place and the veneration of spirits thought to reside in trees, pools and rocks. If we remember that these people dwelled in a quite unspoilt landscape of unsurpassed beauty, this aspect of Celtic religion becomes understandable and almost attractive. There are hardly any visible traces of this religion. Small rectangular temples have been unearthed within the ramparts of South Cadbury hillfort (a beautiful place) and at Heathrow airport; but far more numerous are the holy wells sometimes found in association with Christian churches. While it is generally impossible to establish the pre-Christian backgrounds of such wells, there are good grounds for thinking that the Christian church took over sites which had been held holy by the old religion.

One of these places may be perpetuated in the name of the pretty riverside Huntingdonshire village of Holywell. The church is early thirteenth-century and Tudor, but in a hollow at the edge of the churchyard, sheltered by a brick canopy built by a nineteenth-century rector, can be seen the crystal waters of the ancient well. Even prettier, especially in the late spring with the pink butterbur flowers all around, is the holy well beside the church of Stevington in Bedfordshire. The church has a Saxon west tower with long and short work; and although the well became a minor centre for medieval pilgrimage it may have been sacred to the Celtic religion. One of the better-known wells, near Madron in Cornwall, is dedicated to the saint of that name. The custom for visitors to decorate the surrounding foliage with colourful bits of cloth may be attributed to a passage in Daphne du Maurier's book *Vanished Cornwall* in which votive offerings of an item of clothing are mentioned. But the custom has far earlier roots than that.

It is certain that some pagan wells were associated with particular deities who could be placated or won over by gifts thrown into the waters – a probable origin for the wishing well. A well at Carrawburgh fort on Hadrian's Wall contained a rich hoard of offerings, including more than 10,000 coins presumably bestowed mostly by legionaries. Some of the holy wells dedicated to St Anne, the mother of the Virgin, may be a civilized corruption of the hideous child-eating Celtic goddess Annis.

Very little is known of the arrival and diffusion of the Christian religion in Britain; it gained official acceptance in the Roman Empire during the fourth century, and it must have been at this time that the first churches were built in Britain. These superseded the private rooms used for more furtive Christian worship in the houses and villas of pagan converts: one room in a villa at Lullingstone in Kent was found to contain Christian murals. The oldest presumed Christian church in Britain is a small rectangular building with a western apse and side aisles found at Silchester in Hampshire in the late nineteenth century and re-excavated in 1961. It measures only 42 feet by 33 feet, and may be typical of small early foundations. It seems to have fallen into disuse after a short time, in around 360. At Icklingham in Suffolk lead tanks bearing Christian *chi-rho* symbols were discovered in the early eighteenth century and in 1939. A recent excavation at this little Roman town has revealed a group of buildings, a small stone font and a cemetery, all of which date from about 350.

There were clearly Christians in Britain before the fourth century

A Cornish holy well, one of 40 known to exist in the county.

because a cryptogram scratched on the wall of a Roman house in Cirencester was found to contain the letters of *pater noster* and *alpha omega* twice repeated, conceivably dating from the second century. (*Pater noster* or 'Our Father' are the initial words of the Lord's Prayer, while *alpha* and *omega* are the first and last letters of the Greek alphabet and relate to the passage in the scriptures: 'I am the *alpha* and *omega*, the beginning and the end'.) The church had certainly gained an organized foothold in Britain before the Imperial Toleration Edict of 314, for in the following year the country despatched three bishops and the representatives of a fourth to the Council of Arles. Possibly as early as the end of the second century, Britain had produced its own martyr, St Alban, whose cult developed at Verulamium (now St Albans), but of whom next to nothing is known. About four centuries later the Saxon cleric Bede dated the legend of the martyrdom of St Alban to the year 301.

One intriguing riddle emerges in the manuscripts known as the Welsh Annals, which consist of three later copies of Dark Age documents. An entry for the year 501 notes that 'Bishop Ebur died in Christ in the three hundred and fiftieth year of his age.' The name of the bishop is clearly confused with that of his see – Eboracum simply means York – so perhaps his unlikely age is that of the see rather than the man. This would date the origin of the See of York to AD 151, which although it is early, corresponds quite closely with the date given by Bede for the first conversion of Britain. He writes: 'In the year of our Lord's Incarnation 156, Marcus Antoninus Verus, fourteenth from Augustus, became Emperor jointly with his brother Aurelius Commodus. During their reign, and while the holy Eleutherus ruled the Roman Church, Lucius, a British king, sent him a letter, asking to be made a Christian by his direction. This pious request was quickly granted, and the Britons received the Faith and held it peacefully in all its purity and fulness until the time of the Emperor Diocletian'. Although Bede was writing about events about as distant in time from himself as the Wars of the Roses are from us, it is clear that legends of very early conversion were current in his time.

More famous, but far less credible, are the legends concerning the mission to Britain by Joseph of Arimathea. Whatever sort of holy city Glastonbury in Somerset may have been in the past, it has for some time been a mecca for the credulous followers of fringe 'archaeology'. These have not been slow to capitalize on the local legend that Joseph of Arimathea (called by John, 'A disciple, but secretly for fear of the Jews', and by Mark,

'An honourable counsellor') visited Glastonbury where he buried the Holy Grail and thrust his staff into the ground where it blossomed into a tree. The missionary – so the legend goes – then set up a wattle church of the same dimensions as the tabernacle. In a more elaborate version of the tale the Boy Jesus is said to have accompanied Joseph to Glastonbury. Although entangled in the mumbo-jumbo of fringe doctrines this legend also appeals to fervent anti-Romanists, for it enables the Church of Rome to be bypassed in the story of the original conversion, casting Bede's Lucius as a deviationist and the Augustinian mission of 579 as an alien intrusion.

The origins of the legend of Joseph in Britain are difficult to trace. Had it been current during the Dark Ages it would surely have been recorded by Bede (c. 673–735) or by the Celtic monk Gildas (c. 500–?). But Gildas dates the conversion to a period when Joseph could have been alive: 'Meanwhile, to an island numb with chill ice and far removed, as in a remote nook of the world, from the visible sun, Christ made a present of his rays (that is, his precepts), Christ the true sun, which shows its dazzling brilliance to the entire earth, not from the temporal firmament merely but from the highest citadel of heaven, that goes beyond all time. This happened first, as we know, in the last years of Emperor Tiberius, at a time when Christ's religion was being propagated without hindrance: for, against the wishes of the senate, the emperor threatened the death penalty for informers against the soldiers of God'. Significantly, Gildas makes no reference to Joseph of Arimathea to support his narrative. He is clearly working in a little-known field of history, for he misses the opportunity to his acid-tongued talents which Tiberius presents, he being utterly debauched and a persecutor of Christians.

The historian William of Malmesbury likewise made no reference to Joseph. He stayed at Glastonbury Abbey in 1125, believing it to have been built in 166 by missionaries from Rome, and it remained to a thirteenth-century editor of his book to add a story that Joseph obtained 12 hides of land and the island of Glastonbury from a pagan king. There is a symbolic thorn tree preserved in the Abbey grounds, but the legend of the blossoming staff may be later still. It is first mentioned in a poem of 1520, in which 3 hawthorns miraculously flower at Christmas. The connection between the thorn and Joseph's staff was first made in 1714. Even the science of archaeology does not support the Glastonbury legend, for excavations at the Abbey have failed to find structures earlier than the mid-seventh century, and there is no fifth- and sixth-century Mediterranean pottery usually associated with pre-Saxon sites in Somerset. A probably Saxon wooden church measuring about 60 feet by 25 feet was destroyed by fire in 1184. A bank which could have belonged to an earlier monastery is seen to cut a Roman well, which must therefore predate it but it is overlain by more recent glass-working debris of the ninth century.

So the date of the arrival of the first Christian in Britain remains mysterious. It may well have been that at some date closely following the Roman conquest and occupation of England, a secret adherent of the faith stepped ashore as a legionary, administrator or merchant. But we will never known the truth. By the time of the Roman withdrawal (about 410) there was a numerous and organized Christian community. Many conversions may have been superficial, with British chieftains inducing the conversion of their subjects more for reasons of political expediency than of belief. Although much of the fabric of Christianity crumbled under the British tyrants and pagan invasion, the light of the church still flickered among the monastic communities of the western mountains, and maybe even in the lowlands. Celtic monks, like the broken-hearted and embittered Gildas of the Arthurian period, recalled a dimly glimpsed period more than a century earlier which appeared almost as a Golden Age. He blamed the foolish British leaders for having ever admitted the Saxons:

the guard – or rather the method of destruction – they devised for our land was that the ferocious Saxons (name not to be spoken!), hated by man and God, should be let into the islands like wolves into the fold, to beat back the peoples of the north. Nothing more destructive, nothing more bitter has ever befallen the land.

But the scenario which depicts hordes of all-conquering scourges of Celtic culture is now giving way to one which emphasizes continuity, and sees a smoother transfer of political control to Saxon lords whose followers may have remained a peasant minority in the lands were they settled. Gildas, who had every reason to mourn the displacement of a church which was probably in flight before the larger Saxon migrations, paints a more colourful picture of the Saxon conquest:

It was sad sight. In the middle of the squares the foundation stones of high walls and towers that had been torn from their lofty base, holy altars, fragments of corpses, covered (as it were) with a purple crust of congealed blood, looked as though they had been mixed up in some dreadful winepress.

But Bede relates how in

about the one hundred and fiftieth year after the coming of the English to Britain, Gregory was inspired by God to send his servant Augustine with several other God-fearing monks to preach the word of God to the English nation. Having undertaken this task in obedience to the Pope's command and progressed a short distance on their journey, they became afraid, and began to consider returning home. For they were appalled at the idea of going to a barbarous, fierce and pagan nation of whose very language they were ignorant.

Bede is wrong about the date, for Saxon communities were established in England years before the Roman withdrawal. And Augustine's fears proved utterly ill-founded, because the mission landed in Kent in 597 and the king, Aethelberht, was swiftly converted, and even gave land near his palace at Canterbury for the building of a cathedral church. The conversion of the pagan English kingdoms followed quite rapidly and almost all of them had accepted Christianity by 660.

How was such a swift change of faith effected? The new religion must have seemed a more powerful, sophisticated and organized faith than the one which it replaced, or the conversion would not have been so easily accomplished. But in addition to this there was the policy of tolerance adopted by the Church. Archaeology has not produced convincing examples of pagan Saxon temples, and this may simply be because they were assimilated into new Christian churches. The pagan holy places are not completely erased from the landscape and place names consisting of, or including 'Stow', which denotes such a place, are not uncommon.

Isolated churches are usually suggestive of lost and shrunken villages, but the church at Stow on the edge of the Fenland beside the A45 seems to be an exception. Although recent ribbon development has linked the church to the core of the old village which is some distance away, there are no traces of the earthworks of abandoned settlement which commonly testify to the drift of a village away from its ancient ecclesiastical focus. Neither can I find fragments of medieval pottery in the land by the church which has been disturbed by recent road-building. It therefore seems likely, especially in view of its name, that the church at Stow always stood apart from its congregation and that it was built on a site considered sacred before the Augustinian conversion. Christopher Taylor quotes the similar case of Maxey near Grantham, where the church stands on a swelling mound isolated from the village but close to a recently excavated pagan Saxon village. The church at Knowlton in Dorset is also detached, and is surrounded by prehistoric earthworks, while the one at Edlesborough in Buckinghamshire lies within the village but on top of a large mound which may be far older than the church.

The lunatic fringe makes rather heavy weather of the location of Christian churches on pagan sites, invoking sinister forms of mysticism which are not mentioned in the mass of documents of the period. In fact the church is anything but silent on the matter, and shows the same practical opportunism which enabled the Roman Empire to assimilate the followers of many creeds, and the Roman church to allow converts to incorporate older pagan festivals in their new religion, particularly in the case of the region of the Andes. Bede provides the keynote in his *History of the English Church and People*, where he gives a copy of a letter from Pope Gregory to Abbot Mellitus on his departure to Britain in 601. It deserves to be quoted at some length because it clearly expresses the policy of the Church:

We have been giving careful thought to the affairs of the English, and we have come to the conclusion that the temples of the idols among the people should on no account be destroyed. The idols are to be destroyed, but the temples themselves are to be aspersed with holy water, altars set up in them and relics deposited there. For if these temples are well built, they must be purified from the worship of demons and dedicated to the service of the true God. In this way, we hope that the people, seeing that their temples are not destroyed, may abandon their error and, flocking more readily to their accustomed resorts, may come to know and adore the true God.

The Medieval Church at Knowlton in Dorset stands inside a prehistoric henge monument.

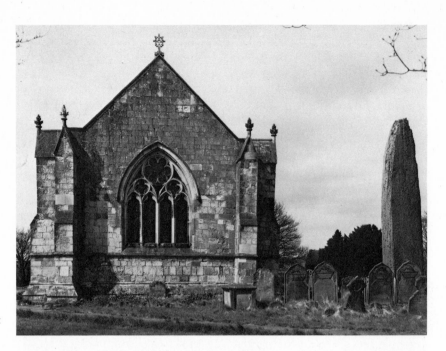

England's tallest monolith surrounded by the churchyard at Rudston near Bridlington.

The letter continues with instructions for pagan sacrifices to be replaced by church festivals and the thought that 'If the people are allowed some worldly pleasures in this way, they will more readily come to desire the joys of the spirit'.

There are plenty of examples of such reuse of sites and structures, although it is unclear whether all were intentional. The examples of Stow, Maxey, Knowlton and Edlesborough may well show a deliberate assumption of a pagan site. Then there is Rudston near Bridlington, where a monolith almost 26 feet (7.8 metres) tall and dating from the Bronze Age stands in the churchyard. Similarly, the Norman church at Knowlton lies within a circular earthwork, and a large menhir appears to have been built into the wall of the church at Llandysiliogogo. In the case of Avebury the Saxon church conspicuously avoided the vast prehistoric ring and was built to the west, while its congregation made periodic attempts to topple and destroy the stones. Whatever goodwill was produced by Pope Gregory's advice to Mellitus, however, there seem to have been cases of later resistance to Christianity. There are numerous local legends describing how the Devil hampered the building of a church. The incompetent mason had an enviable array of excuses available to him in this age of superstition. But at Rudston and Boroughbridge in Yorkshire the huge standing stones are said to be missiles which the Devil hurled at the church, and may be identified with a force of opposition.

In some respects the strength of medieval paganism has doubtless been exaggerated by more recent writers on the 'Old Religion'. But the sheila-na-gigs found in the fabrics of a number of churches are so much an exception that their presence needs an explanation. These obscene pagan fertility symbols, plainly tolerated by the church authorities, were either incorporated from older structures into new churches, or were carved later on their walls. Tolerance of pagan symbols does not seem to accord with the explicitly worded laws of Canute in the eleventh century which forbade every heathenism: 'Heathenism is that men worship idols; that is, that they worship heathen gods, and the sun or moon, fire or rivers, water-wells or stones, or forest trees of any kind; or love witchcraft or promote morthwork of any wise'. Although reports of pagan revivals exist, for example in 1303 when the Bishop of Coventry was accused before the Pope of Devil worship, it is hard to believe that pagan rites took place in all the churches where fertility symbols are now found. It seems more likely that the Church took its responsibility to the community seriously, and was ready to take risks. In exchange for the one tenth of village produce they took as tithes, they were expected to ensure that the crops flourished. If obviously pagan symbols were sanctioned by the church, for a blatant sheila-na-gig would hardly escape the notice of a bishop, this suggests that the church was hedging its bets by being seen to placate the old gods too, just in case their supporters believed this was necessary.

One of the most striking of these symbols is built into the Norman part of the tower of the charming church at Whittlesford in Cambridgeshire. It very much seems that the carved slab of imported stone was removed from an older monument, for unlike the quoins of the church, it is not of carefully dressed stone. To the left of the female fertility figure is a human-headed goat or bull, maybe the Devil. This could have been transferred from a pagan temple, but although Roman settlement traces abound in the locality, the head of the animal seems to show Celtic influences. Not far away, at Royston in Hertfordshire, an artificial cave contains carvings, probably medieval, which represent both pagan and Christian symbols. Various fertility symbols have been found beneath the altars of Welsh churches. It would be worthwhile to investigate the claim that sheila-na-gigs do not represent the survival of pre-Christian pagan cults, but a separate development of early-medieval fertility sects; for although the Whittlesford earth mother figure may be Celtic, one like it at Kilpeck in Herefordshire seems to belong to the twelfth century.

Besides these Earth Mother symbols, there is a second category of figures known as Green Men, who are usually demon-headed figures, clothed or masked in leaves. At Melbourne in Derbyshire, where the Green Man appears on a carved capital, and at Crowcombe (Somerset) on a much later bench-end, he has a cap of leaves, and vines issuing from his mouth. While the adherents of paganism and lunatic fringe archaeology have various reasons for seeking to perpetuate the view that the medieval church was merely a veneer masking the practices of pagan religion, if the church in this period deviated seriously from Christian practices, it was in the direction of selfish materialism. Perhaps another form of pragmatism was evident in the incorporation of pagan symbols in the church fabric – for to the simple and superstitious they might seem to provide a double insurance against the failure of crops. The Green Men might in part be decorative motifs, for the use of hideous gargoyles in church architecture does not denote that devils were worshipped.

In the chapter on Boundaries and Barriers (pp. 149–50), I described how the modern parish is in many cases based on a much older estate and village

The sheila-na-gig in the
churchtower at Whittlesford near
Cambridge.

Christian and pagan symbols
carved in an artificial cave at
Royston, Herts.

unit. Early missionaries founded an organizational framework of local ecclesiastical centres or 'minster churches'. Cathedrals and monastic establishments were at the top of the church hierarchy, while the minsters were staffed by secular clergy under a head priest. Local minster churches despatched preachers to the rural backwaters to conduct services in the open air, often under preaching crosses until a proper building could be provided. Somewhat later it was the estate, with its central village church, which often furnished the territorial framework for the parish. Just how many parish churches there were in pre-Conquest England we may never know, although the figure of 400 surviving Saxon churches is widely quoted. Of these 400, only 50 are near-complete Saxon buildings, and the rest merely contain elements of Saxon work. It is likely that thousands of churches have Saxon origins. Saxon stonework, such as at Earls Barton in Northamptonshire or Wing in Buckinghamshire, was of high quality, but many of their churches were of timber, the only surviving example of which is at Greensted-juxta-Ongar in Essex. It is much altered and restored, and its vertical oak logs may or may not be typical of the period.

A Saxon roundel, incorporated high in the wall of Edenham Church in Lincolnshire.

Any church listed as 'Saxon' in the guidebooks can expect regular streams of visitors and contributions. Those listed above are splendid national monuments, but most churches are glorious accretions of centuries of endowment and reconstruction, and hosts of churches not described as Saxon contain tantalizing little fragments which betoken an older foundation. Edenham in Lincolnshire, for example, has a Saxon cross roundel built high in one of the interior walls.

This can be illustrated by my observations in village churches of the Cam valley south of Cambridge. The valley between Little Shelford and Ickleton is 6 miles long and has 7 riverside churches, all bearing names which suggest that they were sited at ancient fords carrying branches of the prehistoric Icknield Way across the river. Only one of these churches could be listed as Saxon, but the Norman and post-Norman church of Little Shelford has at least 2 Saxon grave slabs built into the flint rubble walls. About 3 miles to the south is Whittlesford, with its possibly Celtic sheila-na-gig set into its tower. There again the oldest walls are Norman pebble rubble. Duxford, originally Duxworth, lies 2 miles to the south of Whittlesford and was created by the early-medieval merging of 2 river ford villages. It has 2 churches as a result, both described as much-altered Norman buildings. But St John's has the tympanum of its doorway decorated with a carved rosette and cross of a quite early Saxon type. Hinxton, across the river and a mile or so away, has a thirteenth-century church which seems to have been built around an older nucleus. Ickleton, lastly, is listed by Pevsner as Early Norman but by others as Late Saxon, although 2 of the columns are believed to have been removed from a nearby Roman villa or temple, and Roman bricks were incorporated. Thus, of the 7 churches in the valley section, 4 or 5 contain strong hints of pre-Conquest predecessors.

Archaeology also suggests that there are far more Saxon churches than was realized. At Great Paxton in Huntingdonshire, researches in 1967 and 1971 revealed Saxon architecture of a design unique in Britain and with only few continental parallels. Its graceful white arches stand on columns with peculiar bulbous capitals, and the Saxon nucleus endows the church with a cool and airy ethos. Hadstock church in the north of Essex is also remarkable, for its wooden door is Saxon and may even have been embellished with elaborate iron tracery. There is also evidence that for centuries it bore the gruesome trophy of a Dane's skin, fragments of which are preserved in Saffron Walden Museum.

The decision to renew the floor of the church gave archaeologists a rare opportunity to ask questions. While it was generally accepted that Hadstock church had a Late Saxon nucleus, the excavations revealed an unsuspected Middle Saxon church, which would date back as far as the seventh century and place the building closer to the Saxon conversion than the Norman conquest. A major rebuilding took place in the Late Saxon period, and this may be the minster of stone and lime constructed by Canute as a memorial to those slain in his defeat of the English king Edmund Ironside in 1016. But it is safer to link the original Hadstock church with the monastery and resting place of Abbot Botolph, who died about 680. According to the *Anglo-Saxon Chronicle*, Botolph founded a monastery at 'Icanho' in 654; and Hadstock was known as 'Cadenho' in the Early Middle Ages. The excavation revealed a number of graves, including a large shallow grave beside the centre of the original east wall, which may once have held the stone coffin of the saint, subsequently opened and his remains dispersed as relics. Equally remarkable was the discovery within the church of a substantial medieval bell foundry which could only have operated when the church was unroofed, perhaps during a restoration. Other remains of bell-casting have also been found in the Old Minster at Winchester, dating from about 980, and within the thirteenth-century chapel at Cheddar. These examples show that archaeological investigations can uncover a wealth of unexpected information about familiar churches and their origins, although of course the opportunity to dig in a flourishing church seldom arises.

The landscape of England is beautifully punctuated by the towers or spires of 13,000 parish churches, which not only provided landmarks and elaborate houses for the bells, but may also occasionally have supported beacons to advertise an island of civilization in the perilous countryside. On the whole, the tower was the least functional part of the church, and the triumph of the decorative over the practical is evidenced in the glorious soaring edifices built in the late medieval Perpendicular manner. But it has long been suggested that the church tower in England originated as that most functional of buildings – a defensive refuge. In a number of Saxon churches the tower was a massive and solid structure, wider than the nave and completely dominating the rest of the building. Perhaps the best example of the mighty defensive tower is to be seen at Earls Barton, where it is thought that the chancel may simply have been a small appendage to the tower stronghold.

A number of other Saxon church towers survive, nearly all of them in Norfolk, an area exposed to Danish coastal and riverine attack. Mainly they are circular and their durability is demonstrated by the frequency of their survival; those at Beachamwell and Cranwich are beautiful examples. Norfolk contains 112 round towers, though many are Norman rather than Saxon. Of the remaining 54 examples, 41 are in Suffolk. The circular form was doubtless developed because of the difficulty in forming corners in flint rubble

without the costly importation of freestone for making quoins, but the round tower may also have been a more difficult structure to attack.

The round tower of Beachamwell Church.

In Ireland a quite different form of slender and lofty defensive tower was developed, usually found in churchyards. A detached member of the Irish group can be seen at Brechin in Angus. It dates from about the year 1000, and a series of wooden ladders originally ascended the 7 storeys of the tower, which like its Irish cousins has a door some distance above the ground. The only other Scottish example is at Abernethy in Perthshire and may be a century or so later. The export of these towers to Scotland must reflect the infiltration of the Columban church into areas of Pictish Christianity following Kenneth McAlpin's union of Pictland and Dalriada in the middle of the ninth century.

In England, after the conquest of 1066, the Normans held down their territory and protected themselves against each other with a series of local fortresses of the motte and bailey type. These simple structures exploited the concept of defence through height, and consisted of a steep earthen mound topped by a tower of timber or stone. The origins of this kind of fortification have provoked much discussion, for it does not seem to be a development of existing Saxon defenceworks. In some Saxon sites the original timber towers were replaced by sturdier, fireproof towers of stone. It may well be that Saxon defensive church towers inspired the Norman stone keep, as David Wilson has suggested. In only a few places can a continuity be seen, with a Saxon tower being surrounded by later earthworks. At Earls Barton, a later motte runs up against the sturdy tower of the beautiful Saxon church; while the imposing defensive churches at Barnack and Barton-on-Humber appear to be the foundations of important landowners who were as preoccupied with defence (perhaps against Vikings) as they were with religion. The Earls Barton defences are now controversial, however, and could be interpreted as an older promontory fort.

One long-standing riddle of the landscape for which we can now suggest some answers is the origin of the isolated church. Few sights are more likely to set the imagination winging on flights of fancy than a lonely church dreaming quietly in some secluded corner of the countryside. But although it invariably has some fascinating story to tell, it is never one of the wonderful or the supernatural – usually one of desertion or failure. A few examples may have been built at sites of religious importance rather than for communal convenience, but generally such churches have simply been robbed of their worshippers, for no patron would consider providing a church where no one lived. Others may have served a population scattered in farmsteads and hamlets; or they may have been chapels of ease for a remote corner of the parish, some distance from the main church. But the vast majority of isolated churches stand in areas studded with villages, so the strange surplus of medieval structures cannot be explained by any of the reasons we have suggested.

In order to understand the true reason we must understand the dynamics of the village. Writers on the British countryside tend to perpetuate the myth of the rock-like village, firmly rooted in the nook or valley of its birth, never growing or shrinking very much and certainly never moving. Quite the reverse is now known to be the case; villages have perished in their thousands. For every two which flourish today, there must be at least one, possibly two, which have withered and vanished since the Conquest. Villages are also prone to shrink, and to wander. The harshness of peasant life in feudal England is difficult to imagine, but at different times any village might perish as a result of environmental adversity or pestilence, or be devastated by a vain or avaricious lord.

Between the Saxon conversion and about the year 1300 the picture was one of a vigorously expanding population. The thirteenth century saw such population pressure that peasant communities were established in some of the least promising environments. But soon after, for complex reasons, including those of economic decline, the impoverishment of poorer soils of the marginal ploughlands, and possibly climatic deterioration, there was a first great wave of village desertion. This succession of misfortunes took on a flavour of foul drama with the first violent outbreak of the Black Death in 1348-9. The pestilence did not entirely cease to prey on village communities until the seventeenth century. But long before this, landowners discovered that sheep rearing made it possible to use their land in a much more profitable manner. So having begun as an expediency to cope with farmland that had lost the men to work it, sheep were discovered to be a better economic proposition than miserable peasant holdings. The nationwide process soon started of evicting thousands of peasants and destroying their villages to make sheep runs, which climaxed during the Tudor era.

By this time, another fashion had begun which destroyed further villages. Particularly appealing to the *nouveaux riches* was the vogue for replacing the old rambling manor house in the village with an opulent mansion set in its own spacious park. Almost invariably the ancient village would be swept away during the emparking. This continued well into the nineteenth century, although by then it had become customary to compensate the dispossessed with a new village beyond the park gates, such as at Houghton in Norfolk where the old church lies stranded in a park laid out by the Prime Minister Walpole.

These are only some of the ways in which a village might be wiped off the map. But in the Middle Ages, when the peasant home was usually little more than fragile sticks, mud and thatch which swiftly disappeared, the church would survive, for it was usually a substantial building of stone. In areas where stone was rare, however, the church might itself vanish almost as quickly once the stone robbers started work. Some churches which survived the demise of their congregations were then maintained by the lord of the manor and remained as a romantic and isolated monument.

At Childerley in Cambridgeshire a declining village received no such help, for it disappeared in the construction of Sir John Cutt's deer park early in the sixteenth century. No trace of the church can be seen, while Sir John's mansion was provided with its own separate chapel. At Pickworth in Rutland the once prosperous village had gone by 1491. A legend attributes its demise to enraged soldiers in 1470 during the Wars of the Roses after the nearby battle of Lose-coat Field, but sheep clearance seems more likely. At least the site of the church is known, for a stone archway still stands sentinel in front of a group of decaying farm buildings, probably built of stones pillaged from the crumbling church. At Egmere in Norfolk, the fourteenth-century church tower remains almost intact despite the removal of the roofing lead during the reign of Henry VIII. Its unusual durability may well be due to the fact that – quoins excepted – the church is of the flint that abounds in north Norfolk, and therefore would not attract the stone robbers. Finally, at Tixover in Rutland the isolated church of a lost village is used and maintained by the people of modern Tixover, a couple of fields away.

Isolated churches can also be the result of village drift rather than actual disappearance. Though the causes of village drift are usually less easy to establish than those of village death, it has recently become plain that it is a very common occurrence. In parts of Norfolk there seems to have been a generalized drift of settlements from original villages towards damp meadows offering common grazing for peasant livestock during the period of medieval population pressure. In the case of Comberton in Cambridgeshire, the village seems to have wandered from its lovely chalk hilltop church to a lower crossroads site some distance away; and the Northamptonshire village of Braybrooke moved more than a quarter of a mile westwards to its present position south of its medieval church. In this case the earlier village is overlain by the complex earthworks of manorial fishponds, perhaps of the thirteenth century, which seem to have elbowed the village out of the way.

Although they appear in all regions of Britain, isolated churches are famous in the county of Norfolk. Of its 904 churches from before the year 1700, 245 are in ruins. Others have probably been lost, but even so Norfolk had the greatest density of medieval churches in England – 1 to every 3 square miles. Although some of these communities had driven their ploughs into lands which could not long sustain a village, Norfolk suffered its share of pestilence, sheep clearances and emparking. The decline of its textile industry in the face of competition from the north of England removed yet another source of economic viability.

The isolated churches of Norfolk have puzzled so many people partly because they lack the characteristic earthworks one would expect to find in association with them. Even where earthworks survive, as at Pickworth and Childerley, they are far from sharply defined and it is plain that a brief spell of ploughing could level them altogether. Since Norfolk is a largely arable county, Peter Wade-Martin decided to base his search for lost villages on pottery rather than on earthworks, and has recovered village traces near a number of isolated churches where other signs of occupation seem to have been removed. The church at West Dereham perches alone on a low hill a little distance from its village; but close examination of the surrounding fields reveals fragments of a type of pottery known as 'Ipswich Ware', pointing to the proximity of a village in Middle Saxon times.

Air-view of the isolated church of West Dereham in Norfolk.

Scotland has so far been rather neglected in this brief survey of church riddles. A shadowy but important figure in the conversion of Pictland is St Ninian, who with St Columba should share much of the credit for the establishment of Christianity in Scotland, although Columba is later and far better known. Columba was born in Donegal in about 521 and was reputedly the heir to the kingdom of Tara. He left Ireland as a trained cleric and was given Iona and permission to preach among the Picts by Bridei, a Pictish king. He probably preached in Scotland well beyond Iona and encouraged the founding of some rather insubstantial churches. Several Columban monasteries were doubtless established in the seventh century on the Scottish mainland, although their locations are uncertain. Deer in Aberdeenshire is a likely candidate. But rather earlier, in the middle of the fifth century, St Patrick had written a letter of rebuke to the soldiers of Strathclyde for massacring Christians during a raid on Ireland. He mentions their associates as being 'Most evil and apostate Picts'. If the Picts were apostate in the middle of the fifth century, they must already have been converted to Christianity and have abandoned it, well before the Columban mission.

Evidence of the work of the shadowy St Ninian in the second quarter of the fifth century may well have been found at Whithorn in Wigtownshire. Bede writes that the Picts had 'abandoned the errors of idolatry' long before the Columban mission, and describes the 'stately church' of Ninian's See: 'The place belongs to the province of Bernicia and is commonly known as *Candida Casa*, the White House, because he built the church of stone, which was unusual among the Britons.' Excavations at Whithorn in 1949 and 1965 produced dark local flagstones covered with an unusual cream coloured plaster – interpreted by many as evidence of Ninian's White House. Among the inscribed stones are the mid-fifth century memorial of one Lord Latinus, and the perhaps later marker of 'The Place of Peter the Apostle'. One is uncertain how to interpret these remains; the plastered ruins could be those of a later church, set up to commemorate the legendary white hut of St Ninian, and the Peter Stone could perhaps be from a chapel housing a relic of St Peter.

The possibility of conversion at the time of St Ninian is underlined by three inscribed stones at Kirkmadrine Church, one of which bears the well-cut inscription, 'Here lie the holy bishops – Ides, Viventius and Mavorius'. It is in good Roman lettering and could mean that there were organized churches in Galloway during the fifth century – the currently quoted date for the inscription.

Arboe Cross, Co. Tyrone. One of the finest crosses in Ireland, it stands on the W shore of Lough Neagh, to the W of Belfast. The church may date from as early as the 6th cent., but the cross is in 10th-cent. style. It stands almost 20 ft high, and bears intricately carved biblical scenes. In later times Arboe became a pilgrimage centre.

Barton-on-Humber, Lincolnshire. The church of St Peter is one of the most remarkable Saxon churches in England. The village lies on the A 1077, 5 miles SW of Hull, on the River Humber. The tower seems once to have been the main structure of the church, and it is of defensive proportions. It is decorated with the characteristic flat band decoration, similar to that at Earls Barton.

Beachamwell, Norfolk. The thatched Saxon church stands at one end of the village green, 5 miles WSW of Swaffham (25 miles W of Norwich). The nave, chancel and tower are Late Saxon. The upper section of the circular flint tower is later and polygonal.

Brechin Round Tower, Angus. The cathedral has been added to a 10th cent. Dark Age tower in the centre of the old city of Brechin (7 miles W of Montrose, NE of Dundee). The tower is topped by a 14th cent. spire, similar in many ways to Irish round towers. The Irish link is certain in the statue of a bishop carrying an Irish T-shaped crozier, standing near the elevated doorway.

Carrawburgh Temple and Well. Lies 7 miles NW of Hexham, (25 miles W of Newcastle). Near the site of the seventh fort from the E along Hadrian's Wall. The Mithras temple contained 3 altars, now in Newcastle University Museum of Antiquities and replaced by copies. The temple contains a remarkable ordeal-pit, in which initiates were interred as part of the conversion ritual. A well, dedicated to the Celtic water goddess Coventina, lay in nearby marshy ground. The temple was desecrated early in the 4th cent., and was lost in advancing marshland until the bog shrank in the 1949 drought.

Collingham, Yorkshire. Lies 10 miles NE of Leeds on the A58. Two 9th cent. crosses discovered in 1840 have been embedded in the S wall of St Oswald's church. One is known as the Apostles' Cross and displays Christ and 11 apostles; the Aerswith Cross is decorated with fantastic beasts and includes runic inscriptions.

Cranwich, Norfolk. One of the most charming of churches – thatched and round-towered in its secluded and tranquil setting. Mostly Late Saxon. It lies in woodland and meadow, not far from the village, 2 miles NW of Mundford (on the A134, 10 miles NW of Thetford and SW of Norwich).

Earls Barton, Northamptonshire. Lies 6 miles NE of Northampton, SE of the A45. Perhaps the most imposing Saxon church tower in the country. It dates from the late 10th cent. and is characteristically decorated with pilaster and stripwork, with long and short work in the quoins.

The Saxon tower (and later parapet) at Earls Barton in Northamptonshire.

Edenham, Lincolnshire. The village church of St Michael lies 3 miles W of Bourne (on the A15, 15 miles NNW of Peterborough). Some 9th cent. work remains in the S wall of the nave. High in the wall above the font, to the right of the entrance, is a Saxon roundel with 4 scrolls. At the W end is part of a 9th cent. cross.

Eyam, Derbyshire. This much-visited village on the B652, 12 miles E of Chapel-en-le-Frith (20 miles SE of Manchester), is best known for the courage of the community when they isolated themselves to prevent the spread of the pestilence to neighbouring villages. The churchyard contains a finely carved Dark Age stone cross. Although the plaque states that it is Celtic, the head is in the Northumbrian style and seems to date from the early 9th cent.

Glendalough, Wicklow. Regarded as one of Ireland's most beautiful corners, near the Wicklow mountains (10 miles NW of Rathdrum, 30 miles S of Dublin). Here are a pair of glacial lakes, the site of the 6th cent. cell of St Kevin and of a cathedral, and one of Ireland's remarkable round towers. This example is 110 ft tall and dates from the Dark Ages.

Greensted Church, Essex. This unique Saxon timber church lies 1 mile W of Chipping Ongar (10 miles W of Chelmsford, S of the A122), within easy reach of London. Amid later additions stands a Saxon church of vertical log walling that dates from around 950. It may have replaced a still earlier timber church. Its oak ground-sill now rests on a Victorian brick plinth.

Great Paxton, Huntingdonshire. This beautiful medieval church with its Saxon core lies in a small village 3 miles N of St Neots on the B1043 (15 miles W of Cambridge).

Hadstock, Essex. Lies 2 miles S of Linton on the A604 10 miles SE of Cambridge. The remarkable church, complete with a Saxon door, dominates the village.

Holywell, Huntingdonshire. The village, one of the prettiest in the area, takes its name from the well in the hollow at the end of the churchyard. It lies beside the Great Ouse, 2 miles E of St Ives (N of the A604, 11 miles NW of Cambridge).

Ickleton, Cambridgeshire. Lies 10 miles S of Cambridge, on the M11. A branch of the prehistoric Icknield way circles the church. One of the finest Early Norman interiors in the country, that also incorporates grey Roman columns. Fire destroyed much of the interior woodwork in 1979.

Ilkley, Yorkshire. On the A65, 15 miles NW of Leeds. Three 9th-cent. carved stone crosses are preserved in the churchyard of All Saints. Their origins are uncertain and all were re-erected in the 19th cent. The churchyard and the flanking roads faithfully preserve the outlines of a Roman military camp.

Lancaster, Lancashire. The church of St Mary lies in the town centre. In the N chapel is a collection of fragments of Saxon sculpture, including a carved cross-head bearing Christ within a circle.

Landbeach Green Man. The church at Landbeach, 4 miles NNE of Cambridge, is one of many to sport a Green Man carving. The author discovered this carving on the horizontal timber roof-beam nearest to the entrance porch, when scaffolding was erected during recent restoration work. Other beams carry similar carvings, but only this one shows vines springing from the mouth in true Green Man fashion. The church is also exceptional because one of the pillars in the aisle was found to contain a desiccated heart.

St Kevin's Church, Glendalough.

Greensted Church, Essex.

Saxon stonework in Great Paxton Church, Huntingdonshire.

183

Black magic is not suspected, for the heart was probably interred at the request of the owner who had died far away – a crusader perhaps. Note also the unusual double-decker village pump, with 2 spouts one above the other, beside the small green opposite the church.

Leeds, Yorkshire. In the churchyard of St Peter, the parish church of Leeds, is a superb Late Saxon carved stone cross standing more than 11 ft high.

Lullingstone Villa, Kent. The villa lies to the SW of London, W of Eynsford village (5 miles S of Dartford, on the A225) in the Darent valley. It survived remarkably well after its burning and abandonment in the early 5th cent. Among its various beautiful mosaics and murals was a wall painting with a *chi-rho* monogram, now restored and in the British Museum. A late 4th-cent. owner had converted one room into a chapel and painted 6 praying figures on the plastered walls. A late 2nd-cent. shrine dedicated to a local water nymph was also found.

Maxey, Cambridgeshire. Lies 7 miles NNW of Peterborough. The church stands well away from the village on a mound which may previously have had pagan significance. Opposite it is the site of an older village of Saxon huts, excavated in the 1970s.

Melbourne, Derbyshire. Lies 7 miles S of Derby. The church has a fine carving of a Green Man, wearing the typical cap of leaves with vines sprouting left and right from his mouth.

Middleton Stoney, Oxfordshire. This village, 3 miles WNW of Bicester (20 miles N of Oxford), has one of the many churches isolated as the result of emparking the original village and rebuilding it outside the gates of an imposing park. The lost village, which lay in the park close to the attractive Norman church, was recently

excavated under the direction of Trevor Rowley, and was shown to contain relics of a far earlier prehistoric settlement. The church is worth visiting for its vigorous Norman decoration. Its font, removed reputedly from the nearby Islip church, is supposed to have been used for the christening of the penultimate Saxon king, Edward the Confessor. An impressive Norman motte mound lies just beside the church.

Monasterboice, Meath. Lies 3 miles E of Collon (30 miles N of Dublin) in Ireland's lovely Boyne valley area. The monastery is said to have been founded by St Buithe, a disciple of St Patrick, around AD 500. There are the ruins of a Dark Age round tower, 2 ruined churches and 3 high crosses. Muiredach's cross is probably the oldest, dating from the early 10th cent., and displaying remarkably rich Celtic carving.

Pickworth, Leicestershire. Lies 5 miles NNW of Stamford (10 miles NW of Peterborough). Pickworth has some of the clearest and most interesting remains of a deserted medieval village. An arch from its church stands over a holloway which marks a street. Another street runs between the arch and the more recent church.

Stevington, Bedfordshire. The church stands 4 miles NW of Bedford, (between Northampton and Cambridge) between the A6 and the A428. An old holy well, which became a minor centre for medieval pilgrimage, lies beside the Anglo-Danish church. The village also contains a market cross and a restored windmill.

West Dereham Church, Norfolk. The church stands somewhat isolated from its village, 3 miles SE of Downham Market (40 miles W of Norwich), in an area dotted with ruined and isolated churches, most of which probably stand near lost and shrunken villages. A spread of Saxon pottery, known as 'Ipswich ware', in the fields around the church indicate that in Saxon times the village stood much closer to the church than it does at present.

White Island Church, Fermanagh. This ruined 12th-cent. church, near Lower Lough Erne in SW Northern Ireland, contains 8 carved figures possibly dating back to the 8th cent. Some of them appear to be pagan. Whatever their origin, they so embarrassed the builders of the church that they were carefully hidden, some of them being incorporated in the church structure until they were found recently.

Whithorn, Wigtownshire. Lies 10 miles S of Wigtown, 30 miles W of Carlisle. The possible site of St Ninian's *Candida Casa*. The Whithorn Priory museum contains the earliest Christian monument in Scotland: the Latinus Stone of about 450, erected by Barrovadus in memory of his grandfather. It also has the St Peter Stone, dated not later than the early 8th cent. Other early Christian inscribed stones can be seen at Kirkmadrine church on the W of Luce Bay, 2 miles SW of Sandhead.

Whittlesford, Cambridgeshire. Lies 7 miles S of Cambridge, E of the M11. The sheila-na-gig is set high in the church tower and binoculars are a help. Best photographed with a telephoto lens in the long shadows of the evening. The village is pretty and has a superb medieval moot hall.

Carved figures at White Island Church, Fermanagh.

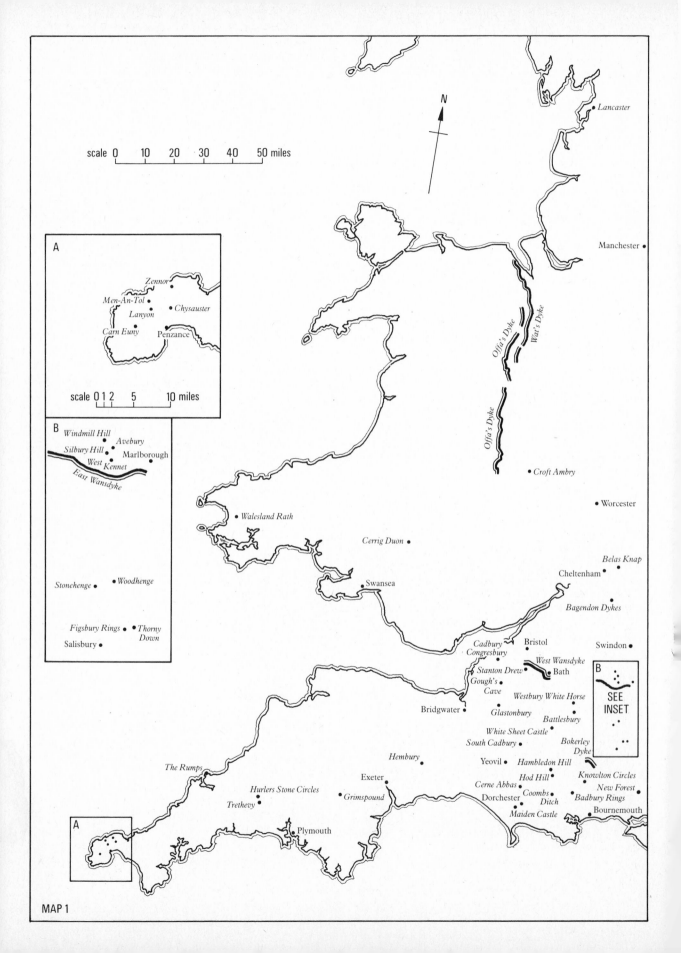

N

scale 0   10   20   30   40   50 miles

A

Zennor

Men-An-Tol   Chysauster
Lanyon

Carn Euny   Penzance

scale 0 1 2   5   10 miles

B Windmill Hill
           Avebury
Silbury Hill   Marlborough
West   Kennet
East Wansdyke

Stonehenge   Woodhenge

Figsbury Rings   Thorny
                              Down
Salisbury

Lancaster

Manchester

Offa's Dyke   Wat's Dyke

Offa's Dyke

Croft Ambry

Worcester

Belas Knap
Cheltenham

Bagendon Dykes

Walesland Rath

Cerrig Duon

Swansea

Bridgwater

Cadbury   Bristol
Congresbury
              West Wansdyke
Stanton Drew   Bath
Gough's
Cave
          Westbury White Horse
Glastonbury
              Battlesbury
White Sheet Castle
South Cadbury   Bokerley
                                    Dyke

Swindon

B

SEE
INSET

The Rumps

Hurlers Stone Circles
Trethevy

Grimspound

Exeter

Plymouth

Hembury

Yeovil   Hambledon Hill
           Hod Hill
Cerne Abbas   Knowlton Circles
Dorchester   Coombs   New Forest
                       Ditch   Badbury Rings
           Maiden Castle   Bournemouth

A

MAP 1

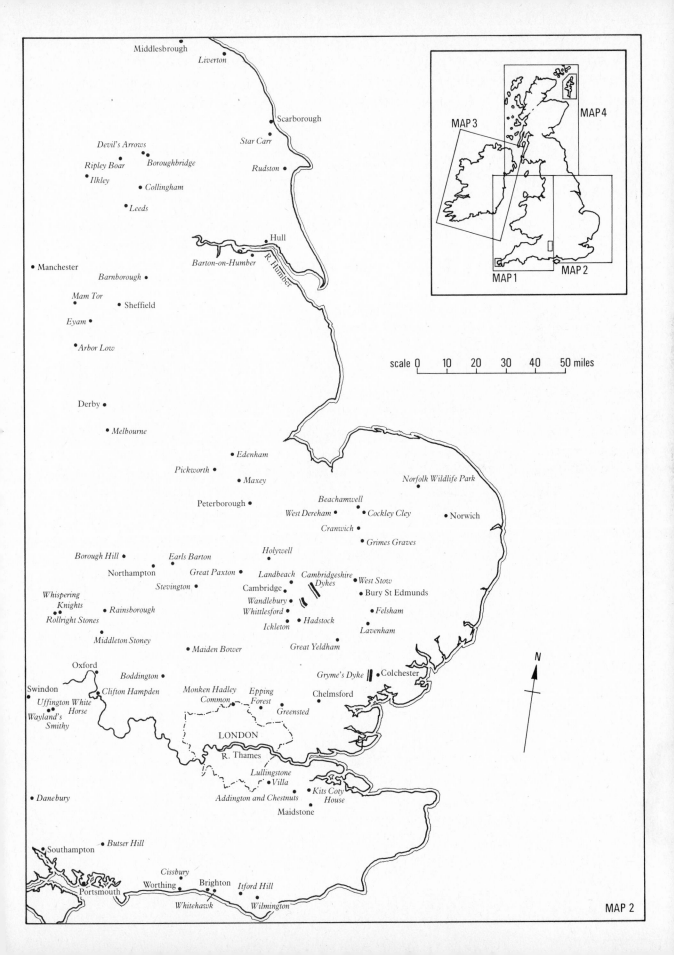

Middlesbrough
Liverton

Scarborough

Devil's Arrows
Ripley Boar   *Boroughbridge*   *Star Carr*
Ilkley   *Rudston*
        Collingham

Leeds

Hull
Barton-on-Humber   R. Humber

Manchester

Barnborough

Mam Tor   Sheffield
Eyam

Arbor Low

Derby

Melbourne

Edenham
Pickworth   *Norfolk Wildlife Park*
        Maxey
Peterborough   *Beachamwell*
            West Dereham   *Cockley Cley*
            Cranwich   Norwich
                        Grimes Graves

Borough Hill   *Earls Barton*   *Holywell*
Northampton   *Great Paxton*   *Landbeach*   *Cambridgeshire*   *West Stow*
        Stevington   Cambridge   *Dykes*   Bury St Edmunds
Whispering   *Wandlebury*
Knights   *Rainsborough*   *Whittlesford*   *Felsham*
Rollright Stones   *Ickleton*   *Hadstock*   *Lavenham*
        Middleton Stoney
                Maiden Bower   *Great Yeldham*

Oxford   *Gryme's Dyke*   Colchester
    Boddington
Swindon   *Clifton Hampden*   *Monken Hadley*   *Epping*   Chelmsford
Uffington White   *Common*   *Forest*
Horse   *Greensted*
Wayland's
Smithy
                LONDON
                R. Thames
            Lullingstone
            Villa
Danebury   *Addington and Chestnuts*   *Kits Coty*
                House
                Maidstone

Butser Hill
Southampton

                Cissbury
            Worthing   Brighton   *Itford Hill*
Portsmouth
        Whitehawk   *Wilmington*

MAP 3
MAP 4
MAP 1
MAP 2

scale 0   10   20   30   40   50 miles

N

MAP 2

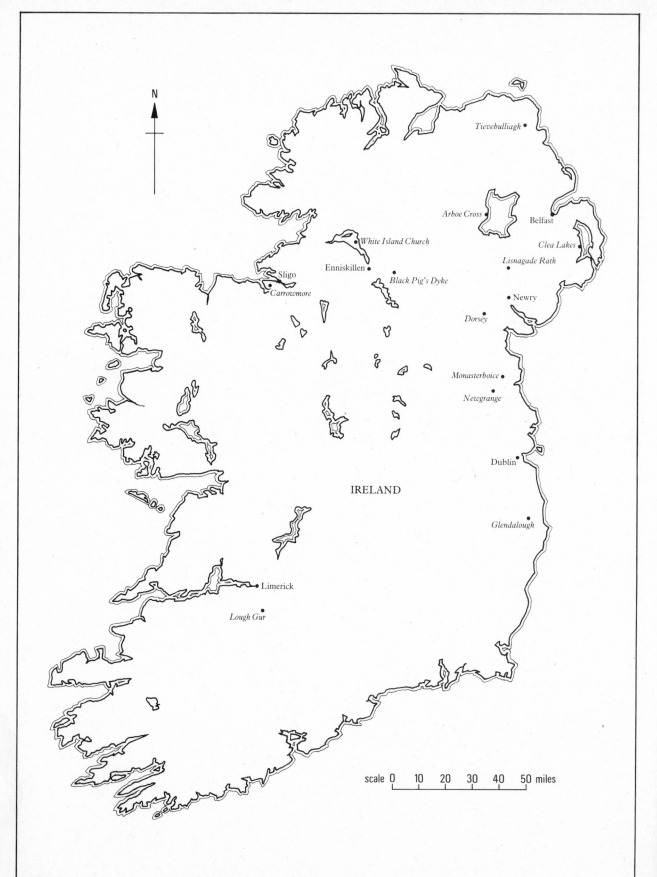

N

Tievebulliagh •

Arboe Cross •   Belfast •

                Clea Lakes

• *White Island Church*

Enniskillen •   *Lisnagade Rath* •

Sligo •   • *Black Pig's Dyke*

• *Carrowmore*   • Newry

Dorsey •

Monasterboice •

Newgrange •

Dublin •

IRELAND

Glendalough •

Limerick •

Lough Gur •

scale 0   10   20   30   40   50 miles

MAP 3

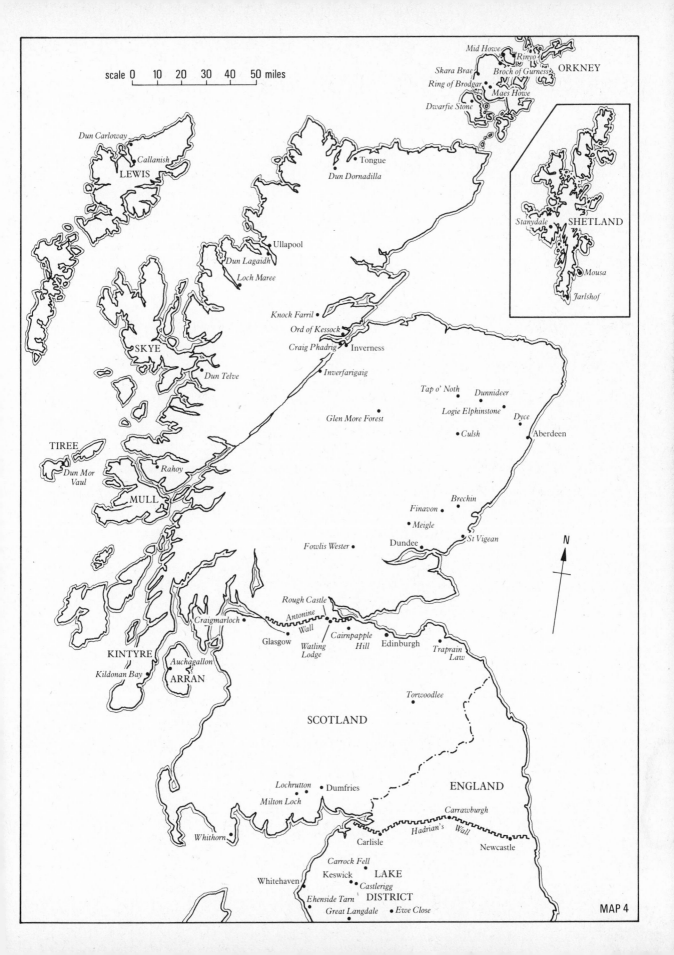

scale 0 10 20 30 40 50 miles

ORKNEY

Mid Howe *Rinyo*
Skara Brae *Broch of Gurness*
Ring of Brodgar *Maes Howe*
Dwarfie Stone

SHETLAND

Stanydale

Mousa

Jarlshof

Dun Carloway
Callanish
LEWIS

• Tongue
Dun Dornadilla

• Ullapool
Dun Lagaidh
Loch Maree

SKYE

Knock Farril •
Ord of Kessock
Craig Phadrig • Inverness

Dun Telve •

Inverfarigaig

Tap o' Noth *Dunnideer*
Logie Elphinstone *Dyce*
Glen More Forest • Culsh
Aberdeen

TIREE

Dun Mor
Vaul *Rahoy*

MULL

Brechin
Finavon
• *Meigle*
Fowlis Wester • Dundee • *St Vigean*

N

Rough Castle
Antonine
Craigmarloch • Wall
Glasgow *Watling* *Cairnpapple*
Lodge *Hill* Edinburgh • *Traprain*
Law

KINTYRE
Auchagallon
Kildonan Bay • ARRAN

Torwoodlee •

SCOTLAND

ENGLAND

Lochrutton Dumfries •
Milton Loch

Carrawburgh
Hadrian's *Wall*
Carlisle Newcastle

Whithorn •

Carrock Fell
Keswick • LAKE
Whitehaven • *Castlerigg*
Ehenside Tarn DISTRICT
Great Langdale • *Ewe Close*

MAP 4

Suggestions for further reading

CHAPTER 1

G. E. Daniel, *The Prehistoric Chamber Tombs of England and Wales*, 1950.

Dendrochronology in Europe, BAR Research Paper S51, 1978.

L. V. Grinsell, *The Ancient Burial Mounds of England*, 1953.

Euan W. MacKie, *The Megalith Builders*, 1977. (A speculative account, like his *Science and Society in Prehistoric Britain*, 1977.)

S. Piggott, *The West Kennet Long Barrow*, 1962.

Colin Renfrew, *Before Civilization*, 1976; he is also editor of *British Prehistory: A New Outline*, 1974.

David Wilson, *Science and Archaeology*, 1978.

CHAPTER 2

Richard Bradley, *The Prehistoric Settlement of Britain*, 1978.

A. Dent, *Lost beasts of Britain*, 1974.

Geoffrey Dimbleby, *Plants and Archaeology*, 1978.

John G. Evans, *The Environment of Early Man in the British Isles*, 1975.

O. Rackham, *Trees and Woodland in the British Landscape*, 1976.

R. C. Steel and R. C. Welch, *Monk's Wood*, 1973.

CHAPTER 3

R. J. C. Atkinson, *Stonehenge*, 1979.

Aubrey, Burl, *The Stone Circles of the British Isles*, 1976.

Peter Lancaster Brown, *Megaliths, Myths and Men*, 1976.

Evan Hadingham, *Circles and Standing Stones*, 1975.

Gerald S. Hawkins, *Stonehenge Decoded*, 1975 and *Beyond Stonehenge*, 1973.

Fred Hoyle, *On Stonehenge*, 1977.

R. S. Newall, *Stonehenge*, 1977.

A. Thom, *Megalithic Lunar Observatories*, 1971.

CHAPTER 4

Barry Cunliffe, *Iron Age Communities in Britain*, 1974.

J. Forde-Johnson, *Hillforts*, 1976.

D. W. Harding (ed), *Hillforts: Later Prehistoric Earthworks in Britain and Ireland*, 1976.

A. H. A. Hogg, *Hill-Forts of Britain*, 1975 and *British Hill-Forts; An Index*, BAR British Series, 1979.

CHAPTER 5

Evelyn Clark, *Cornish Fogous*, 1961.

J. D. G. Clark, *Star Carr*, 1963.

J. M. Coles, *Archaeology by Experiment*, 1973.

J. R. C. Hamilton, *Excavations at Jarlshof, Shetland*, 1956.

Lloyd Laing, *Late Celtic Britain and Ireland*, 1975.

G. Sievking, I. Longworth and K. Wilson (eds), *Problems in Economic and Social Archaeology*, 1976.

F. T. Wainwright, *Souterrains in Southern Pictland*, 1963.

CHAPTER 6

Evan Hadingham, *Ancient Carvings in Britain*, 1974.

I. Henderson, *The Picts*, 1967.

T. C. Lethbridge, *Gog Magog*, 1957.

K. E. Maltwood, *A Guide to Glastonbury's Temple of the Stars*, 1964.

M. Marples, *White Horses and Hill Figures*, 1949.

P. Meldrum (ed), *The Dark Ages in the Highlands*, 1971.

F. T. Wainwright, *The Northern Isles*, 1962 and (ed), *The Problem of the Picts*, 1955.

CHAPTER 7

R. Feachem, *Guide to Prehistoric Scotland*, 1977.

Euan W. MacKie, *Dun Mor Vaul: An Iron Age Broch on Tiree*, 1977 and *The Brochs of Scotland* in P. J. Fowler (ed), *Recent Work in Rural Archaeology*, 1975.

B. H. St. J. O'Neil, *The Date and Purpose of the Brochs* in W. D. Simpson (ed), *The Viking Congress*, 1954.

I. A. Richmond (ed), *Roman and Native in North Britain*, 1958.

CHAPTER 8

O. G. S. Crawford, *Archaeology in the Field*, 1953.

E. Fowler, *Field Surveys in British Archaeology*, 1972.

P. J. Fowler, *Continuity in the Landscape* in P. J. Fowler (ed), *Recent Work in Rural Achaeology*, 1975.

Sir Cyril Fox, *Offa's Dyke*, 1955.

P. A. Jewell (ed), *The Experimental Earthwork on Overton Down*, 1963.

E. Pollard, M. D. Hooper and N. W. Moor, *Hedges*, 1974.

CHAPTER 9

L. Alcock, *Arthur's Britain*, 1971.

The Anglo-Saxon Chronicle, translated by G. N. Garmonway, 1953.

Bede, *A History of the English Church and People*, (Penguin) 1971.

Gildas, *The Ruin of Britain and Other Documents*, (Phillimore) 1978.

Francis Jones, *Holy Wells of Wales*, 1954.

Lloyd and Jennifer Laing, *A Guide to the Dark Age Remains in Britain*, 1979.

Lloyd Laing, *The Archaeology of Late Celtic Britain and Ireland, 400–1300 AD*, 1975.

H. Mayr-Harting, *The Coming of Christianity to Anglo-Saxon England*, 1972.

P. H. Sawyer, *From Roman Britain to Norman England*, 1978.

P. Wade Martins, *The Origins of Rural Settlement in East Anglia* in P. J. Fowler (ed), *Recent Work in Rural Archaeology*, 1975.

Index

Numbers in *italics* refer to illustrations.